The Changing World of Bali

The glossy guidebook images of Bali as a timeless paradise whose people are devoutly religious and artistically gifted hides a very different reality. *The Changing World of Bali* analyses the religious and social changes in Bali and the impact of tourism in the context of political and economic developments in Indonesia from the colonial period to the present day.

A hundred years of colonialism, war, Indonesian independence and tourism have produced modernising changes, but also generated images of Bali as 'traditional'.

Incorporating up-to-date ethnographic fieldwork, the book investigates the myriad of ways in which the Balinese have responded to the influx of outside influence. The Balinese have seen the emergence of a much more fluid and contested religious scene, generating dynamic connections between religious practice, ethnic identity and artistic activity. However, Howe argues that these developments have been complicated by a concern for the integrity and authenticity of Balinese culture. Exploitation of the island by the tourist industry, especially after the 2002 Bali bomb, has created a sense among the Balinese that they are being robbed and their culture contaminated.

In documenting these diverse changes, Howe critically assesses some of the work of Bali's most famous ethnographer, Clifford Geertz, and demonstrates the importance of a historically grounded and broadly contextualised approach to the analysis of a complex society.

Leo Howe is Senior Lecturer in social anthropology at Cambridge University. His books include *Hinduism and Hierarchy in Bali* (James Currey, 2001) and *Being Unemployed in Northern Ireland* (Cambridge University Press, 1990).

The Modern Anthropology of Southeast Asia

Editors
Victor T. King, University of Hull
William D. Wilder, University of Durham

The books in this series incorporate basic ethnographic description into a wider context of responses to development, globalisation and change. Each book embraces broadly the same concerns, but the emphasis in each differs as authors choose to concentrate on specific dimensions of change, or work out particular conceptual approaches to the issues of development. Areas of concern include nation-building, technological innovations in agriculture, rural–urban migration, the expansion of industrial and commercial employment, the rapid increase in cultural and ethnic tourism, the consequences of deforestation and environmental degradation, the 'modernisation of tradition', ethnic identity and conflict, and the religious transformation of society.

The Modern Anthropology of Southeast Asia: An Introduction
Victor T. King and William D. Wilder

The Changing Village Environment in the Southeast
Applied anthropology and environment reclamation in the northern Philippines
Ben J. Wallace

The Changing World of Bali
Religion, society and tourism
Leo Howe

The Changing World of Bali
Religion, society and tourism

Leo Howe

LONDON AND NEW YORK

First published 2005
by Routledge
2 Park Square, Milton Park, Abingdon, Oxon, OX14 4RN

Simultaneously published in the USA and Canada
by Routledge
270 Madison Ave, New York, NY 10016

Routledge is an imprint of the Taylor & Francis Group

Transferred to Digital Printing 2009

© 2005 Leo Howe

Typeset in Times New Roman by Bookcraft Ltd, Stroud, Gloucestershire

All rights reserved. No part of this book may be reprinted or reproduced or utilised in any form or by any electronic, mechanical, or other means, now known or hereafter invented, including photocopying and recording, or in any information storage or retrieval system, without permission in writing from the publishers.

British Library Cataloguing in Publication Data
A catalogue record for this book is available from the British Library

Library of Congress Cataloging in Publication Data
Howe, Leo.
　The changing world of Bali: religion, society and tourism / Leo Howe.
　　p. cm. – (The modern anthropology of Southeast Asia)
　Includes bibliographical references and index.
　1. Bali (Indonesia: Province) – Civilization. 2. Bali (Indonesia: Province) – Religion. 3. Tourism – Indonesia – Bali (Province)
　I. Title. II. Series.
　DS647.B2H68 2005
　959.8'604–dc22   2005002518

ISBN10: 0-415-36497-3 (hbk)
ISBN10: 0-415-54674-5 (pbk)

ISBN13: 978-0-415-36497-3 (hbk)
ISBN13: 978-0-415-54674-4 (pbk)

Contents

	List of illustrations	*vii*
	Acknowledgements	*ix*
	A note on foreign words	*x*
1	Introduction: The Kuta bomb and Balinese culture	1
2	Colonialism, caste and the beginnings of tourism	18
3	Balinese character assassination?	38
4	The efficacy of ritual action and the transformation of religion	56
5	The new religions of Bali: Agama Hindu and Sri Sathya Sai Baba	91
6	Controversies about hierarchy	111
7	Tourism, culture and identity	131
	References	*147*
	Index	*157*

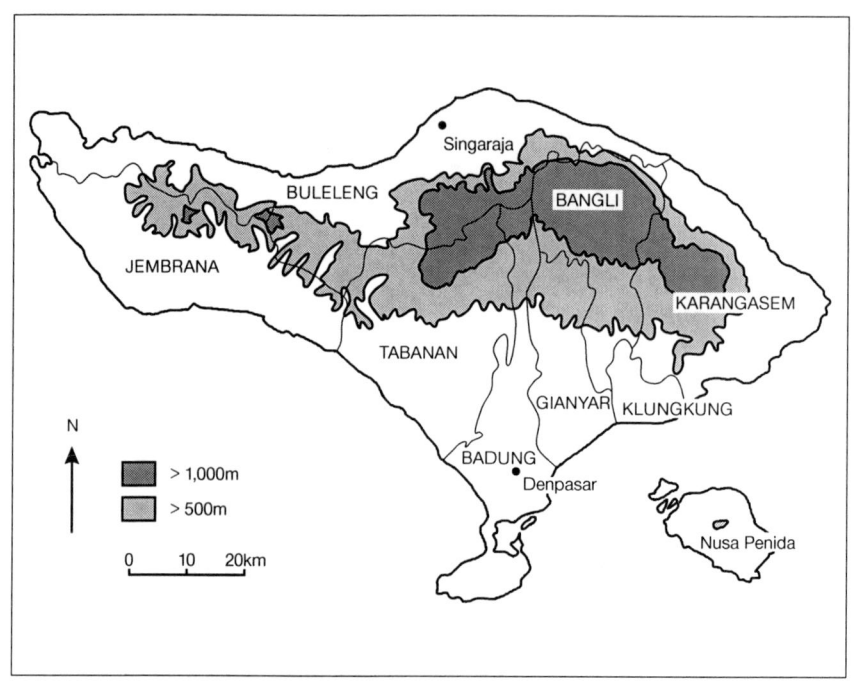

Regional map of Bali

Illustrations

Figures

1.1	The *nawa sangga*	11
1.2	The layout of buildings in a Balinese walled compound	12
1.3	Crossroads and buildings at the centre of a Balinese village	13

Map

Regional map of Bali   vi

Plates

1	Balinese terraced rice fields	75
2	Low-paid female workers sanding and varnishing woodcarvings for the tourist market	75
3	Market day in the village of Pujung, northern Gianyar	76
4	High-caste men in Corong indulging in the typical early evening pastime of discussing the merits of their fighting cocks	77
5	Cockfighting preceding the annual temple ceremony at Samuan Tiga, Gianyar	77
6	Seven-roofed cremation tower (*badé*), Ubud village	78
7	Last-minute details being added to sarcophagus (*patulangan*) in which a body is cremated	79
8	Bull sarcophagus for a high-caste Balinese, Ubud village	80
9	Doorway to the palace (*puri*) of Cokorda Pemayun, Corong village	81
10	Snacking in the late morning at the local coffee shop (*warung*) in Corong village	82
11	Welcoming Rangda (the fearsome mask) during an annual temple ceremony in Corong	83
12	Stately procession (*mapeed*) of hamlet women to the temple, Corong	83
13	Preparation of food for guests and offerings on the morning of a tooth-filing, Corong	84
14	Some of the many offerings for the tooth-filing ceremony, Corong	85
15	The eleven young men and women about to undertake the tooth-filing ordeal, Corong	85
16	Low-caste couple getting married in Pujung village	86
17	The proud fathers of the bride and groom	87
18	Two couples receiving admonishing advice about marriage from a priest in the temple, Pujung	87

19	The Sai Baba temple in Denpasar	88
20	The Hare Krishna ashram on the outskirts of Denpasar	88
21	A view of some of the shrines at Besakih, Bali's 'mother temple'	89
22	Street scene in Kuta, the tourist mecca on Bali's south coast	89
23	Garbage disposal scarring Bali's tropical landscape	90
24	Western tourists waiting for a ritual in a temple ceremony to begin	90

Acknowledgements

I have undertaken research in Bali on many occasions between 1978 and 2002, funded variously by the Economic and Social Research Council, the Evans Fund of the University of Cambridge Faculty of Archaeology and Anthropology, and the University of Cambridge Travel Fund. I am very grateful to all these bodies for their generous assistance.

I wish to acknowledge the kind help of the officers of the Lembaga Ilmu Pengetahuan Indonesia (Indonesian Institute of Sciences), under whose auspices my research in Bali was conducted. I have been fortunate at different times to enjoy the sponsorship of three remarkable individuals in Bali – the late Professor Gusti Ngurah Bagus, Anak Agung Madé Jelantik, and Professor Gedé Pitana. I am tremendously grateful to them all for their warm friendship, encouragement and wise counsel. Special thanks also go to Professor James J. Fox for help in arranging research visas.

Some of the material which appears in this book has previously been published elsewhere. Chapter 5 is a revised version of 'Sai Baba in Bali: identity, social conflict and the politics of religious truth' which appeared in Vol. 33 of the *Review of Indonesian and Malaysian Studies* in 1999. I have also adapted and rewritten some sections from an earlier book, *Hinduism and Hierarchy in Bali*, published by James Currey in 2001. I am grateful to the publishers for permission to use this material here.

Many friends and colleagues have given of their time and expertise to comment on various chapters of this book. I particularly wish to thank Declan Quigley, David Gellner, Marilyn Strathern, Stephen Hugh-Jones, Susan Bayly, Michel Picard and Martin Ramstedt, who have provided incisive comments and much sound advice. I am also indebted to Bill Wilder, whose meticulous reading of the final draft has rendered the text considerably more reader-friendly than it would otherwise have been.

In Bali I have resided in three different places, and wish to record my gratitude to all those Balinese friends who made life in Bali enjoyable. Special thanks go to Wayan Gina and his family, in whose house in Pujung my wife, son and I lived for eighteen months. Our many neighbours and friends in Pujung helped us in ways too numerous to record, and it has been wonderful to see their children grow up, get married and have children of their own. Ketut Mijil, the late Jero Kubayan, Jero

Mangku Dalem and Jero Mangku Pandé all allowed me to benefit from their expert knowledge as they patiently explained various aspects of Balinese society. In Corong my thanks go to Gung Oka, Gung Alit, Cok Gedé Pemayun, Déwa Gedé Ngurah, Gus Nyoman Oka, Ketut Togog and many others who have been very good friends, even if they later came to regret teaching me rather too well the popular card game *ceki*! In Denpasar I wish to record my thanks to the lay officials and devotees of Sri Sathya Sai Baba, who allowed me access to all their services and spoke frankly about many contemporary aspects of Balinese religious practices.

Finally, I would like to thank my wife, Elizabeth, and our three children, Tom, Jo and Dan, for their unstinting love, generosity and fun.

A note on foreign words

I have tried to keep the number of words in foreign languages to a minimum, but where translations would be clumsy, inelegant or simply impossible I have retained the indigenous terms. Words in the Indonesian language are denoted by the abbreviation 'Ind.'. All other foreign words in the text are Balinese apart from a few in Sanskrit, Dutch and Arabic. Words from these latter three languages have not been specifically noted since the context usually makes it clear that the word is not Balinese.

There are some Balinese terms, such as *anak agung*, *déwa*, *brahmana* and *cokorda*, which can cause confusion because they carry multiple meanings. These terms designate descent groups, the status titles of members of those groups, and form a part of the personal names of the group's members. The following convention has therefore been used to distinguish these different senses: the capitalised and unitalicised term refers both to the group as a whole and to the names of members of the group, while the title of the members of this group when referred to separately is given lowercase and italicised. Thus Anak Agung Gedé Alit is the full personal name of a member of the Anak Agung descent group, while members of this group possess the title *anak agung*. The capitalised form is also used for several words which refer to classes or categories of Balinese, such as Brahmana, Satria, Wésia, Sudra, Triwangsa, and so on, and I retain this convention when these terms are used adjectivally – thus a Brahmana priest or a Sudra woman.

1 Introduction
The Kuta bomb and Balinese culture

On the night of 12 October 2002 a bomb exploded outside the Sari Club in the tourist village of Kuta on Bali's south coast, eventually killing over two hundred people. Within hours news of the tragedy had reached most areas of Bali and was being reported by the media throughout the world. In the first few days after the bomb there were many theories as to who the terrorists were. In the West, for example, it was widely assumed to be the act of an al Qa'ida terrorist cell, while among many Muslims in Indonesia it was believed to be the American CIA trying to discredit Islam. On the island, many blamed fanatical Muslims for trying to extend the communal violence in Ambon, Kalimantan, Lombok and other areas of Indonesia by inciting religious and ethnic violence in Hindu Bali, ultimately with a view to securing an Islamic state by destabilising the fragile incumbent one. However, though I am introducing the book in this way I am less interested in who the actual culprits were than in using the event to sketch some social and cultural themes that will later receive more detailed treatment.

There have been Balinese Muslims, especially in north Bali, for hundreds of years, but it was more recent migrants, mostly Muslims from Java and elsewhere in Indonesia working and living in the tourist areas and towns of south Bali, who quickly became targets for retaliation by Balinese Hindus. For several decades these migrant workers have been blamed for most of the crime, drug abuse, prostitution and other social ills besetting modern Bali. Ask many Balinese about these issues and the stereotypical reply is that 'Balinese people do not do such things, it must be "*orang jawa*"' – other Indonesians, though not necessarily Javanese. On occasion such migrants, when discovered in villages at night, have been killed by massed gangs of villagers on the assumption that they had commited or were about to commit a robbery.

An important issue lurks behind such killings. This is the idea, voiced both by some Balinese and by outside observers, that Balinese culture is being 'sold' for tourist dollars, thus debasing it and reducing it to a commodity. Over the years Balinese have displayed their artistic accomplishments – particularly music, dance and drama, often in truncated and impoverished forms – for the delight of tourists. They also willingly invite tourists into their homes and temples to witness a variety of colourful ceremonies such as cremations, weddings and tooth-filings. Most Balinese accept that it is this rich and sumptuous spectacle which brings tourists, both foreigners and other Indonesians, to Bali. People come to see Balinese culture, and therefore it must be accessible and tailored to tourist requirements. This orientation to tourist desires, which goes back to late colonial Bali, has encouraged Balinese to develop what to anthropologists appears a rather narrow concept of culture (*kebudayaan*, Ind.), consisting solely of these artistic and material productions. While many performances are part of everyday life and would be enacted whether or not tourists were present, others are specifically designed for an exclusive tourist audience, performed in special arenas – often hotels, have no religious significance, and are organised by entrepreneurs, businessmen and state tourist agencies for profit. This has fostered the notion that *kebudayaan* is a kind of object which Balinese possess but over which they no longer have sole control, because it is being shaped partly to suit the interests of the market and foreign investors. Balinese are the authors of this culture and are proud that others are willing to pay to experience it, but by putting it into the market place sole effective control is relinquished. If this culture has to some extent become a commodity, it implies it can be bought and sold, and even that it can be stolen. The purchase of precious agricultural land for tourist development – golf courses, theme parks, statues and hotels – mostly by non-Balinese, who turn a profit by utilising Balinese cultural themes to adorn and advertise their products, creates among Balinese a sense that they are being exploited and robbed, and that their culture is being contaminated. This leads to misgivings about the place of culture in tourism, and dilemmas about how to sustain tourism without debasing and losing Balinese culture.

Whatever the guidebooks say, it is important to guard against the view that in the past Bali was an isolated society enjoying an unchanging tradition free from outside interference, but which is now irretrievably breaking down under the onslaught of external and modernising influences. Bali has always been part of larger changing political and economic structures, and beset by internal conflict throughout its history. Though Bali is regularly described as a timeless and traditional paradise, it is essential to be aware of the very modern reasons – to keep the tourists coming for example – that such partial images are maintained and perpetuated. Once the image of unchanging tradition became influential, it proved hard for Balinese to resist its seductiveness and, as a result, to become concerned about the uncertain future of their society. The irony, as will become evident in later chapters, is that the attempt to maintain an ostensibly unchanging and 'authentic' culture itself creates change. Thus what is in fact novel may be interpreted by Balinese as the rediscovery and reinstatement of something old, and in this way the new becomes 'traditionalised'. As Vickers (1996: 31) notes: 'One can see more "traditional" rites and dances on Bali now than could have been observed in the nineteenth century.' A hundred years of colonialism, war, Indonesian independence and tourism have certainly produced modernising change, but have also generated images of Bali as 'traditional'.

As we shall see, the notion that Balinese possess a unique culture which is exclusively theirs and which needs to be kept intact, authentic and protected emerged during the colonial period. More recent incidents, however, help us recognise just how far this process has gone. Balinese tend to understand their social life as predicated on the central importance of certain kinds of material objects – sacred relics, masks, magically powerful daggers, ritual paraphernalia and other valuables – mostly kept in temples, and because there is occasional theft of such objects it has been common for a few men to keep watch overnight (*makemit*) within the temple precincts. Following some highly publicised temple thefts during the 1990s, and rumours of many more, all allegedly committed by non-Balinese, this form of security has been dramatically extended. Many villages now have a kind of civilian vigilante force (*pacalangan*), members of which gruffly patrol the village, act as guards at temples and ritual events, direct traffic, and so forth.

Temple thefts were always reprehensible and entailed much work – the specialist labour to replace the stolen objects and elaborate rituals to sacralise them – but they did not have wider repercussions. Now, however, they have assumed a more sinister undertone. Temple theft has become symbolic of stealing from, violating, and polluting not just a specific temple site, but Balinese culture as a whole (Santikarma 2001). Previously an isolated event, temple theft has come to be seen as a manifestation of a much wider process – the alienation of Balinese 'culture'. Since it is difficult to blame foreign capitalists or tourists for these thefts, it has been the highly visible, poor and defenceless migrant Indonesians who have borne the brunt of Balinese violence. Given this increasingly exclusivistic notion of their threatened culture, Balinese have begun to draw the boundary between themselves and others much more tightly, their culture and religion becoming an ever more significant marker of ethnic identity and ethnic pride. After the bomb exploded, therefore, it was no surprise when Balinese – and many Westerners living in Bali – predicted that mobs of angry Balinese would soon begin attacking these Muslim outsiders.

In the event the anticipated retribution never happened. Almost immediately after the bombing Balinese politicians, religious and community leaders, and members of the middle class intelligentsia came out to plead that Balinese should not react with communal and ethnic inspired violence. However, such apparently altruistic calls for peace and moderation should not necessarily be taken at face value. Tourists – and with them their tourist dollars – had already embarked on a mass exodus. Kuta, Legian, Sanur, Nusa Dua, Ubud and other tourist areas in south Bali fell quiet as planes left the airport full but arrived empty. Since tourism accounts for about half the island's economy, communal rioting, it was widely agreed, could only make this disastrous economic situation even worse. Such exhortations were clearly motivated by the recognition that a tolerant and peaceful response would facilitate a quick resumption of tourism and the money it earns.

Such a response, however, cannot just have been about vulgar economic interests. If one set of forces has created insecurity concerning the relation between Balinese and their culture, requiring violent retaliation against outsiders seen as the cause of social disorder, another set has painted a picture of Balinese people as deeply religious, tolerant, peaceful, and with a dislike of confrontation. These two images, created and internalised by Balinese and outsiders alike over a long period of time, are both partial. While many Balinese voice concerns over the effects of mass tourism, those off the tourist routes rack their brains to think of ways to bring the tourists in so that they too can enjoy some of the benefits. Thus instead of automatically blaming foreigners for the Kuta bombing, an alternative response for many Balinese was to turn inwards and consider their own culpability. Part of this response meant resorting to forms of action that they would usually use in such circumstances – ritual and the pacification of spirits thought to have engendered the crisis in the first place. And here we see Balinese living up to the images others have been partly responsible for creating. How else should Balinese behave when it is their ritual and religious life that has been put on a pedestal for everyone to admire (Couteau 2003)?

Thus, in direct contrast to those who blamed terrorists and outsiders for this monstrous crime, there were others who began to articulate a rather different discourse, in which they blamed themselves for the tragedy. In setting out ritually to cleanse and purify the bomb site, and indeed the whole of the island, Balinese asked themselves why this terrible catastrophe had chosen to benight them. Events on such a scale – earthquakes, volcanic eruptions, war, plagues of pests – are often explained as the anger of the gods and ancestors who have been neglected or insulted in some way. Even if it was an Islamic terrorist group which exploded the bomb, the perpetrators could be seen as merely the instruments of the unseen supernatural power of Balinese ancestors who wished to punish their living descendants and shock them into an appreciation of what was wrong with their society.

But what had the Balinese done to deserve this? According to Professor Suryani, a noted Balinese psychiatrist, many Balinese had forgotten a fundamental axiom of modern Balinese religious belief, the idea that there should be a harmonious balance between man and god, between man and nature, and between men, a balance known as Tri Hita Karana. Tempted by the tourist economy into becoming ever more greedy and materialistic, they had turned a blind eye to the commodification of their culture, the ecological degradation precipitated by tourism, and the unsavoury behaviour of some visitors. They had thus become responsible for morally unbalancing the cosmos, leaving the gods no alternative but to act as they did. An alternative explanation was that because of the increasing violence in Indonesia, and the lax moral attitudes of the Balinese in their own island, the gods had fled Bali, leaving the area unprotected and thus vulnerable to malign influences. In either case the Balinese had only themselves to blame, and the solution was a return to their religious roots and a thorough overhaul of how the tourist economy is managed. Consequently, many Balinese have argued that Kuta must not be allowed to revert to its previous ways. The bombing has created confusion for many Balinese – some blame outsiders, some blame themselves. Whoever was responsible, there is no doubt that the resulting upheaval has created massive unemployment, and led to a turning inwards as people cope with economic hardship and try to come to terms with a shocking event.

This picture of Balinese as both violent and tolerant, kind-hearted and cruel, religious and materialistic, inclusive and exclusive, is thus far more complex and ambivalent than the usual glossy images found in the guidebooks, which for the most part present the Balinese as a peace-loving, spiritually-developed people who assiduously perform their colourful religious ceremonies, make beautiful music, mount vivid dramatic performances, and care lovingly for their famed rice terraces. Almost relentlessly, tourists are told that Bali is the 'last paradise', the 'land of a thousand temples', and that 'every Balinese is an artist'. Such images are myths, and like most myths they tell only a partial truth. Most visitors to Bali witness a cremation or a temple ceremony, and hear a *gamelan* orchestra or see the *legong* dance. But this aspect of Bali, without doubt alluring and seductive, belies the strains and tensions in the underbelly of Balinese society.

The truth is that Balinese are often in dispute with their relatives and neighbours, sometimes violently; men may beat their wives and squander money at cockfights; priests may be accused of exploiting their clients; rising expectations cannot be satisfied by the economy, thus leaving many young people unemployed, frustrated and marginalised; the commodification of Balinese culture leads to accusations of immorality and cosmic imbalance; and the smiling face is often a mask hiding turbulent emotions (Wikan 1990). If the guidebooks portray Bali as peaceful, harmonious and highly religious, this is only achieved by ignoring the riots which swept Bali in 1999 when Megawati Sukarnoputri was denied the presidency of the republic after winning most votes in the national elections, and by passing over in silence the slaughter of some 50,000 Balinese alleged to be communists during 1965–6 after the downfall of Sukarno and the rise to power of General Suharto, these killings themselves being the culmination of years of chaos and violence across Indonesia. Such a romantic myth is only possible if Bali's war-torn precolonial history is ignored.

The image of Bali as a paradise, and of the Balinese as practising a colourful version of Hinduism in a sea of austere Islam, was generated in colonial times. It supplanted other earlier and different images, both theirs and ours (Vickers 1989), so it is important to explore how such a representation was produced, and what effects it has had. It is clear that portraying Bali in this particular way has enhanced its appeal as a destination for mass tourism. What is less clear are the myriad ways in which the Balinese have responded to such an image (Picard 1996), and to the waves of outside influence breaking on the shores of their island society. Conceiving of themselves more and more as Hindus, and thus distancing themselves increasingly from Muslims, has triggered struggles of ethnic identity leading to communal tensions. It has involved constructions of 'otherness' which have implications for cultural purity and boundedness at a time when anthropologists are at pains to point out that the notions of 'a people' and 'a culture' are to a large extent figments of the imagination. The progressive Hinduising of Bali over the last hundred years has produced massive and complex religious change, which has had ramifications throughout Balinese society. Moreover, if the advent of mass tourism has produced new ideas about what culture is for the Balinese and how it may be marketed, advertised and displayed, it has also had an enormous economic, political and environmental impact as the infrastructure creaks under the weight of traffic, water runs out, agricultural land is converted to hotels, art shops, golf courses and theme parks, plastic rubbish overlays lush countryside, inequality grows, and resistance movements targetting Jakartan and other foreign capitalists get into gear. The complex relationship between tourism, economy, culture and religion has become one of Bali's most fascinating issues.

An interesting phenomenon emerged in connection with the many rituals which were performed subsequent to the Kuta bombing. Because the bomb killed many foreign tourists, especially from Australia, the relatives of the deceased were invited to attend the ceremonies. These rituals were of various kinds. Some were dedicated to the gods and ancestors to ask for peace, forgiveness, safety and prosperity. They were what might be called ecumenical, in the sense that Balinese Hindus asked those of other religious persuasions, primarily Muslims and Christians but also Jews, Buddhists and others, to pray together to help both the worshippers and the souls of the dead. These ceremonies of common worship served several purposes – healing the psychological wounds of the bereaved, re-establishing trusting relationships with westerners in the hope that tourism could be renewed more quickly, and demonstrating the tolerance of the Balinese towards those thought to be the perpetrators so that communal rioting and violence could be avoided. These were ceremonies in which friends and relatives could participate, and which they could appreciate and understand. Other rituals however, purificatory ceremonies known in Bali as *caru*, involved the sacrifice of animals – chickens, ducks, dogs, goats and even water buffalo. Some of these animals had their throats slit – the usual manner of sacrificial slaughter – and were then thrown in the sea. Others were turned into disembowelled carcasses; a live water buffalo with its legs bound was heaved into the ocean to drown. The bereaved and other visitors were invited to these ceremonies, but apparently were not given much explanation as to what was going on, and it has been reported that some were shocked and disgusted that innocent animal life could be sacrificed to atone for human death. While the Balinese probably understood what was going on, it must have been hard for the outsiders to come to terms with such apparent barbarism.

Reflections on these purificatory rituals were aired in an online discussion forum, The Bali Arts and Cultural Newsletter (see Darling 2003 for a summary). An initial message from Garrett Kam suggested that the bombing could be a springboard for further reform of ritual practice in Bali. Some Balinese already find the sacrificial slaughter of animals distasteful, believing it to be morally wrong and an affront to the deity, while others complain that such rituals are too expensive. Kam reported that an influential Brahmana priest, concerned about the killing of endangered turtles for ritual purposes, had proposed that it would be appropriate to use a drawing as a substitute for the real turtle. Similar solutions were suggested – using a part of an animal, its fur for example, to represent the whole animal. Such alternative procedures are endorsed by Balinese who have joined new Hindu movements of a devotionalist nature – Sathya Sai Baba, for example – which denounce cockfighting and the ritual slaughter of animals, and encourage vegetarianism. There followed further messages for and against the initial suggestion, and the discussion turned into one about cultural relativism. The debate was ended by the only contribution from a Balinese, Dégung Santikarma, who noted that the 'ritual in Kuta may have been watched by an international audience, but it was not staged for them ... Balinese are very pragmatic – they want their rituals to work. And most Balinese still think that demons prefer blood to pictures.'

This may seem an arcane issue, but such an ethicised reworking of Balinese religious ideas has provoked debates whose significance is central to many aspects of religious and political change in Bali. I shall discuss the issue of animal sacrifice in more detail in Chapter 4; for now all I need say is that the argument about the ritual use of animals is part of a broader and continuing debate about the efficacy of ritual action. One of the most significant aspects of religious reform in Bali concerns the belief, held by a minority, that most of the time, money and materials consumed by ritual are wasted, since ritual cannot accomplish what many think it can. What really influences the fate of the soul after death, this minority believes, is not the expensive paraphernalia and large scale offerings of cremation, most of which are destroyed, but the right conduct of the person while they are still alive. Such reform amounts to what might be seen as a 'protestantisation' of Balinese Hindu religion, a belief in the importance of ethical conduct and inner spirituality rather than in external ritual and magical action, a trend also seen in other parts of the world (for example Gombrich and Obeyesekere 1988 on Protestant Buddhism).

Religious reform, stimulated during the colonial period and later by the incorporation of Bali into the mainly Muslim Republic of Indonesia in 1950, also involved attempts to change the hierarchical nature of Balinese social organisation. In the nineteenth century Balinese society was organised around nine small kingdoms. At the head of each kingdom were regional overlords (*raja*, or kings), who controlled large tracts of land cultivated by their subjects, who also served as soldiers and provided labour for ritual spectacles and building projects. Kings and their kin, nobles of lesser rank, and court priests all had prestigious titles – as a category they were 'insiders' (*anak jero*). Peasants or commoners were collectively 'outsiders' (*anak jaba*) – subjects, servants and slaves. Comprising nine-tenths or more of the population, commoners had to show deference to their lords through forms of bodily posture, linguistic etiquette, and in many other ways. Among the *anak jero* this structure was reminiscent of the caste societies of India, in that the hierarchically ranked descent groups conceived of themselves as exclusive, and entitled to ritual and other privileges. The higher the rank the more exclusive they considered themselves to be, and tended to marry their women endogamously or hypergamously (that is, to men of even higher status). While it was always possible for commoners of ability to rise to positions of influence in the noble courts, the system was largely based on ascription by birth rather than on achievement through talent, wisdom and hard work.

During the colonial period, however, some commoners, especially in north Bali, the seat of colonial rule, became administrators in the colonial bureaucracy, teachers, and other kinds of functionary. Some were educated in Dutch schools, where they began to imbibe European notions of democracy, equality before the law, and advancement by merit – even if the Dutch, while expounding these principles, did not necessarily practise them in relation to their colonial subjects. Similar ideas could be found in Balinese religious literature – books of inscribed palm leaves – and in the sacred books of India such as the *Bhagavadgita*. Here, for example, it is argued that a Brahmana is not someone who happens to be born of Brahmana parents, but anyone who lives up to Brahmana ideals. Armed with such notions, these commoners began to articulate a challenge to the ruling elite. Status and privilege, they argued, should be founded on wisdom, talent, ability and achievement, rather than on the status of one's parents. This challenge to hierarchy was intimately related to religion, since commoners argued that the traditional caste hierarchy was unfair and an obstacle to progress in a modern society, and abolishing it would help to invigorate religion (*agama*) regardless of status and hierarchy. The elite insisted that the traditional and hierarchical social order, from which they derived their privileges, was inescapably bound up with religion. It was in the context of this debate that commoners began to claim that many ceremonies placed too much emphasis on status-sensitive offerings and ritual equipment, and on blindly following the high priests, all of which served to legitimate and justify the hierarchy. They argued that Balinese should aspire to a religion more like Islam and Christianity – religions which stress a relationship with a high god, a set of revealed ethical teachings, and an ideal of social progress. This debate continued throughout the twentieth century, and is still evolving.

This concludes the tally of main themes around which this book is organised:

- the colonial period and its long-term legacy;
- the reform of ritual and the transformation of religion and identity formation;
- the contemporary dynamics of hierarchical social relations and the challenge to caste; and
- tourism in relation to the commodification and objectification of culture.

Village, house and caste

The small tropical island of Bali lies in the middle of the Indonesian archipelago at about 8° south. A ridge of active volcanic mountains, stretching from Mount Batukaru in the west to Mount Agung in the east, separates the narrow coastal strip on the northern edge of the island from what is sometimes referred to as the heartland of Balinese society on its southern side. Periodically these volcanoes erupt in devastating fashion – Mount Batur exploded in 1917 and Mount Agung in 1963. The Agung eruption killed over two thousand people and took thousands of hectares of paddy land out of cultivation, causing widespread poverty. From the south coast, where Denpasar, Bali's present day capital, and the main tourist areas of Kuta, Sanur and Nusa Dua are situated, the land is relatively flat for a few miles, then begins to rise steadily. Twenty kilometres north of Denpasar is the village of Ubud, the inland centre of cultural tourism, especially for young back-packers. From here the land begins to rise more steeply. Roads wind along narrow ridges separated by deep valleys, making east–west travel difficult but creating the wonderful panoramas of terraced wet-rice cultivation for which Bali is justly famous. Above 700 metres, irrigation – from rivers fed by mountain lakes – becomes increasingly difficult, and wet rice farming gives way to gardens in which many varieties of fruit and vegetables are grown. To the north of the mountains is a precipitous drop to the port town and old colonial capital of Singaraja.

Bali is very densely populated, particularly in the southern plains – its population nudges three million. The vast majority of Balinese now call themselves Hindus, though there is a significant minority of Balinese Muslims in the north, and small scattered communities of Balinese Christians. In a state which is overwhelmingly Muslim – Indonesia is the most populous Muslim country in the world – this allegiance to Hinduism has created chronic uncertainty and insecurity. Many economic migrants, mostly Muslims, come to Bali from other islands in search of work, mostly in the tourist and construction sectors.

Most Balinese still live in nucleated villages (*désa*) ranging in size from 500 to 5,000 people, surrounded by paddyfields and coconut groves. Fifty years ago most Balinese were farmers, working their own land or that of others, and growing two crops of rice each year on well irrigated soil. Since the beginning of mass tourism in the early 1970s, however, economic activities have greatly diversified. Many Balinese now work in the tourist sector as hotel and restaurant employees, in the many businesses – transport, construction, commerce, professions, health and leisure – which support tourism, in state bureaucracies, the armed forces and manufacturing. While farming is still practised by many, it is now less lucrative and carries less prestige. In many villages in central south Bali those who own land – even plots as small as half a hectare – rarely now work it themselves, preferring to do other jobs. Many work in the tourist and associated sectors, while others are full-time woodcarvers, silversmiths, painters and stone sculptors, creating an array of art objects which are sold to tourists and to foreign dealers who ship them all over the world.

In order to describe Balinese villages and houses, we need to consider the cosmological principles governing the value of different kinds of space. Things which are above are superior to and purer than things which are below. Balinese deities, very pure beings, are imagined as being above the human realm with their abodes in the mountains. Things which are polluted, such as the remains of ritual offerings, are thrown into rivers to be carried to the sea, which is the great absorber of pollution. Consequently the most important axis for Balinese is that which connects 'towards the mountains' (*kaja*) and 'towards the sea' (*kelod*). Within the human realm – villages, houses and bodies – above and upstream are therefore purer than below and downstream. This leads to a great many rules concerning the placing of objects. When sleeping, the head should be oriented to *kaja*. Drying clothes should be arranged so that headgear and blouses are hung above trousers, skirts and sarongs, while underwear should be placed on the ground. Offerings to deities are placed in high altars, whereas those to low spirits are laid out on the floor. Corpses are impure and should be buried beneath the ground, and graveyards are usually sited at the downstream end of a village, while within graveyards higher status people are buried upstream of those of lower status. With one exception – meetings of village associations – in social gatherings Balinese arrange themselves so that people of lower caste are not physically above those of higher caste. In the precolonial period inferiors had to grovel at the feet of superiors and not look at their faces; very severe punishment could ensue should a commoner touch the head of a prince.

Kaja–kelod is augmented by an east (*kangin*) and west (*kauh*) axis, which is also hierarchical though in less dramatic fashion. East and sunrise are linked to beginnings, and the path of the sun through the sky is metaphorically associated with the passage of life. One Balinese word for 'afternoon', *lingsir*, also means 'old people'. Cremations should be carried out after midday and burials at dusk, and when a corpse is washed prior to burial its head should be propped up to face west. The first ploughing of fields, planting rice and transplanting seedlings are activities ideally carried out at sunrise.

The combination of these two dimensions provides a topographical rather than a cardinal grid, because while *kaja* aligns with 'north' in south Bali it aligns with 'south' in north Bali. This grid is used extensively by Balinese, who rarely use the terms for left and right. Instead they speak about 'going to the east', objects being 'further north', and things being 'in the west'. Within this grid the most sacred direction is *kaja-kangin*, since it combines the values of mountain peak and east, while the least sacred is *kelod-kauh*. This fourfold grid, with a centre (*puseh* or 'navel'), also provides a mandala for the laying out of offerings in a great many rituals. This four-around-the-centre scheme can be augmented by the incorporation of the four intermediate directions (*kaja-kangin*, *kelod-kauh*, etc) to produce an eight-around-the-centre model which has the name *nawa sangga*, and which is the template for offerings in larger and more complex rituals (Fig. 1.1).

Balinese live in agnatically related, extended families occupying large, walled compounds which comprise a houseyard temple (*sanggah*), sleeping quarters, open pavilions, kitchens, granaries, back garden, pigsties and chicken coops. These buildings are laid out according to the same cosmological rules, which dictate that the most sacred structure (the temple) occupies the *kaja-kangin* space, whilst the least sacred buildings (kitchen and pigsties) are placed *kelod-kauh*. Other ritually important buildings, such as the *balé dangin* and the *metén*, occupy intermediate areas (Fig. 1.2, and Howe 1983). A household shares a kitchen if it comprises only parents and unmarried children. Daughters usually marry out of the compound, while sons bring wives in. Once a household comprises more than one nuclear family, agricultural land may be divided so that father and married son each have their own share, an event which triggers the building of a second granary to store the divided product. Additionally, a second kitchen is usually built so that the two nuclear families may cook independently. Further division and separation may occur when other children marry and bring in new wives. When people die or divorce buildings may lose their function and be converted to other uses.

The term *désa* (village) denotes the consecrated ground (*tanah désa*) on which residential houses, village temples, communal meeting pavilions and markets are built. The authority over this territory ultimately lies with the village's ancestral founders, now converted into deities worshipped in the village temples. There is

kaja-kauh	kaja black Wishnu	kaja-kangin
kauh yellow Mahadéwa	puseh multicoloured Siwa	kangin white Iswara
kelod-kauh	kelod red Brahma	kelod-kangin

Fig. 1.1 The *nawa sangga*

also an association (*krama désa*) which is composed of the senior married couple from each compound built on village land. In many villages this association meets regularly, and is responsible primarily for the maintenance of village temples and the performance of ceremonies held in them. Villagers are also members of another very important association known as the *banjar* ('hamlet'). The members (*krama banjar*) comprise all the married couples living in the houses belonging to that *banjar*. Like the *krama désa*, the *krama banjar* meets regularly and is responsible for a wide range of secular and religious activities. It is particularly important as the group which organises the cremation rituals of its members. In many cases a village's population is divided into several *banjar*, which may or may not be territorially discrete (Howe 1989b, Guermonprez 1990).

Like houseyards, the spatial layout of villages also conforms to cosmological rules, but there are many exceptions, sometimes quite startling ones. Ideally, the centre of the village should be formed by a crossroads with the 'palace' (*puri*) of the ruling prince at its north-east (*kaja-kangin*) corner, and a market (*pasar*), meeting pavilion (*wantilan*), and field (*alun-alun*) to the south and west of the crossroads. There is often a large shade-providing banyan tree (*waringin*), a temple, and often the home (*gria*) of a Brahmana priest (*pedanda*) adjacent to this area (Fig. 1.3, and Schulte Nordholt 1991a: 146). There are in fact few villages in which all these buildings are found in their 'correct' places, and in modern Bali it is often difficult to discern where the old crossroads used to be, given that village growth and development often proceeds in a haphazard manner. Certain other

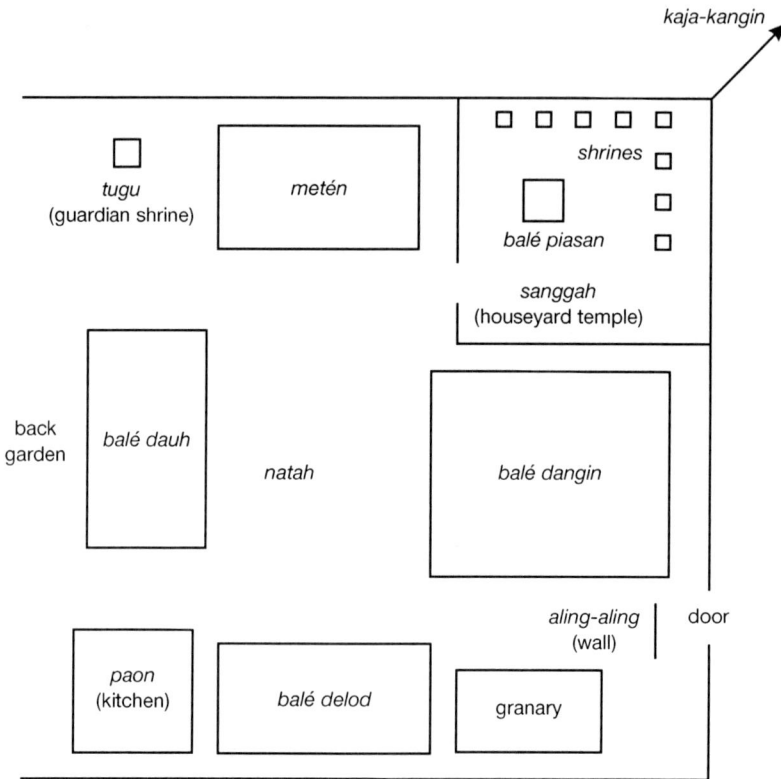

Fig. 1.2 The layout of buildings in a Balinese walled compound

temples are often thought to be obligatory (Swellengrebel 1960; Geertz 1959). These are the *pura puseh*, dedicated to the village founders and located at the upstream (*luan*) end of the village, the *pura balé agung* located in the centre, and the *pura dalem*, the temple dedicated to the goddess of death and situated near the graveyard, at the downstream end (*tebén*). There are, however, villages in which the cemetery and *pura dalem* are at the opposite end of the village from where they ideally should be, and many villages do not have a full complement of supposedly obligatory temples.

Further details of spatial arrangement will be discussed later, but at this point it would be useful to look at Balinese hierarchy and its caste system (*sistim kasta* or *catur warna* – the latter meaning 'the four *warna*'). Louis Dumont (1980) has written extensively about the Indian caste system, and there can be little doubt that the Balinese version was influenced by ideas transported from India to Indonesia millennia ago (van Leur 1955). The so-called *varna* system of Indian hierarchy, combining the four-fold classification of people (Brahmin, Kshatriya, Vaishya and Sudra) with associated occupations (priest, ruler, merchant, servant), is found in Bali, where it is known as *warna*, *wangsa* or *bangsa*, the corresponding Balinese terms being Brahmana, Satria, Wésia and Sudra. While this classification

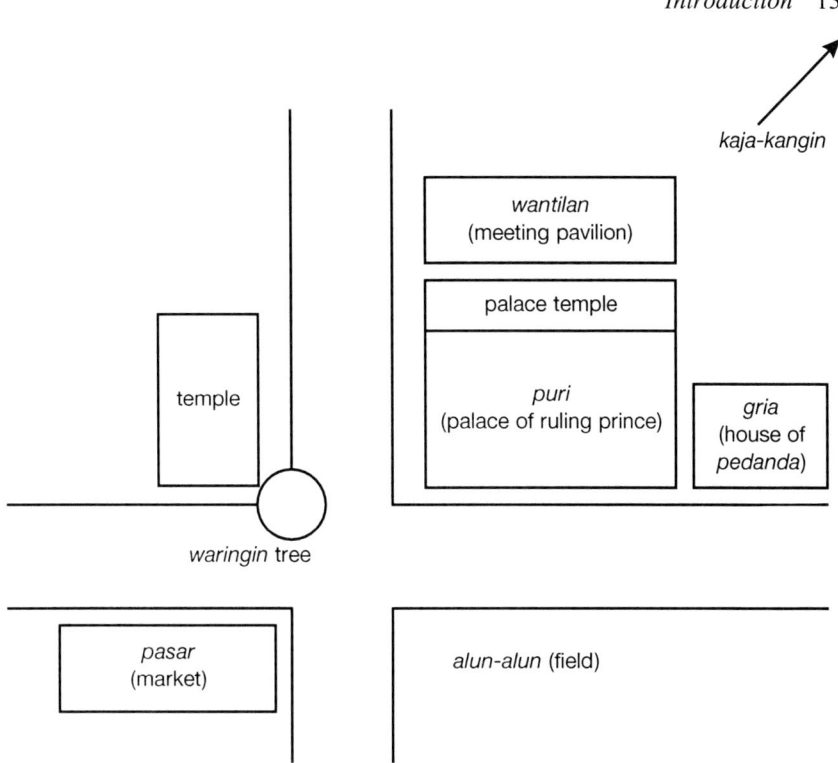

Fig. 1.3 Crossroads and buildings at the centre of a Balinese village

into general categories of people is significant in Bali, what is more important is the ranking of the patrilineal descent groups, which are the smaller local components of the encompassing *warna* categories. I use the term 'hierarchy' to describe the linear ranking of these smaller component groups, since it reflects contemporary Balinese usage; it is rather different from Dumont's more theoretical and complex definition of hierarchy.

Balinese make a distinction between the top three categories of the *warna*, collectively designated as Triwangsa and accounting for less than ten per cent of the population, and the rest of the population, who since colonial times have been designated Sudra. These terms are not in fact much used by Balinese themselves, except when explaining the system to non-Balinese. Balinese prefer the terms *anak jero* ('insiders') and *anak jaba* ('outsiders'). In this book, following Geertz and Geertz (1975), I often refer to the two categories as 'gentry' and 'commoners'.

The Brahmana category is further divided into five groups, supposedly descended from the five different wives of the first – Javanese – ancestor of Brahmana, but distinctions of status between these groups are not very significant. In the Satria and Wésia categories there are, however, numerous groups which actively vie with each other over relative ranking. Within the large Sudra category there are also many groups, but they are not overly concerned with ranking among themselves. Nonetheless, because some of these Sudra groups held hereditary offices and privileges in pre-colonial times, which were removed when the Dutch reorganised the system (see Chapter 2), in post-colonial Bali such groups sometimes attempt to reactivate dormant claims to gentry status. Thus the most important conflicts concerning relative ranking usually revolve around commoners trying to elevate themselves to gentry levels, rivalry among Satria and Wésia groups, and ambiguity over the relative ranking of Brahmana and the highest Satria groups, descendants of pre-colonial rulers, both of whom claim pre-eminence (Howe 2001: Ch. 6).

The hierarchy is perpetuated in various ways. Children of gentry are themselves gentry, and by and large tend to marry other gentry, so that the category as a whole remains fairly exclusive. Gentry men may, and often do, marry commoner women; these women become elevated by the adoption of an honorific such as 'jero', designating their new insider status. The children of such mixed marriages take the status of their father. If, however, gentry women oppose the wishes of their parents and marry commoner men, they are decasted (*nyerod*) to the level of their husband, lose their original gentry title, and become commoners. In the past a liaison between a Brahmana or other very high caste woman with a commoner man could be punished by death; today her parents are likely to disown her by referring to her as having been 'thrown away' (*makutang*). It is quite possible that a reconciliation will occur later, with the appearance of children and a lessening of the parents' disapproval. In economic terms the highest gentry in a village, often the descendants of pre-colonial ruling families, usually enjoy much greater landed wealth than commoners, and in contemporary Bali have used this wealth to finance a range of enterprises which keep them wealthy (Geertz 1963b). Politically this is also the case, with these gentry often holding the major village political offices and being disproportionately represented in the higher echelons of the modern administrative bureaucracy which governs the island. While there are many exceptions, the pre-colonial ruling elite has reproduced itself as a modern political and economic elite, which helps to maintain and reinforce its pre-eminent status. It is thus not surprising that lower groups often attempt to elevate their position in the hierarchy through converting newfound wealth into ritual status, an issue discussed in Chapter 6.

Finally, gentry keep themselves exclusive through the temple system. Each descent group has a temple dedicated to its founding and now deified ancestors, which is called its *kawitan*, or 'origin temple'. Unless they marry into this group, and hence take leave of their own ancestral origin temple, Balinese of higher caste are not allowed to worship in the temples of lower castes. This means that each title group has its own ancestors, and thus its own gods, who are exclusively worshipped by their descendants, and who are superior to the gods of lower castes. The concept of origin is enormously important to Balinese because it connects them to their ancestors who are the ultimate source of life, prosperity and safety. If Balinese do not know their origin point or have discovered – through a spirit medium's revelation, for example – that they are worshipping at the wrong one, they may go to great lengths to find their true origin (Howe 2001: 50–56). Moreover, ancestors are jealous and demanding and, if they cannot establish relations with their descendants through the proper channel, the *kawitan* temple, they resort to direct and dangerous methods such as afflicting them with misfortune and illness, events which then trigger a visit to a spirit medium to find out why they are suffering. By anchoring Balinese in the past the *kawitan* establishes their place in the present, and thus the proper forms of relationship they have with others of different status. Attempts to raise status are thus often prosecuted by the 'discovery' of genealogical texts (*prasasti*), which may have been fabricated, and which claim that the group in question has an origin status which is hierarchically superior to that which it presently enjoys. During the last two hundred years other kinds of genealogical chronicles (*babad*) have been composed by many different descent groups, gentry and commoner alike, for a variety of reasons – some to validate their origins and justify their current high status, others to claim that even if they are considered commoners they nonetheless have origins as illustrious as Brahmana.

High concentrations of gentry, sometimes reaching twenty-five per cent, are usually only encountered in the large villages of the southern plains, particularly those that were the seat of minor princes in pre-colonial Bali. In villages above the line of irrigation gentry are often completely absent, allowing ideologies of equality to develop (Howe 2001: Ch. 4). In villages with large populations of gentry, hierarchical relations are very important, and become visible during life-crisis rituals such as cremations, in temple ceremonies, and in social gatherings and rituals where members of different status interact. For example, in rituals many offerings contain food which can be consumed after the ceremony has finished. However, hierarchically superior Balinese refuse to consume the food of offerings from a ceremony carried out by, or dedicated to, an inferior, on pain of being decasted to the level of the latter, though the reverse is of course allowable. Nonetheless, it should not be assumed from the many rules by which Balinese are separated that interpersonal behaviour between members of different groups is always difficult and strained. In contemporary Bali, though linguistic, ritual and other caste-linked forms of distinction are preserved in village life, relations between neighbours and friends of different status are often informal, co-operative and friendly (see Chapter 3).

Hierarchical relations thus prevail in many domains of Balinese life, though they are rarely unambiguous and are still regularly contested in a variety of ways. Hierarchy dictates that within the same title group men are superior to women, husbands to wives, and elder siblings to younger ones. It dictates where buildings are located and what their purposes are; influences how people interact and speak and how they spatially position themselves; and determines how rituals are conducted and what kind of offerings and structures are appropriate. The vertical axis of the body and relative head height encode relations of hierarchy to a remarkable extent. In the past subjects bowed before the ruler, averted their gaze, and drooped their heads.

> Kings were referred to as Sang Prabu, the "Head," their lords and retainers, as their *kaki tangan* (Indonesian), "feet and hands." Rulers or priests could also

be referred to as *sesuunan*, "borne on the head," like the seats of deities when carried in processions.

(Wiener 1995: 154)

Purified ancestors are *leluur* (from *duur*, 'above') or *lelangitan* (from *langit*, 'sky'). The most dramatic form of subordination is to juxtapose one's feet with another's head. This occurs in various contexts – when a Brahmana priest touches the head of his pupil with his foot during the latter's consecration; in the gesture of *masulub*, when juniors walk under the raised corpse of their deceased senior relative; and in the act of *ngenjékin*, when a person treads on the head of another prostrated on the floor to enforce subordination, which usually occurs only between close kin.

There is also a related scheme of classification concerning centre and periphery. The gods live in the centre of the island, so that what is highest is also most central. Ritual offerings are often oriented above and below, but when in the horizontal plane they are placed, as we have seen, according to the four-around-the-centre schema, with the centre symbolising unity and totality. Away from the centre of the island *kaja* assumes a hierarchical relationship with *kelod*, as above to below, but on the mountain top *kaja* becomes centre and *kelod* the periphery, so that hierarchy – above, below – and centrality – inside, outside – are different but related schemas. The king's palace is ideally at the centre of the capital town, itself ideally at the centre of the realm, and the actions of the ruler determine the condition of the realm, symbolising an identity between them (Schrieke 1957; Anderson 1972; Geertz 1980). Where gentry are numerous they usually occupy the centre of the village by arranging their house compounds around the *puri*, the house of the pre-colonial prince, while commoner houses are distributed beyond them. In this way village spatial organisation articulates cosmological schemes of centre and periphery and ideological schemes of superiority and inferiority.

Centrality is also configured in terms of the superior inside and the inferior outside. The architectural design of temples and houses demonstrates these distinctions. The innermost courtyard of a temple, physically a step above the others, is the *jeroan* (the 'inside'). The middle courtyard is the *jaba tengah* (the 'middle outside'), and the outer courtyard, if there is one, is simply the *jaban* ('outside'). Palaces are similar – the innermost area is again the *jeroan*, and is the most secluded and intimate region where the king ate and slept. The king of Klungkung, the highest ranking king in pre-colonial Bali, was the Dalem ('inside'), the 'ultimate insider' (Wiener 1995: 153). As we have already seen, gentry are the *jero*, the 'insiders', who live in houses called *jeroan*, even though these houses are virtually indistinguishable from the houses – *umah* – of commoners, who are *jaba* ('outsiders').

As a result of economic growth many Balinese now live in towns and in the cities of Denpasar and Singaraja. Because the *banjar* is such an important institution, much of the population of these towns is also divided into *banjar*, which function in much the same way as their village counterparts. Those who have permanent homes in towns construct them according to the same principles as village houses, with houseyard temples in the most auspicious space. Many other Balinese have their main home in a village but live most of the time in the town to be close to their place of work. In this case they may build functional homes which only have a simple shrine which connects ritually with their houseyard temple in their natal village, and to which they return frequently for family ceremonies. The attraction of the home village is still very strong for most Balinese, since it is construed as a place of safety. When they are ill, for example, Balinese often go home to recover and recuperate, since it is a common belief that the rice grown on village land and the water from its springs have particular health-giving properties.

In recent years there has been very rapid urbanisation in parts of Bali, especially along the south coast. What were once villages separated by agricultural land are now linked in a largely unplanned sprawl of shops, hotels, businesses, factories and administrative buildings, creating massive problems for a creaking infrastructure. Road and telephone networks, waste disposal, water supplies and other essential services are all working at or above their limits. Water is a particularly severe problem, with many areas, inland as well as on the coast, suffering water shortages on a daily basis in the dry season. It is estimated that within a few years groundwater supplies will be damaged by the intrusion of seawater as far as five miles inland, and surface water from the mountain lakes and from rain will be insufficient to meet demand (Suasta 2001).

Even before the Bali bomb of 2002, and the SARS scare and Iraq war of 2003, the concern in the minds of many Balinese was whether tourism was sustainable. The upmarket end of tourist development is funded by Jakartan and foreign capitalists who export the profits and who seem to show little anxiety about the long term effects of resource depletion and inadequate infrastructure. Although the new era of openness and democratic politics in Indonesia has triggered increasingly vigorous protest from many sections of the Balinese population, the politics of tourism and environmental control (Chapter 7) is complex and its trajectories uncertain (Warren 1998, Suasta and Connor 1999).

2 Colonialism, caste and the beginnings of tourism

Colonial beginnings

There were to be no plantations or factories in Bali, indeed virtually no commercial exploitation at all, certainly not the kind that occurred in Dutch-colonised Java (Geertz 1963a), northern Sumatra (Stoler 1985), and the Spice Islands (Ricklefs 1981). In fact, the main reason for Bali's incorporation into the Dutch colonial empire was more strategic than economic. To protect and consolidate Dutch interests in Java against interference from the English after the Napoleonic wars, when Java was governed temporarily by Sir Thomas Stamford Raffles (later to found Singapore) the Dutch felt it expedient to control Bali, situated a few miles east of the larger island. Economics played a part too, but only insofar as the Dutch wanted to stop Balinese piracy and the plundering of shipwrecks. The colonial project they set in motion in Bali – what came to be called by the Dutch '*Baliseering*' or the 'Balinisation of Bali' – amounted to a reconstitution of what the Dutch thought Balinese society must once have been. This is a strange notion, and I shall try to explain the colonial thinking behind it.

Although the Dutch had been active in the archipelago since the seventeenth century, there had been only intermittent and casual contact with Bali. When the island's strategic importance was reassessed, however, the colonial government persuaded some of Bali's regional lords to sign treaties recognising Dutch colonial authority, although internal sovereignty remained with the Balinese. These treaties also included agreements to end the plundering of shipwrecks. Subsequently, the continuation of this practice in defiance of the treaties provided a pretext for invading the north of the island (Vickers 1989: 26–9). It took three 'punitive' expeditions in the 1840s (Hanna 1976: 41), with much loss of Balinese lives, to pacify the area. In 1906, under a similar pretext, the Dutch invaded the southern kingdom of Badung, and in 1908 that of Klungkung in east Bali. The conflicts in north Bali can be seen as uncomplicated wars, since Balinese aggressively fought the Dutch military. However, those in south Bali were radically different. When the Dutch marched on the palace of Badung, situated in what is now Denpasar, they were met outside by the raja, his priests, nobles, kin and servants, indeed the entire court, all dressed in their finery and carrying lances and daggers. At first they walked in procession towards the Dutch, and then ran at them. When the

Dutch opened fire the Balinese, in a frenzy, began to kill themselves, each other, and any Dutchmen they encountered. This appalling sacrifice was repeated two years later at the court of Klungkung. The Balinese term for this is *puputan*, 'the end' (Wiener 1995).

News of these horrific events brought protests in Holland, and became part of the reason for a greater commitment to the new 'ethical policy' officially adopted by the Dutch in 1901, a central theme of which was a moral obligation to govern the Indies in the interests of its subject peoples (Ricklefs 1981: 143). As far as Bali was concerned this meant two things – reforming Bali in the cause of peace and order (*rust en orde*), and studying and preserving its culture. These two aims may appear incompatible, but there was a peculiar twist to the notion of preservation. Since colonial thinking diagnosed Balinese culture as having degenerated, what they meant by preservation 'was not so much preserving the culture as they found it, as restoring it to what they thought was its original integrity' (Picard 1996: 21). As Picard explains, the objective was to teach the Balinese 'how to be authentically Balinese' by making them aware of the wonderful richness of their language, literature and traditional arts, and simultaneously by preventing 'any improper expressions of modernism' (1996: 21). This preservation policy allowed the Dutch to present Bali as a showcase of enlightened colonial rule, on the grounds that they were protecting Balinese culture. Simultaneously, however, it also gave them the opportunity to reform Balinese political organisation, since in order to revitalise this culture they had to remove certain political obstacles. One of these was the Balinese rulers, since they were construed as oriental despots whose rule had suffocated real Balinese culture. The process of Balinisation also retrospectively justified the *puputan* atrocities, because in removing the rulers a wonderful and unique culture could be regenerated.

Balinisation had its problems, however. In trying to restore Bali to what the Dutch imagined it should be, their policy came up against not just those modernisms which had already appeared, but also against those Balinese who actually wanted to be modern. Bali was a dynamic society embedded in a wider civilisation, and was changing all the time (Vickers 1989). Balinese wanted education, they wanted to explore new ideas, exploit new economic opportunities, and develop new forms in dance, painting and literature (Vickers 1996). Some wanted to abolish the caste system because it was outmoded and feudal. All this was dangerous to Dutch control because such demands were often the first indications of nationalist movements and calls for self-government. Forcing the Balinese to be more Balinese than they were, to keep them 'properly Balinese' rather than allowing them to engage actively with the modern world, had the effect of dampening opposition. Leaving nothing to chance, and to enforce *rust en orde*, they outlawed 'modern' movements and clamped down on dissent. The Balinese had to be taught to be 'Balinese'. They had to dance, paint, and write in traditional style. All their buildings had to be constructed according to ancient Balinese conventions, with no new motifs. They must study Balinese literature and practise all their ceremonies. Nothing must change (Pollmann 1990). Indeed, things which had been 'lost' (in fact discarded and changed) had to be brought back and fostered. While many Balinese wanted to be modern, the Dutch forcibly traditionalised them. Many Balinese recognised this as a policy of conservatism, an attempt to keep Bali static (Pollmann 1990: 15). Promoted as an enlightened colonial policy designed to protect an incomparable culture, it turned out to be an oppressive form of political domination. 'Yes, the temples are beautiful, but the stomachs are empty' said one Balinese; another 'Bali is a paradise. Yes, I answer, but for whom?' (Pollmann 1990: 14, 17).

'Balinisation' raises two further issues. The first is that keeping Balinese in 'their' culture meant keeping them in 'their' subsistence rice economy, and therefore impoverishing them. Geertz makes the more general point that Dutch colonial policy was designed to bring Indonesian products into the modern world, but not its peoples (1963a: 140). The second is that Bali may have been a paradise for the many expatriate artists, writers and musicians from Europe and the United States who lived in Bali during the interwar years, but it was not a paradise for the mass of Balinese. Whether some of these expatriates might be branded as 'sex tourists' is a moot point – certainly some liked to paint nude women and indulge their homosexual inclinations with young boys, practices which Balinese found unacceptable but were powerless to prevent. In the end Dutch patience with these activities ran out, and Roelof Goris in 1938 and Walter Spies in 1939 were arrested and tried for sexual offences with minors (Vickers 1989: 124).

One of the images of Bali that facilitated Balinisation was that the island was seen as a 'living museum' (Picard 1996: 20), a repository of customs once found throughout Java but which had now disappeared. Java once had a developed 'Hindu–Buddhist' culture – witness the spectacular Buddhist monument Borobudur and the Shivaite temple of Prambanan in central Java, both built in the ninth century (Holt 1967) – but the spread of Islam through the Indies after 1300 submerged and in part eradicated it. However, there is a legend pervasive in Bali which claims that this culture came to Bali in the sixteenth century, carried there by Javanese nobles when the kingdom of Majapahit in east Java, the symbol and culmination of that Hindu heritage, succumbed finally to Islam. Subsequently, a nineteenth century colonial image of Bali was constructed which portrayed it not just as the last bastion of Hinduism in the archipelago, and therefore as a barrier to an expansive and aggressive Islam, but also as the preserver of a once glorious Hindu-Javanese past. That Bali could then be interpreted as a contemporary manifestation of what Hindu-Javanese society had previously been meant that the organising principles underlying ancient Javanese society could be reconstructed by reference to what was still visible and functioning in Bali. Conversely, in what was a beautifully circular argument, the analyses and descriptions of village structures in Bali (Korn 1933, Grader 1937) were heavily influenced by the highly conjectural theories of social organisation in ancient Java advanced by W.H. Rassers (1922; King and Wilder 2003: 36).

Being descended from Javanese invaders, the nineteenth century Balinese aristocracy was seen by the Dutch as alien and tyrannical, ruthlessly oppressing the indigenous Balinese people. The latter, by contrast, were portrayed as independent, manly and proud, essentially democratic folk who governed themselves in independent 'village republics' (Korn 1933, Covarrubias 1937). They were really not very different from their pragmatic colonial masters. With its dams, dykes and canals, Bali reminded the Dutch of their homeland, and could thus be seen as 'little Holland' (Boon 1977: 15). Such a perspective justified reform of the caste system so that the autocratic rulers could be reined in. Here we witness European style separation, alien to the Balinese, between politics and culture. By reforming political institutions the Dutch could argue that they were leaving culture alone, even restoring it to what it should be.

But if Bali was occasionally 'little Holland', more frequently it was 'little India'. Even if there were many differences between Bali and India (Howe 1987), important aspects of Bali's religion and social organisation had originally come from there, perhaps via Java, nearly two millennia before, and were still recognisably Hindu. There was, and still is, the division of people into the four great classes of the Indian *varna* scheme. If the Balinese system did not exactly mirror its Indian counterpart, since there was only a tenuous link between caste and occupation, it nevertheless boasted Brahmana high priests who performed the daily worship of Siva, consecrated holy water, and acted as kings' counsellors. The wife of a ruler was expected to perform the Indian sacrifice of *sati* – to immolate herself on her husband's funeral pyre. Higher status groups enjoyed many privileges in ritual, language and under the law, and notions of purity and pollution were reminiscent of those in India.

Consequently, reforming Balinese social and political institutions through 'enlightened' Dutch colonial rule seemed to require the demotion of autocratic rulers and the removal of 'excesses and excrescences that [had] fastened themselves onto [authentic Balinese culture] through the sheer despotism of those in power' (de Bruyn Kops, quoted in Schulte Nordholt 1986: 28). If this could be achieved, it would release the Balinese to follow the customs of their ancient culture. In this way, by interfering with Balinese political organisation, the Dutch could reveal and then protect and foster true Balinese culture and religion.

This put the Dutch in a quandary. The aim of restoring Bali to its pristine state was hampered because colonial policy was being pulled in two different directions. The caste system, with despots occupying the top positions, seemed central to Balinese life. Linked to it was the Hindu religion, viewed as 'the foundation of Balinese society, the guardian of its cultural integrity and the inspiration of its artistic works' (Picard 1996: 20). However, preserving religion and therefore culture meant supporting these despots, and though Dutch sensibilities were offended by the privileges enjoyed by the princes and nobles, they needed them to act as the local representatives and agents of colonial domination, since the Dutch did not have the means to run Bali themselves. In the event colonial policy became a contradictory mix of idealism and pragmatism. While the Dutch outlawed what they considered the most disgusting practices, such as *sati*, slavery and the opium trade, it was decided to 'uphold the caste concept, being the principle foundation of Balinese society' (quoted in Schulte Nordholt 1986: 28).

The reform of Balinese caste

The Dutch believed in 'upholding the caste concept', but what exactly were they going to preserve? The caste system they saw on the ground did not match their expectations of what caste was or should be (Bagus 1969, 1975). What was probably perfectly clear to the Balinese perplexed the Dutch, who, in 'reforming' caste, actually changed it into a much more rigid system than it had been before, leading to a great deal of anger and resentment, and some loss of life.

Social organisation in pre-colonial Bali, as in many other areas of lowland Southeast Asia (Adas 1981; Tambiah 1985), was a fluid hierarchy. Followers – often subordinate kin – depended on their overlords who gave them land, prestige and titles, delegated control to them over commoner subjects and slaves, and provided them with security and booty in time of war. But equally rulers depended on their followers, without whom they were powerless. Lesser ranking nobles were under the nominal authority of a higher ruler, but had their own entourage of followers which provided them with a separate and partially autonomous power base. These patron–client relationships were highly personalised, yet often characterised by distrust, intrigue and competition. They fragmented regularly, and new combinations of alliances emerged. Unreliable or unsuccessful followers faded away and lost titles. Subordinate rulers occasionally became more powerful than their overlords, and claimed autonomy or incited rebellion. Rulers defeated in war lost land and subjects, and were demoted in status or exiled. Men with obscure origins sometimes accumulated followers and resources, converted these into rank and titles and, through war, marriage alliances and other means, established their own little kingdoms in competition with others (Geertz 1980, Schulte Nordholt 1996 Ch. 2).

When the Dutch encountered this fluid and complicated hierarchy they found it difficult to understand. Since it supposedly originated in India, they presumed it to be similar to Indian caste. Influenced by the orientalist scholarship of the time into thinking that Indian caste was an immutable order in which everyone had a fixed position, they concluded that the Balinese system must have broken down and become confused. They were puzzled by the existence of a large number of titled descent groups each claiming precedence over others, who in turn did the same, and by the fact that classifying these groups in terms of the *warna* scheme was controversial. Assuming the system was in disarray, colonial officials set about putting it to rights.

To bring order into the situation colonial officers sought the advice of high priests (*pedanda*) from the Brahmana groups, particularly those in Klungkung, the highest ranking kingdom in Bali. These literate priests were considered the most knowledgeable custodians of Balinese culture. With their help, but also in line with their own ideas of the Indian caste system, the Dutch endeavoured to codify and simplify the titles attaching to descent groups, and to put them in some sort of order. This was of course heavily influenced by Brahmana ideology, since it was essentially these priests who worked out the finer details of 'who could use which title, and what the proper moral duties and ceremonial rights were for each caste' (Vickers 1989: 148).

This is a good example of how colonial practice in Bali enhanced the position of the Brahmana. In the pre-colonial period the relation between kings and high priests was highly ambiguous and contextual, each group claiming to occupy the highest position in the hierarchy, a situation that remains to this day (Howe 2001 Ch. 6). Assuming incorrectly that Brahmins were unequivocally the highest category in India (Parry 1980, Fuller 1984), the Dutch believed this was also true in Bali. Consequently, Brahmana priests played a major role both in explaining Balinese society to the Dutch and, since they were very heavily represented in the new law courts, and in implementing the reforms they themselves recommended. As a result many ordinary Balinese, if not the ruling elite, gradually began to view the Brahmana as superior to all other groups, and thus to validate the Dutch perspective.

The most significant change the Dutch introduced was a clear distinction between the three highest status categories (Brahmana, Satria and Wésia – collectively Triwangsa) and the large residual population who were classified as Sudra despite the many differences between them. The Triwangsa were the nobility, the 'twice-born' (*dwijati*), while the Sudra were the low folk, the 'once-born' (*ekajati*) (Boon 1977: 41). In establishing these categories, the Dutch also prohibited movement between them.

Unsurprisingly, this policy had the opposite effect of what was intended. Instead of bringing order to a confused situation they introduced confusion where, in Balinese minds, none had previously existed. In trying to determine once and for all who had rights to which titles, many Balinese moved quickly to establish themselves as high caste (Triwangsa) before the door was permanently closed on them (Schulte Nordholt 1986: 148). Consequently, the reforms created an arena in which claims to high rank and titles flourished (Vickers 1989: 147), precisely the situation the Dutch were seeking to eliminate. In the past, rulers decided on conflicts about status and titles, but in the new Dutch-imposed system the only route open to aggrieved or opportunistic commoner groups was through newly instituted courts presided over by *pedanda* priests. Many of the cases heard in these courts were brought by commoners attempting to claim gentry titles. Some groups ignored the negative judgements handed down and refused to undertake corvée labour, as a result of which there were occasional violent clashes with the (Balinese) police in which some Balinese were killed (Vickers 1989: 149).

A principal motive for these claims was that in the new system those designated Triwangsa were exempted from performing unpaid labour for the colonial state, while Sudra, whatever their origins and previous positions, were obliged to contribute labour to projects such as the construction of roads, bridges and harbours. Prior to the colonial period many able commoner Balinese, being less likely to be involved in palace intrigues, achieved high administrative positions in noble courts, and had hereditary titles and privileges conferred on them. With the Dutch reforms many of these positions, and thus the associated privileges, disappeared. Those that remained, many fewer in number, were allocated to members of the Triwangsa who were considered to be the natural rulers, an idea inconsistent with the view of the aristocracy as an alien imposition. This interference resulted in a much more marked distinction between gentry and commoner, and the newly instituted barrier between them became harder to cross.

Since the Dutch had neither the manpower nor the expertise to rule the Balinese on their own, they enlisted the traditional elite to rule as their agents. It was the *raja*'s assistants, the *punggawa, perbekel, sedahan* and other gentry officials of the pre-colonial states, who had to coerce the ordinary Balinese peasant to contribute labour and taxes for the colonial regime. The irony of this was that, although the Dutch initiated and enforced the system, its detailed implementation was in the hands of the Balinese who were its local agents, and who could therefore manage it for their own – usually traditional – ambitions. For example, under the new system a lord in Mengwi district managed to complete the building of a royal temple because he now had control over more labour than he had been able to mobilise under the previous system (Schulte Nordholt 1991a: 153). Moreover, as managers of this new and more exploitative system of enforced labour, it was the Balinese who became the targets of sporadic rural unrest, rather than the distant and often invisible Dutch. Protestors were sometimes fired on by the native police force, and tried according to Balinese law. Not surprisingly, little overt anti-Dutch sentiment was expressed, but relations between elites and commoners grew increasingly fractious (Robinson 1995: 69).

Even though the colonial regime did not introduce plantation schemes, which had taken such a toll in Java and elsewhere in the Indies, this was still a harsh and unremitting time. Peasants were worse off under the Dutch than they had been under their own lords. They were required to provide a greater number of days of unpaid labour, and taxation on land, trade and the slaughter of animals increased (Robinson 1995: 54–64). These taxes had to be paid in scarce cash. Since many Balinese were unable to meet the demands they either increased production of cash crops or sold land, often both. In some areas this resulted in numerous transfers of land from small to large farmers (Schulte Nordholt 1988: 273). This increasing inequality was probably one of the main causes of conflict over land reform in the 1950s and 1960s.

It is ironic and disturbing that the image of Bali as an exotic paradise and a land of plenty, in which most people spent their time performing ceremonies, dancing and making music, was being generated during a period when many were mired in deep and growing poverty. As well as colonial oppression, a severe earthquake and volcanic eruption in 1917, the influenza epidemic of 1918, and the world depression of the 1930s all exacerbated the situation. If Balinese commoners seemed happy, assiduous enactors of their 'traditional' culture as Dutch colonial officers liked to present them, it was because there was little else they could do. As part of the colonial policy of 'peace and order' the Dutch ran an elaborate spy network which imposed severe sanctions on Balinese who showed dissent (Pollmann 1990: 21). Beneath the apparent tranquillity of Bali, which later visitors misrecognised as a feature of an easy-going, peaceful Balinese personality, lay the stranglehold of Dutch power.

Images of Bali and the beginnings of tourism

It is simplistic to argue that the Dutch alone created the representation of Bali as an exotic paradise, since similar images of other places – Tahiti and other South Sea Islands for example – had been extant in Europe for a long time, and 'Bali's ecological compactness, its striking relief, and the profusion of visual-spatial symbolism' (Fabian 1983: 135) made the island eminently suitable to being similarly classified. Moreover, the image of exotic Bali competed with other representations of the island. So how did the image of 'exotic Bali' become the favoured one?

Before colonisation, Bali as exotic paradise was not the predominant image. Late eighteenth- and early nineteenth-century European descriptions portrayed Bali as savage and warlike, anything but peaceful and harmonious (see Vickers 1989, on whose work much of the following is based). It was said to be ruled by decadent, opium-smoking, warmongering despots, heavily involved in the Indies slave trade, and in piracy and smuggling. Within Bali there was chronic warfare among the nine little kingdoms. However, during the period that Raffles governed the colony for England (1811–16) he introduced the idea that these despots were foreign invaders, under whose alien rule could be discerned real Balinese society – the autonomous Asian village. Ordinary Balinese were characterised as independent and proud, assimilated by Raffles into the Enlightenment idea of the noble savage, and thus very different from the Javanese who he claimed had become listless, lazy and corrupted. Moreover, Bali's colourful and vibrant Hinduism was contrasted positively with Javanese Islam, portrayed as austere, drab and threatening. This image of independence and defiance did not suit the Dutch when they resumed control of their colony. Trying to trade and make treaties with Balinese rulers, they found them hard to deal with. It is not surprising that the image of the Balinese as wild and deceitful came to the fore, a representation of the islanders which began to play an increasingly important role in decisions to colonise and pacify a people viewed as recalcitrant and unruly.

After the military operations of the 1840s, north Bali was governed by P.L.van Bloemen Waanders. He despaired of bringing order to what he viewed as the chaotic state of the region in which he could see 'not a trace of an ordered administration' and 'a situation contrary to all principles of government' (quoted in Vickers 1989: 32). The blame was heaped onto the 'lawless' Balinese rather than being seen as the outcome of protracted warfare. Two further military expeditions had to be sent from Java to quell revolts in 1858 and 1868. With van Bloemen Waanders the first scholarly accounts of Balinese social life began to appear, though these are heavily inflected by the assumption that the Balinese were not fit to rule themselves, and could only benefit and prosper under benevolent Dutch government. In outlawing slavery and widow burning he thought he was taking the first steps in reducing the tyrannical grip of despotic rulers.

This view of the Balinese as warlike, savage and fierce was seen as a positive contrast with the supine and lethargic Javanese. In the context of Dutch colonial interests this image veered towards one of despotic potentates who governed arbitrarily, their perfidiousness making rational trade and treaties impossible. Yet these same despots were heirs to a glorious Javanese heritage transported to Bali, where an extravagant Hindu culture had blossomed which was now seen as a bulwark against an expanding and threatening Islam. Complicating the situation further was the image of ruthless rulers purportedly subjugating noble and independent Balinese peasants, who needed to be released from bondage to revitalise their authentic culture.

It thus seems pointless to look for a consistent and neutral description of the Balinese, for most images of them are constructions owing much to the economic and political interests of Dutch colonial expansion and little to disinterested observation. As Picard points out, 'before their conquest, the Balinese had to be perceived as savages to be *pacified*; once the conquest was accomplished, they could become an exotic curiosity to be *gazed at*' (1996: 27, his emphasis).

After the conquest of south Bali there were real efforts by Dutch scholars and officials to understand Bali in a more objective and systematic way. These men produced important accounts of Bali, especially its literature and its Hinduism (Vickers 1989: 78–85). Although they exhibit many differences in emphasis, what united them was a deep appreciation of Balinese culture. However, this appreciation saw the culture as almost wholly derived from elsewhere – its religion from India and its literature from Java, or again from India. Consequently the only Balinese who were of any real interest to these writers were the Brahmana high priests, who were seen as the experts in these matters.

From this scholarly activity testifying to the uniqueness of Balinese Hinduism emerged the view that Bali had one of the most important cultures in the Indies, an idea which neatly dovetailed with the image of Bali as the living museum of ancient Java, and thus a culture which needed to be both studied and preserved. The image of Bali as exotic paradise now came to predominate, because it best fitted complex and often contradictory Dutch colonial interests. Emasculating the despots served to justify the *puputan* atrocities and legitimated large scale political reform; keeping them in place as puppet rulers concealed political domination. Enforcing traditional Balinese ritual, arts and religion made it look as if no change had taken place, thus validating the policy of cultural preservation. Eulogising the rice terraces masked poverty, and glorifying Bali as exotic and beautiful facilitated tourism. In less than forty years a great deal had changed in south Bali, but the Balinisation policy encouraged outsiders to believe that nothing had changed, or if it had changed it had changed for the better. Ironically, soon after this image of Bali as exotic paradise had been consolidated the growth of tourism elicited the anxiety that the 'last paradise' would soon turn into the 'lost paradise' (Picard 1996: 34).

Tourism in the Netherlands East Indies began in 1908, and was at first limited to Java. By 1914, however, it had been extended to Bali, described in brochures as the 'Gem of the Lesser Sunda Isles'. A few intrepid tourists landed at Singaraja, and in a three-day visit saw some of the temples, the panorama of the volcanoes from the mountain village of Penelokan, and a number of other sites of interest. The tourists of the first ten to fifteen years were probably lured there by Bali's growing image of beauty. Two of the 'image-makers', as Picard (1996: 28) calls them, were W.O.J. Nieuwenkamp and Gregor Krause. Both published lavish albums containing photographs, drawings and paintings, Krause in particular concentrating on the physical attractions of bare-breasted Balinese women. But it was not just physical beauty that intoxicated Krause; he also saw in the Balinese an exuberant love of life manifested in their joyful ceremonies, devotion to their gods, and a seemingly uninterrupted happiness.

Books like those of Nieuwenkamp and Krause stimulated tourism, and during the interwar years encouraged a number of artists, novelists and musicians to visit and live in Bali. They carried on this image-making tradition with barely less enthusiasm. Among the most notable were the German painter Walter Spies (de Zoete and Spies 1938), the Mexican artist Miguel Covarrubias (1937), the Austrian novelist Vicki Baum (1937), and the Canadian composer Colin McPhee (1947), all of whose works still sell widely. These men and women lived a bohemian life of luxury amid what we now know was grinding poverty for the mass of ordinary Balinese. They recorded social and religious life, plastic arts, and dance, music and drama, and took a keen interest in re-establishing artistic forms that had fallen into disuse. Walter Spies was especially prominent, for it was from him that others often took their lead in how they portrayed Bali.

These artists revelled in describing Bali's rich culture as though it had grown out of its lush tropical landscape, but they also sounded a warning note about its precariousness. Conveniently forgetting the transformations pushed through by the colonial regime, or just not aware of them, they also saw Bali as an unchanging, traditional culture, so far luckily bypassed by the ravages of western modernity. Spies and his fellow bohemians were grateful to the Dutch for letting them live in Bali to carry out their artistic and other activities, and tended to accept uncritically Dutch descriptions of the Balinese. The fear of complaints reaching Dutch ears made Balinese reticent to speak their mind to these Euro-Americans, who were often seen as politically naive. In an interview in the 1980s, the Balinese man who acted as a long-time assistant to Margaret Mead said that he saw many gaps and erroneous ideas in her knowledge of Bali, but believed it was too dangerous to be frank with her (Pollmann 1990: 19). Spies and his friends became anxious that over-ambitious marketing of Bali as a tourist destination would entail the disintegration of its culture. Like most things that are valuable and rare, it was thought to be fragile and its continuing existence uncertain. If not properly cared for, as they thought the Dutch had done, it would quickly succumb to Islam, to the corrosive effects of mass tourism, or to western materialism. If the intricate, finely tuned culture of Bali was to be maintained as the island's main attraction for tourists, then tourists themselves represented the biggest threat to it. Of course it was too late to prevent tourism, so brochures of the 1930s cynically exploited the concern by arguing that people should not wait to visit the island since it would soon be spoiled by tourism (Picard 1996: 37)!

Early anthropologists: a glimpse

The first trained anthropologists to visit Bali were the newlyweds Margaret Mead and Gregory Bateson in 1936–8. Mead had already conducted fieldwork in Samoa and New Guinea, and had become famous for her radical views on child-rearing, adolescence and sexuality, which she argued were relative and culturally constituted, and in Bali she hoped to elaborate her theory of the connection between culture and personality. Under the influence of Spies, who they went to see as soon as they arrived in Bali, they decided to concentrate on the 'ordinary' Balinese, eschewing the study of elites and their textual tradition which had largely monopolised the attention of Dutch philologists. Mead readily accepted Spies' assertion that in the villages one could find Balinese life untouched, preserved and protected by the Dutch (Vickers 1989: 121).

With Bateson she lived in the cold mountain village of Bayung Gdé, where they spent much time taking thousands of photographs, filming the Balinese in their everyday life and writing copious notes on their observations, but not actually speaking to the villagers very much (Bateson and Mead 1942). On the basis of these data they interpreted Balinese childrearing practices as producing a kind of bipolar personality. A mother would play with her baby intensively until it was highly aroused and then abruptly cut off the interaction, leaving the child frustrated. Mead claimed that this behavioural sequence produced adults who were normally calm and restrained. However, because socialisation involved repression, they would sometimes erupt into aggressive outbursts, curiously the kind of character description which fitted well with the *puputan* events of thirty years earlier. In fact, hardly any of the photographs provide convincing evidence that their views have much validity, and it is more likely that Mead's interpretation was based on the assumptions she already held about cultural relativity and psychoanalytical theory.

While Mead was interested in the repressed side of Balinese character, which she associated with witch figures, trance and the underbelly of Balinese life, Bateson, in some independently written works (1970a, 1970b), focused not just on the harmonious aspect of individual personality but on the 'steady state' of their entire social organisation. He agreed with Mead that mother–child interaction did not build to a climax but was prematurely stifled, an idea that they also borrowed from the musician Colin McPhee, who argued that Balinese music did not achieve a climax (Vickers 1989: 123). Seeing this deep-rooted restraint as a general template for interpersonal behaviour, Bateson argued that it provided an explanation for the avoidance of conflict and the emphasis on achieving harmony purportedly characteristic of Balinese society. As Vickers (1989: 123–4) points out, such a theory reinforced the view of Bali as a peaceful and essentially traditional society, which implied there was little to gain from studying Balinese history – what is history in a steady state? Moreover, stressing child-rearing, socialisation and religious ritual in the formation of Balinese character made it look as if 'culture' was the driving force in Balinese life, and that political and economic factors were of little significance. Both conclusions fitted neatly with the colonial regime's own version of its impact on Bali, and endorsed the tourist image-making rhetoric.

By the time war broke out in 1939 this master-image of Bali – the last paradise, every Balinese an artist, land of a thousand temples – was not simply descriptive hyperbole. It had become an axiomatic truth. The rice terraces, which formed the backbone of the island's economy and covered almost every square inch of available productive land, were appreciated more for their aesthetic beauty than as an index of how close the islanders were to a subsistence margin. The image seemed immune to historical contextualisation. Even if the island's turbulent and violent history was acknowledged, it could be explained as the result of foreign despotic rulers who suppressed 'real' Balinese culture, or by arguing that social ruptures were the inevitable but occasional outcome of a Balinese character which otherwise produced a harmonious and peaceful society. Most often, though, this history was unknown, ignored, or simply deemed irrelevant. Dutch colonial policy, expatriate agents of representation and scholarly anthropological research combined to traditionalise what was in truth a highly dynamic society.

Independence and its aftermath

Bali was occupied by the Japanese for three years between 1942 and 1945, after which there were five further years of conflict between the Dutch and Indonesian pro-Dutch forces on the one hand and republican forces on the other (Robinson 1995). Political and economic chaos across Java and Bali only partially abated when the Dutch gave up their intention to regain the colony, and the Republic of Indonesia, first declared by Sukarno in 1945, was finally ratified at the beginning of 1950. The first few years of the new republic, based on western models of representative parliamentary democracy, saw the revival of mass-based political parties formed during the colonial period but banned by the Dutch (Shiraishi 1990). In Bali, growing political factionalism between the nationalist and socialist parties and later between the nationalists and communists centred on challenges to the elites, conflict over religious reform, and land redistribution. During the early 1960s the first president of the republic, Sukarno, himself half-Balinese, attempted to preserve a precarious balance between the four major forces vying for political ascendancy in the new Indonesian state – the army, the nationalists, the communists and the Muslim parties (Feith 1962; Lev 1966; Sukarno 1965; Legge 1972). As economic conditions deteriorated the army and the communists grew increasingly polarised and, as the militant peasants' organisations affiliated with the communist party began to agitate for land reform, violent confrontations between rival forces were frequent. In Bali this was aggravated by poor harvests, rat plagues, insect infestation, and the 1963 eruption of Mount Agung which took 62,000 hectares of land out of production. Though supposedly a land of plenty, in these years Bali became dependent on large subventions from central government (Robinson 1995: 244).

By 1965 tensions across the archipelago were high, especially as persistent rumours circulated that a shipload of guns was on its way from China to equip the communists. On 30 September an alleged communist coup in Jakarta, in which six army generals were kidnapped and murdered, was crushed by General Suharto. The following nine months saw the massacre of hundreds of thousands of suspected communists, especially in Java and Bali, by the army and allied Muslim groups, and the imprisonment of many others (Crouch 1988, Cribb 1990, Robinson 1995). In 1967 Suharto, as the new president, ushered in the dictatorship known as the New Order (*Orde Baru*), and reversed most of Sukarno's policies. While Sukarno stressed his own brand of socialism – the continuation of the revolution, politics above economics, and strong ties with China and the newly emerging post-colonial states – the New Order emphasised economic development, capitalism and alliance with the west, a process greatly helped by the steep increase in revenues from Indonesian oil (Robison 1986; Hill 1994).

To consolidate his control of the state Suharto began to curb party political activity. The communist party was banned, and all Muslim political parties, which had very different aims, were forced to form a single and consequently ineffectual party (Hefner 2000: 100). It became illegal to engage in active politics outside short periods prior to general elections to be held every five years, elections which were a figleaf barely concealing the dictatorial nature of the military regime (Suryadinata 1989; Budiman 1990; Schwarz 1994). The emasculation of opposition political parties was further entrenched by the use Suharto made of Golkar (*Golongan Karya*, 'functional groups'). Initially a loose federation of anti-communist groups such as civil servants, business associations, women's groups and professional organisations, Suharto transformed Golkar into a political party in everything but name (Reeve 1985). Because civil servants, police, armed forces and all other government employees had to be members, Golkar became his vote-winning election machine. During Suharto's reign state control penetrated into almost every aspect of Indonesian village life. Local government was reorganised and local officials were incorporated into the lower rungs of the ever-expanding state bureaucracy. To the *Pancasila*, the five ideological principles on which the state is notionally based – belief in one god, humanitarianism, the unity of Indonesia, democracy through deliberation and consensus, and social justice for all (Feith 1963; Morfit 1986) – were added other New Order ideologies. Among the most important were 'development' (*pembangunan*, Ind.), 'advancement' (*kemajuan*, Ind.), 'order and discipline' (*tata-tertib*, Ind.) and 'cleanliness' (*pembersihan*, Ind.). These ideologies were disseminated in compulsory indoctrination courses for government workers, community leaders, and business and private company employees. The school curriculum became strictly controlled and began to act as an important means of creating a new sense of Indonesian identity (Leigh 1991, Parker 1992a).

For most of the New Order period Bali appeared to be a Golkar stronghold. Despite much dissatisfaction voiced privately, especially by the poor, there were positive reasons for Balinese support of the regime – its antipathy to the aspirations of Muslims for an Islamic state, and the island's sustained and rapid economic growth, particularly through tourism. The fact that much-needed presidential and other government grants for schools, markets, running water and electricity could only be channelled through village leaders, themselves state employees, added to the pressure to vote for Golkar. Any opposition, which was anyway disorganised and sporadic, was often subjected to blatant and sometimes violent intimidation (Schulte Nordholt 1991b; Wenban 1993).

Suharto was removed in 1997, and in 1999 the first genuinely free elections for 45 years were held. Many new political parties contested these elections. Bali had 2.04 million registered voters, of whom 1.5 million voted for the Indonesian Democratic Party of Struggle (*Partai Demokrasi Indonesia-Perjuangan*) led by Sukarno's daughter, Megawati Sukarnoputri, while only 200,000 voted for Golkar. Since then, despite the Bali bomb, the island has remained relatively peaceful. Unfortunately that has not been the case elsewhere in the archipelago. Once the claustrophobic pressure of the military regime was removed, ethnic and religious conflict in areas such as Ambon, Aceh and Lombok emerged in murderous forms (Aragon 2001; Klinken 2001; Siegel 2001).

Clifford Geertz and Bali

It was during 1957 and 1958, after they had spent two years in central Java in 1953–4, that Clifford and Hildred Geertz carried out nine months of fieldwork in two areas of southern Bali. The extensive corpus of Clifford Geertz's work on Bali has advanced the anthropological study of the island enormously, and much subsequent work has been built on, developed from, or been a reaction to this remarkable anthropologist's many insights and analyses. His work on Balinese social organisation (1959), kinship (C. and H. Geertz 1975), the nineteenth century state (1980), the meaning of the cockfight (1973d), religious change (1973b) and much more both illuminated his general theoretical statements, which helped reorient an entire discipline, and generated a broad research agenda for empirical research in Bali within which many others have continued to work.

Nonetheless there is a downside to Geertz's *oeuvre*. Just as others have followed in his footsteps and worked with ideas he first enunciated, so Geertz too worked within an already established set of issues, concerns and assumptions about what Bali was like. While he was highly critical of some of the Dutch scholarly research, he was rather less disapproving of the basic position that Mead and Bateson had taken, especially their views on Balinese character. Moreover, many of his writings about Bali give the impression, perhaps unintended, that the political turmoil of the time was of little direct significance to many of the issues he was writing about. Though conflicts were mentioned, they were not always seen as factors which might play a significant role in an historically constituted explanation of a specific institution. Often such factors were marginalised, so that the interpretation – whether of the cockfight, Balinese personhood or the pre-colonial state – appeared to render Bali as timeless and unchanging (Tambiah1985; Wikan 1990; Crapanzano 1986).

To illustrate this criticism, and to show how colonial images influenced academic accounts, a brief look at Geertz's celebrated interpretation of Balinese personhood is instructive. The essay *Person, Time and Conduct in Bali* (1973c) was written in 1965, some months before the Suharto anti-communist killings began but at a time when political conflict and violence were nevertheless intense. In this influential essay, Geertz examines Balinese symbolic ideas about personhood, time, and typical forms of interaction, in all of which he finds a basic similarity. According to Geertz, in symbolic terms Balinese do not treat other Balinese as though they are individuals with specific biographies. Rather they consider them as 'stereotyped contemporaries, abstract and anonymous fellowmen'; apparently they have attenuated social relationships, somehow they 'do not meet'. What is culturally played up is their social location in an eternal, metaphysical order. Paradoxically Balinese 'formulations of personhood are depersonalising' (1973c: 389–90). In relation to conceptions of time, Geertz argues that Balinese time is not durational, but punctual or particulate, in the sense that Balinese calendars do not tell you what time it is, but what kind of time it is. There are full days when important things go on, and empty days when not much happens. Geertz asserts that Balinese do not use their calendars to count time (though in fact they do: see Howe 1981), but use them to determine whether a day is auspicious or inauspicious in relation to some important undertaking. The paradox here is that Balinese time is being detemporalised – stasis is emphasised and change is underplayed. Interpersonal behaviour, whether between strangers, neighbours or friends, is seen as structured by extreme forms of etiquette. Balinese play out standardised roles as though they are permanently performing on a public stage. If this is botched 'the moment is felt with an excruciating intensity and men [are] locked in mutual embarrassment' (1973c: 402). The anonymisation of personhood, the immobilisation of time, and the ceremonialisation of conduct are all of a piece, and constitute what Geertz calls a 'cultural triangle of forces' (1973c: 389).

In the whole of this fifty-page essay there is not one reference to social and political conditions in contemporary Bali, nor to any past issues of political violence. There is a final footnote which informs the reader that dramatic changes occurred later in the year, seeming to imply that the violence came out of nowhere, and that the chaos of the period between 1945 and 1965 was of little relevance to the analysis. Geertz makes approving reference to Bateson's description of Bali as a 'steady state', and to Mead's 'acute' perception that neither interpersonal relations nor collective activity (religious, artistic, political or economic) build to consummation. Echoing Mead, Geertz maintains that Balinese culture is characterised by an 'absence of climax' (1973c: 379, 401). It would appear, at least in their symbolism, that Balinese character and society are immune to change.

Geertz and the Balinese state

Apart from his famous essay on the Balinese cockfight (1973d), perhaps the most seminal and influential of all Geertz's writings on Bali has been his study of the pre-colonial Balinese state (1980), the *negara*. In this section I take issue with Geertz's conceptualisation of the *negara* as a 'theatre state', arguing that it is more appropriately seen as a 'contest state'. Perhaps ironically, I show that the notion of a 'theatre state' makes more sense in relation to the colonial and post-colonial periods in Bali than it does to the pre-colonial period.

Earlier I described pre-colonial Balinese polity as a fluid hierarchy based on highly personalised patron–client relationships. Such polities have been called 'contest states' (Adas 1981, Schulte Nordholt 1996) because at their heart they involve conflict and competition. This competition occurs among leaders who struggle for control over followers, whom they use as soldiers to fight for land and other resources. It also occurs between leaders and their followers, the leaders trying to bind followers to them by supplying protection, privileges, status and land in return for support, and followers seeking to become leaders themselves or to switch allegiance to a different leader who can provide better rewards. This kind of structure is often found in upland societies with low density populations, in which a combination of personal charisma, ambition, oratorical skills and individual accomplishment often propels people into temporary and informal leadership positions (Atkinson 1989, Tsing 1990). It is also sometimes discernible in lowland societies with high population densities based on wet-rice irrigation, such as Bali, the Buginese (Errington 1989) and the Javanese (Keeler 1987). In these societies, men – and sometimes women – become leaders both by virtue of their personal qualities and by being senior members of large scale kin groups which supply a ready source of followers. Once achieved, such leadership – because it brings ownership of property – can be converted into more formal and institutionalised statuses with associated ranked titles. At this point the structure becomes more intricate. Both descent and inheritance assume significance as the leaders, styled as *raja*, pass on prerogatives to their children, and descent comes to be seen as the most important criterion for legitimising leadership.

Descriptions of such a society at one particular moment in time can make that society look rigidly structured, because statuses appear fixed and governed by descent. Elites remain elites, and commoners remain commoners. There are many Balinese myths and legends which tell of an apparently ordinary and humble commoner overcoming many obstacles to become a king, eventually to be revealed as the rightful royal heir who, through the evil act of a covetous relative, was farmed out as a baby to be brought up as a commoner. Quality will out. However, while descent is clearly essential for succession, it can be used as an ideology which retrospectively ratifies a change in leadership which has been accomplished in a different way. Thus there are historical cases in which men from unpromising beginnings come to positions of leadership, or usurp hereditary claimants, and then have court scribes write dynastic chronicles (*babad*) to provide the necessary genealogical connections to make the usurper appear the rightful ruler (Geertz and Geertz 1975: 119–122; Worsley 1972; Boon 1977; Schrieke 1957). What appears to be a stable hierarchy in the short term begins to look, in the long term, far more flexible, unstable and intricate.

Despite Geertz's claim to provide a historical account of the Balinese *negara*, his critics argue that he is actually describing what he sees as an unchanging and timeless structure. Three major problems mar Geertz's analysis, and when these issues are seen in a different light suggest that the notion of the contest state is considerably more apt. One issue concerns the relationship between lords and their subjects; a second concerns his overemphasis on the king as the silent, exemplary centre; the third relates to the point and purpose of ritual.

Geertz argues that many Balinese peasants privately owned their own land and were thus largely independent agents who willingly supported their lords' rituals, building projects and wars. Anthropologists and historians such as Robinson (1992: 79–80), Schulte Nordholt (1992, 1993, 1996), Connor (1982: 312) and MacRae (1999: 153, n.25), on the other hand, claim that lords controlled extensive tracts of land which enabled them to exert considerable control over the peasants who farmed that land as tenants. These accounts all agree with Geertz that the king was at the apex of the hierarchy and the centre of a magico-political realm, an 'exemplary centre' who mediated between heaven and earth and gave the state its shape. While Geertz implies that this ideology was implemented in such a way that peasants voluntarily supported their lord in the enactment of a cosmic scheme, his critics assert that political practice deviated from the ideal, often involving the coercion of peasants who had little power of their own.

Geertz argues that the *negara* cannot be interpreted with the conventional tools of western political science, for it was neither an organisation of command, nor did it have a monopoly over physical violence, nor was it really about control. According to Geertz, while such ethnocentric interpretations emphasise material power and physical coercion over the symbolism which legitimates and disguises it, in the Balinese *negara* symbolism was the substance of the state, not simply its trappings. The *negara* was thus a 'theatre state' dedicated to spectacle, ceremony and ritual. Kings were the impresarios, priests its directors, and peasants the supporting cast, stage crew and audience.

> Court ceremonialism was the driving force of court politics; mass ritual was not a device to shore up the state, but rather the state, even in its final gasp, was a device for the enactment of mass ritual. Power served pomp, not pomp power.
>
> (Geertz 1980: 13)

In this formulation, elites and peasants appear almost to inhabit two different worlds, and Geertz claims that elites did not intervene much in village life. Government was largely a local level affair, conducted through a set of autonomous peasant institutions – village (*désa*), hamlet (*banjar*), irrigation society (*subak*), and temple congregation (*pamaksan*). In this view, 'power was not allocated from the top, it cumulated from the bottom' (1980: 63), and was therefore surrendered upward.

There are both theoretical and ethnographic problems with this interpretation. Until 1950 many Balinese lords possessed or controlled very large holdings of land, a major cause of the violent campaigns for land redistribution after independence. In the pre-colonial period lords also organised and controlled many aspects of irrigation, and could use flooding or drought as a weapon in their wars against rival lords (Schulte Nordholt 1996). They collected taxes on land, opium, water use, and trade (Hanna 1976: 98), and possessed and traded in slaves (de Kat Angelino 1920; van der Kraan 1983; Schulte Nordholt 1996: 41–4). Though Geertz claims that status and government were separated between elites and peasants, they were in fact conjoined in the person of the ruler, and commoner institutions were subordinate. Peasants did not therefore willingly support their lord, but were coerced into doing so to gain access to land and thus their means of subsistence. In return for this they had to provide service at the lord's court, help in his ritual extravaganzas, and act as soldiers in time of war.

But the lord was not completely omnipotent. To prevent peasants deserting, he too had to provide services (Korn 1932: 306). Physical security was important, but he was also deemed a religious head, and had to maintain peace and order so that people could serve the gods. It was his duty to encourage the religion, maintain certain important temples, and ensure that a person's soul reached its destination via cremation. If descendants were missing, he had to take on the job of cremating the deceased himself. This meant that a large part of the revenue he enjoyed was consumed by his religious and communal obligations – organising purification ceremonies, maintaining Brahmana priests, and ensuring good order in his realm. While in practice the king may have been a burden, as many Dutch thought, his subjects also conceived of him as an exceptionally potent (*sakti*) personage whose death or unrighteous behaviour entailed a magical imbalance throughout the whole realm, manifested through plagues, drought, pest infestation and earthquakes. It was not an equal exchange, since what the lord extracted was usually greater than what he redistributed. As Sahlins (1974: 205) once said, 'in its true historic setting *noblesse oblige* hardly cancelled out the *droits de seigneur*'. One reason for the ever greater intricacies of the etiquette governing interaction between people of different rank in nineteenth century Bali was the opportunities it gave to lords to impose fines for trivial infractions of the rules. These enabled lords to put people into debt slavery, and provided the money to buy guns, opium and other luxuries (Schulte Nordholt 1996: 43).

Geertz is certainly correct in depicting the king as a silent, exemplary centre. However, this can only be a partial description. Given the competition and struggle among leaders and between leaders and their followers, rulers clearly had to be active agents as well as silent centres. From indigenous literature, especially the genre known as *geguritan* which provides historical accounts of actual events, and from Dutch sources and historians' research, we can see that rulers periodically had to defeat rebellions, embark on conquests, seize land and slaves, and bind the peasantry to him through generosity (Worsley 1979; Schulte Nordholt 1992, 1993, 1996). Kings and other leaders throughout Indic Southeast Asia strove to consolidate their positions as rulers, but their states were fragile. Suffering from weak administration and poor communications, they were often in conflict with other rulers, plagued by intrigue and internal rebellion among their own supporters, and prone to their peasants deserting to another lord (Schrieke 1957; Moertono 1968; Ricklefs 1974).

A more balanced view of the doctrine of the exemplary centre, therefore, is that the Balinese king had two modalities. He 'turns a terrifying aspect towards his and

36 *Colonialism, caste and the beginnings of tourism*

his subjects' enemies, within and without the realm, and his gentle aspect he turns towards the loyal and the virtuous' (Worsley 1979: 112). Leaders *aimed* to become immobile icons, but in order to achieve this end they had to mobilise vast resources. Consequently, the idea that the king was an exemplary centre, a 'sign in a system of signs' (Geertz 1980: 131), was only part of a wider and more dynamic conception of kingship whose other dimension was the king as charismatic leader and warrior (de Heusch 1997: 228). The sacred king was thus not the start but the end product of a struggle conducted through political and symbolic means. Warring king and silent centre were not contradictory modalities, but two aspects of a single, unstable process.

For Geertz ritual is the end, not the means, of state activity: 'the state ... was a device for the enactment of mass ritual' (1980: 13). Geertz even discusses warfare as little more than a ritual, sometimes involving large numbers of people, in which after a brief skirmish involving some wounding, the opposing parties withdrew (1980: 65, 252–3). This contrasts strikingly with Schulte Nordholt's description: 'War was no knightly sport; it was a scourge that deeply scarred local life' (1996: 68), and he provides sufficient examples to demonstrate that war was often bloody and violent.

This should not be taken to mean that mass ritual and spectacle were not of great significance, but it does suggest that ritual was not just an end in itself, as Geertz claims, but a means to a different end. Rituals, whether the small ceremonies conducted by householders or those of leaders and kings performed on a gigantic scale, have always had several purposes. They are conducted to ensure that the gods and ancestors bestow protection, long life and prosperity on their mortal supplicants, and make the fields fertile. At the same time, ceremonies – because of their paraphernalia, their size and the number of people involved – are status sensitive, and thus at the heart of competition over rank. Spending more, inviting more prestigious guests, slaughtering more animals and making more elaborate offerings – these are all ways of outdoing rival households and leaders. Those who lose out in this game of prestige suffer from the complex combination of shame and anger which Balinese refer to as *jengah* (Howe 2001: 93–108). Ritual thus becomes a weapon in status competition.

Kings and leaders needed to be active agents in the contest state, and this activity centred around the mobilisation of peasant labour to build palaces and temples and to fight wars. The performance of mass ritual was, and still is, in the same category. These rituals – especially cremations which often took months to prepare and weeks to complete – were more than mere dramatisations of the king's status and power. In organising a major ceremony the king had to bring together a vast array of material and human resources. Success in this confirmed the king's capacity to control, coerce and protect his subjects, and showed him to be a potent leader who could attract the followers of other leaders who competed inadequately. Failure, on the other hand, indicated a loss of such capacity and potency, and could result in his subjects drifting away to more successful leaders. Viewed from this perspective, major rituals were dangerous and high risk events threatening the king's position (Vickers 1991; Howe 2000). In performing a ritual the king put himself on trial and threw down a challenge to other leaders. Rather than war being a form of ritual, it is perhaps more pertinent to understand ritual as a form of war.

Conclusion

This chapter has shown how colonial knowledge about the Balinese, constructed for specific political and economic interests, was assimilated by expatriate artists, writers and musicians who developed and generalised it to produce an image of Bali as a harmonious paradise, unchanging and exotic. They appreciated and reinforced Dutch accounts because their continued and privileged presence in Bali depended on Dutch favour. When Mead and Bateson arrived they went straight to Walter Spies, who instructed them about what Balinese people were like. Through this mediation, colonial knowledge was converted into apparently disinterested academic and scholarly accounts of the nature of Balinese character and society. Mead and Bateson's theories subsequently influenced Geertz's early descriptions of Balinese institutions and character. And it did not stop there.

In Geertz's acclaimed study of the pre-colonial Balinese state colonial knowledge was recycled yet again, even though he painted a very different picture of the elites. In Geertz's account they are not tyrannical despots – elites did not govern, rule or command as they do in western states; they were consumed by the status imperatives of ritual and spectacle in a 'theatre' state. Order and government were left to peasants in their supposedly independent villages. Thus we meet again the colonial separation of politics and culture, for which Geertz has been heavily criticised.

Many aspects of Geertz's account of the pre-colonial state only make sense if it is seen as a description of Bali *after* the changes effected by colonial reforms. In the colonial period the political power of rulers was much diminished, so all that was left to them was ceremonial and artistic activity, which the Dutch positively encouraged. This left the villages disconnected from elite control, so it looked as though they ruled themselves through peasant institutions. Geertz's view of the self-governing Balinese village is little different from colonial ideas of the village as an autonomous little republic, ideas originally brought into existence through reforms which severed the connection between village and court. Similarly the Dutch represented the *subak* – the irrigation society which distributes water to the rice fields – as though it was a democratic association of farmers independent of royal control. Again, however, this only occurred after considerable effort had been made by the colonial regime to 'restore' the *subak* to its supposedly 'original' state (Schulte Nordholt 1996: 246–54). Clifford Geertz's book *Negara*, presented as a description of Bali in pre-colonial times, is better seen as an interpretation of what Bali had become during the colonial period.

None of these expatriates and anthropologists actively connived with colonialism, but whether they knew it or not their frameworks, perspectives and accounts were deeply influenced by it.

3 Balinese character assassination?

Introduction

In this chapter I explore the issue of Balinese character, not to prove writers like Margaret Mead, Clifford Geertz and Unni Wikan wrong and substitute my own ideas, but because it is useful to explore some of the theoretical and ethnographic problems involved in the enterprise. Since descriptions of Balinese character have often revolved around issues of fear – either the anxiety surrounding conduct on the public stage or to the possibility of attack by witches and sorcerers – I have deliberately kept this chapter relatively light-hearted. This is both to counter the impression that everyday life for Balinese people is dominated by tension and worry, and to give the reader a flavour of how ordinary Balinese people think, talk and act in response to these concerns.

When Margaret Mead and Gregory Bateson arrived in Bali in 1936, the topic of Balinese character shifted from colonial image-making to a subject of scientific inquiry. Mead's conclusion, deriving from her direct observation of specific practices of socialisation, was that Balinese exhibited a bipolar personality, for the most part calm and restrained, but occasionally prone to violent outbursts (Bateson and Mead 1942). The absence of climax in mother–child interaction was extended by Bateson to a description of their society as a 'steady state'. Clifford Geertz later linked these ideas to what he saw as the depersonalisation of personhood, the detemporalisation of time, and the ceremonialisation of conduct, to produce a rather startling vision of Balinese character (1973c: 390–1). This vision was later subjected to severe criticism by Unni Wikan (1987, 1990), who advocates a very different approach to the understanding of fear among Balinese.

This chapter concentrates on the two most prominent descriptions of Balinese interaction, those of Geertz and Wikan. I emphasise 'interaction' rather than 'character' because that is what is stressed by these observers, and the specific forms of interaction they dwell on stem from particular ways in which Balinese character is portrayed. Despite significant differences between their interpretations there are also underlying similarities. Echoing Bateson's and Mead's conclusion that Balinese character is based on fear (1942: 47), both Geertz and Wikan continue to stress, though in quite different ways, the centrality of fear as the main organising principle of interpersonal behaviour. This emphasis on fear results in a neglect of other important dimensions of interaction. While the neglect of diversity which produces uniform and essentialist descriptions of Balinese people is fairly clear in Geertz's account, the failing is not immediately obvious in Wikan's case, for she sets out to do the opposite (1990: xviii). Nevertheless, worried about the general tenor of her analysis, she writes that 'the Balinese of my [1990] account ... seem so plain and ordinary, so nonexotic ... Why was my study lacking ... in exotic features?' Concerned not to essentialise the Balinese, she is troubled that she has made them insufficiently exotic. Yet at the end of a discussion of translation and fieldwork practice she wonders if she has 'portrayed them as more exotic than is justified' (1992: 460–1, 476). Can the processes of essentialising and exoticising be decoupled in this way?

Wikan approaches the issue of Balinese conduct in terms of simple differences – the Balinese differ from 'us' ('us' is never defined, but it is assumed that 'we' are Euro-Americans) in some significant way, which is then deemed an exotic feature. But describing something as exotic carries costs. It cannot be merely a matter of identifying differences as such, since real differences abound. The problem lies in transforming differences into essential defining features of a category of people conceived of as bounded, then counterpointing this 'culture' with a hypothetical other treated as equally homogenous and defined by an opposite set of features. Exoticising the other implies an equivalent exoticisation of 'us'. Despite denouncing Geertz's essentialism, Wikan frequently collectivises 'the Balinese', attributing to the whole population a uniform set of ideas and concepts producing similar behavioural outcomes.

Essentialist constructions usually involve several related mechanisms. One is to start from a central but often unstated assumption that the society being studied has a cohesive and homogeneous 'culture' (Keesing 1987). A second is the selection for emphasis of specific forms of behaviour, deemed significantly different from 'our' behaviour, thus filtering out what is similar because it is of little analytical interest (Keesing 1989). A third is the comparison with a largely unexamined 'us', usually Euro-American. Thus the comparison involves two 'cultures'. Carrier (1992) points out that this third mechanism is itself a form of essentialising, which he dubs 'occidentalism', both to differentiate it from 'orientalism' (Said 1978) and to show the parallels with it. The 'other' is constructed dialectically by opposition to a reified 'us' – each generates the other by reversing all the terms. It becomes an exercise in typologising, since the differences are mapped onto whole societies, conceived of as integrated cultures.

Constructions of Balinese interaction

Geertz argues that Balinese cultural patterns 'depict virtually everyone ... as stereotyped contemporaries, abstract and anonymous fellowmen' (1973c: 389), rather than as 'consociates', people who have immediate face-to-face relationships and whose life courses constantly impinge on one another. In their relations with others, Balinese individuality is suppressed and a standardised identity is projected. As contemporaries, rather than consociates, Balinese share a community of time but not of space, and have, often very attenuated, social relationships with one another, but they do not – at least in the normal course of things – meet. They are linked not by direct social interaction but through a generalized set of symbolically formulated (that is, cultural) assumptions about each other's typical modes of behaviour.

(Geertz 1973c: 365–6)

Balinese are presented as primarily concerned with the aesthetics of their own behaviour – its gracefulness, refinement and style. Like Javanese people, Balinese make a most important distinction between *alus* (delicate, refined, formal) and *kasar* (rough, informal). The former connotes smoothness, calm, poise, beauty, obliqueness, while the latter connotes coarseness, noise, ugliness, agitation, directness. Almost anything – language, behaviour, physiognomy, physical objects – can be described using these terms. What is thus pleasing to Balinese is refined language, a calm, considered and measured approach to interaction, and an avoidance of confrontation, shock and direct disagreement.

In the light of this, according to Geertz, the main controlling emotion of interaction is *lek* ('stage fright' or 'shame'; Keeler 1983), the anxiety that ones polished, socially distant and standardised public identity will crumble. If the formal etiquette of public performance is botched, the personality of the individual will break through and then 'the immediacy of the moment is felt with an excruciating intensity and men [are] locked in mutual embarrassment' (Geertz 1973c: 402). Using a theatre metaphor, close to Geertz's heart, it is as if 'the audience (and the actor) loses sight of Hamlet and gains it, uncomfortably for all concerned, of bumbling John Smith painfully miscast as the Prince of Denmark' (1973c: 402) – what should be *alus* suddenly becomes *kasar*. What Balinese fear is their own inability to perform adequately on the public stage.

This description is considered fundamentally flawed by Unni Wikan, who claims that what really troubles Balinese is the morality, not the aesthetics, of interaction. According to her, Balinese personhood is precarious and

constantly dependent on the moral and emotional approval of others, and conceptualized by the North Balinese themselves in a rich imagery dominated by the spectre of illness caused by sorcery and/or mental confusion. Behind a surface of aestheticism, grace, and gaiety, we found social uneasiness, great concern with the individual thoughts and intentions of others, and ubiquitous fear. Fear, not so much of the gods or the demons, but of fellow human beings, individual ones at that.

(Wikan 1987: 338)

In this account the sorcery and black magic of nearby others – kin, friends and neighbours – is the source of fear. Wikan does not dispute Geertz's description of Balinese interaction as highly stylised, but while for Geertz the outward form *is* the substance (he says little about what lies behind the façade), for Wikan the distinction between outer appearance and inner disposition is crucial. The complex rules of etiquette demand the concealment of inner thoughts behind an inscrutable public face. However, interaction is not choreographed to prevent individuality seeping through its casing of protocol as Geertz would have it, but to avoid giving offence to others who might retaliate with sorcery. Balinese thus put on a 'bright face', smile, use elegant speech and maintain poise and calm, all in order to hide their real feelings (Wikan 1990: 49–55). Because others behave in the same way, an inability to divine others' intentions results which generates anxiety and turbulent emotions (Wikan 1987: 338). Not knowing what others really think requires precautionary action to guard against causing displeasure. Wikan believes that these fears and dangers are ubiquitous, diffuse and pervasive: 'Balinese seem ... to live perpetually on the verge of disaster' (1990: 32).

Wikan's stress on the everyday life of Balinese people provides many brilliant insights into their behaviour, and allows her to pinpoint the weaknesses of Geertz's more formal symbolic analysis. Nonetheless, her own account is not immune from some of the same failings. Geertz does not qualify 'Balinese' at all. Wikan appears to do so by confining herself to material from a small number of villages in north Bali. However, arguing that it is a difference in theoretical approach between herself and Geertz which produces divergent interpretations, Wikan presents her account as a general one which has 'captured broad commonalities' (1990: xxiii). They also agree, but for different reasons, that the nature of Balinese social interaction is extremely fragile and based on fear, Geertz singling out stage fright, Wikan emphasising fear of others. Both stress the negative and threatening qualities of interpersonal behaviour, and both claim that complex etiquette mediates social interaction.

Geertz reduces Balinese interaction to a single type delineated in terms of a contrast with an equally flat Western type (we have consociates, they have contemporaries), a strategy characteristic of some of Geertz's other work on Bali (Thomas 1989: 25–7, 1994: 93–4). Wikan also argues explicitly for Balinese 'otherness' on the basis that they differ from 'us' in critical ways. For example, she argues that Balinese have a monistic conception of the self and thus make no distinction between 'thinking' and 'feeling' (1990: 35); they fashion 'feeling–expression–body–soul into a coherent *conception*' (1990: 151, her emphasis). This may be true in certain contexts, but distinctions are often made between the body and the 'spirit' which flows through and animates it, and between the material body and the invisible 'soul' (Howe 1983). Parry has criticised similar essentialist constructions of the Hindu self, and makes the important point that the assumed 'emphatic contrast between their monism and our dualism does little justice to the real complexities of either conceptual world' (1989: 513).

According to Wikan, Balinese postulate monism, and thus suggests that 'we' cannot understand the profound healing properties of laughter. Balinese are regularly told not to express grief in public since it weakens the self and lays it open to supernatural attack. Grief and sadness are also contagious, so making others vulnerable. Balinese should put on a 'bright face' and laugh. Laughter, Wikan tells us, 'works' in ways it would not do with us ... We do not seek out situations that would make us glad when we are sad, nor do we like people to laugh and joke in the face of our distress. We do not recognize the sweetness of the taste of laughter as something soothing as sun to a freezing body; it is not appealing to our senses as a tonic that can 'take sadness away' or make one 'forget' ones sadness. We tend to be skeptical of such connections, for ours are differently constituted body-selves.

(Wikan 1990: 151)

Here difference is posited between societies, not within them. Yet English has a veritable battery of maxims and sayings encouraging people to put on a brave front and laugh in the face of pain and distress – even among 'us' laughter is supposed to be the best medicine. A generalised Balinese conception is thus contrasted with a generalised Western one, implying that both are natural, stable and timeless, and that they are unrelated to broader economic and political issues, subjects Wikan almost completely ignores.

Powerful people and witches

If, for Wikan, interaction with others is dominated by the fear of causing offence, these others should be part of the analysis. Often, however, they are not, implying that the status of the source of the fear – high priest or lowly commoner for example – is irrelevant. When others are mentioned, they tend to be unspecified kin, friends or neighbours. In Corong, a large village in south Bali, I found that villagers listed nobles, priests, officials and healers as prominent figures to be wary of. They referred to them as *anak sakti*, 'powerful people', a category of Balinese which rarely appears in Wikan's account.

Core line descendants of Bali's nineteenth century ruling families, many of whom occupy important local government positions, are credited with an inherently greater amount of *sakti* – 'supernatural power' or 'effectiveness' (H. Geertz 1995b) – than those born into less prestigious groups. Because of their high caste status, their initiation ceremonies, their ritual and textual knowledge, and their ability to curse, Brahmana priests (*pedanda*) are also assumed to have great *sakti*. These two categories of people are potentially dangerous to those who displease them, so they must be treated with considerable caution. Elaborate rules of language, etiquette and deference enable ordinary Balinese to maintain a safe social distance from rulers and priests while interacting with them (Zurbuchen 1987).

Other Balinese, gentry and commoner alike, can increase their stock of potency by becoming specialists – temple priests, puppeteers or healers for example – in magical lore. They are then credited with a knowledge of texts, spells, medicines and poisons with which they can both cure and afflict. Others may become powerful inadvertently. Illness may lead to the acquisition of a spirit helper providing access to the 'unseen world' (*niskala*), the zone where hidden connections between apparently unrelated events in the 'visible world' (*sekala*) become revealed. Sometimes a person near death may pray all night in a temple, and be given a blessing (*ica*) by god which can then be used in various ways. People with disabilities such as dumbness or deafness may be credited with powers enabling them to repel witches, and to safeguard others in danger from witches. Any Balinese can purchase talismans, amulets and love magic, or perform various ascetic activities to make him or herself invulnerable (*kebal*).

Healers and priests almost always claim to use their power to help those bewitched by others, but stories abound that, clandestinely and for a price, they are willing to initiate attacks. *Sakti*, then, is essentially a morally neutral power (Anderson 1972). It makes no difference that a priest is supposed to serve the gods, because the powers that a priest accumulates and wields are identical to those used by a witch – only the intentions are different. This is as it must be, because 'to defeat an enemy one uses a superior form of his own power' (Wiener 1995: 199). Balinese are therefore ambivalent about these categories of people, because their 'inner intent may not be outwardly apparent' (H. Geertz 1995a: 23).

Witches (*léyak*) act out of envy, greed and revenge. Some claim that witches will attack anyone, because it is their nature to hate people, others that witches like to attack other witches to test their powers. Witches possess the ability to change their bodily form to attack the unwary and the vulnerable. These can either be animal forms, particularly pigs, monkeys and bats – though there is usually something strange about the form, such as large teeth, oversize genitalia or protruding intestines, which helps identify the animal as a witch – or more bizarre forms. A friend told me a story in which a group of men were returning from a neighbouring village late at night when they were assailed by a vagina as large as a jackfruit – they fled for their lives.

Given that many Balinese cultivate powers of one kind or another and to varying degrees, some simple but important questions arise. Are *anak sakti* ('powerful people') prey to the same fears as those less potent than themselves? Do powerful people all elicit the same intensity of fear in others, and is this more or less than that elicited by witches? What resources, if any, do Balinese have to repel attacks? Many Balinese are sensibly concerned about priests, healers, and others, but does their ambivalence mark their relationships with kin and friends?

The short answer is that there is immense variation in the extent to which Balinese inspire fear in others, and in the extent to which they respond with fear to the possibility of witchcraft and sorcery. Both Geertz and Wikan considerably underplay the degree to which Balinese have trusting and intimate relationships, often with many others and over long periods of time; Balinese enjoy the company of consociates, not just contemporaries. In general, Balinese are not paralysed by a pervasive fear of sorcery, and can successfully suppress feelings of anxiety concerning what others think and might do (see Jensen and Suryani 1992: 78, 88, who specifically repudiate Wikan's assertion that fear is pervasive and ubiquitous).

According to Wikan, refined (*alus*) linguistic and bodily etiquette lessen the possibility of sorcery attack. But the lack of an analysis of political and economic relations blinds her to the fact that deference, sometimes obsequious deference, is a kind of reverse social control. Servile behaviour can be used by inferiors to cajole superiors into acceding to requests for favours and access to the resources they control, or risk losing face (Appadurai 1990: 97). Though several of my high caste friends have been mortified by the immoderate and coarse (*kasar*) language sometimes used towards them by their commoner friends, I have never encountered a case of witchcraft for which this lack of respect was given as a cause.

As Geertz rightly argues, there are many occasions where the aesthetics of interaction are clearly important. At public meetings and marriage negotiations, for example, speeches have to be made, and groups use their best orators to score points through the quality of their speech and their command of high Balinese (Zurbuchen 1987: 63–81). When commoners use the correct forms of high Balinese when relating to superiors, it is not just to show respect and deference – it is also to elicit it in return (Howe 2001: 84–93). In addition, while individuals may present themselves in a uniform manner, their intentions may vary. Balinese often try to appear polite, unemotional and composed. This may be motivated by a desire to reduce vulnerability to illness and sorcery, and thus to the control of others, but the same behaviour can also be an outward sign of inner potency, and thus the capacity to exert control over others. Etiquette also has economic and political dimensions. For all these reasons it is unnecessary to choose between aesthetics and morality of action to characterise Balinese behaviour. Both are important.

Witches, powerful people and the night

A common attitude of many Balinese is to be vigilant in one's daily life, monitoring things like how one speaks to others, where one eats, where one goes, whom one befriends and when one moves about the village. It is irresponsible to cause unnecessary offence, particularly to those assumed to be powerful, or to attract their unwanted attention. The degree of fear demonstrated and the nature of responses to the possibility of attack vary greatly in both incidence and intensity. It is possible to discern a correlation between fear of others and specific categories of Balinese – women tend to evince more fear than men, for example – but variation within categories is often much greater than between them. Rich, influential, high status men are less likely to admit that others can harm them, because they themselves are powerful, but some nevertheless worry that their success may provoke the witchcraft of envy. The sometimes lavish redistribution of their wealth by affluent Balinese in the form of spectacular ceremonies and large donations to temple renovation is, at least in part, a matter of self-preservation. Much of the time, therefore, we need to examine responses in relation to specific individuals and their biographies.

Like many other villagers in Corong, Déwa, a 25-year-old minor gentry man, was very deferential to his caste superiors – priests and village notables. On several occasions he accompanied me to the house of a renowned healer (*balian*) so that I could interview him. Because healers are dangerous and others might think my intention was to learn how to perform black magic, Déwa was unhappy about these excursions and wanted to keep them secret. When I suggested visiting the healer in the evenings so that others might not notice, Déwa flatly refused because after dark the *balian* would be more threatening. When our regular visits ceased for a time, Déwa became troubled, thinking the healer might be offended at our unexplained absence and take punitive action. He demanded that we either resume our visits or give him an expensive present and formally take our leave.

On another occasion I accompanied a commoner friend to watch a performance of the shadow theatre in the middle of Corong. Usually these finish at about three o'clock in the morning, but around one o'clock my friend decided to go home. He returned twenty minutes later in an agitated state. Having reached the village crossroads he took fright at the very dark road he had to negotiate to get to his house, a road which at one point is within a hundred yards of the village cemetery. He asked to borrow my torch, which I would not lend him since I needed it to keep the dogs at bay as I went home. In the end I had to accompany him to his house. His was not a fear of specific individuals, but rather of the capricious spirits of the newly dead which wander along dark roads and molest the unwary. Such generalised fear of the night leads Balinese to be concerned about sleeping alone. Children and young unmarried men and women almost always have same sex sleeping partners with whom they share a room and frequently a bed. I was often asked why I did not request anyone to sleep with me – was I not afraid to be on my own?

Déwa's anxiety, however, is not experienced by everyone. Some Corong friends told me that there were no villagers who could properly be described as *sakti*, even if they had existed in the past. Oka, in whose house I lived, said 'How do you know if someone is *sakti*? You have to have proof; it's got to be apparent. If you see someone who is dead, no pulse, no breathing, and someone brings him back to life, then you have proof. If a person is wounded and someone can heal the wound quickly, this is proof.' Since Oka had never seen anything like this, he remained skeptical. His view was that one had to take simple, sensible precautions to avoid unwanted encounters with powerful forces (Jensen and Suryani 1992: 88).

Men, who are supposed to be 'brave' (*bani*) in comparison to women, will still warn others that it is foolhardy to move around the village alone at night when witches and other malevolent forces are most active, yet in practice few men take this very seriously. Occasionally I played cards at a friend's house until after midnight. When the game broke up, I was always cautioned to hurry home, but others exhibited little fear for themselves. On no occasion did anyone admit to being so frightened about going home alone that they would not play into the small hours, or tell me the following day that something peculiar had happened. Even so, when I left my own house after dark I was frequently asked who was going to accompany me, and sometimes a younger member of the family was ordered to go with me. Having returned late at night, the following morning I would be asked who had brought me home; but it was always the same one or two people who were concerned about my reckless disregard.

At night the company of others is preferred, because loud talk and laughter generate a safety zone, and witches are reticent to assail groups. Balinese often talk about strange night time noises and sights, and wonder about the causes. Flashes of light or fire may be attributed to contests between sorcerers, and the sighting of a pig or monkey may in reality be that of a witch. Unfamiliar sounds and sights are often dismissed as unimportant, but sometimes they are so singular they attract collective attention. Twice in the south Bali village of Pujung strange noises resulted in meetings and a decision to hold small ceremonies to appease the relevant spirits.

One of Wikan's main points is the fear which Balinese display towards their co-residents, friends and neighbours, since any of these may be a witch. I simply did not perceive Balinese relationships in this way. For the most part everyday behaviour in both Pujung and Corong is quite relaxed. Balinese work, joke, play, bathe, and gamble with friends and family. They swap food, razor blades, combs, clothes and myriad other things. Members of the same sex are extremely intimate – they hold hands, drape themselves over each other, hit one another playfully, and eat and sleep together. There are many strong friendships which cut across caste boundaries, characterised only by the most rudimentary forms of linguistic etiquette. These people have grown up together, and trust is taken for granted unless there is some specific reason to doubt it. Jensen and Suryani (1992: 90–1) argue that typical patterns of childrearing induce a sense of trust and easy familiarity rather than fear, and I would concur. While some villagers admitted that close kin and affines – especially in-marrying women who stereotypically sow dissent between brothers – can be dangerous because they are most likely to hold a grudge, others argued that it is your close kin who are most likely to protect you. Moreover, judged by the frequency with which my friends ventured to interpret others' behaviour, Balinese are quite adept at reading each other's intentions.

Standardised public identities may be on display for strangers, but they are virtually absent with close friends and kin. It is very noticeable how unself–conscious behaviour with friends quickly switches to polite and formal conduct with little known acquaintances. Some people are much more transparent than others. Many of my friends, especially in the heat of the moment, did not maintain composure, but were quick to show resentment, anger, disappointment or distress. A man I regularly played cards with, known to be a hothead, sometimes got so annoyed when he hit a losing streak that he ostentatiously ripped up the cards and walked angrily across the low card table, thus insulting everyone present – this was behaviour of a very *kasar* character. I well remember a young woman in Pujung who moped around the village for weeks because her parents forbade her to marry the man she loved, a form of conduct almost the very opposite of Suriati, the woman whose sad tale is told at the beginning of Wikan's account (1990: 3–11). While some of my classificatory 'mothers' in Corong were exceedingly formal towards me, using very elevated and flowery language, others, of identical caste status, almost entirely dispensed with such formality. This is a very different world from that portrayed by Geertz, in which Balinese are depicted as 'contemporaries' who have 'attenuated social relationships' and who rarely 'meet'. His account is accurate if confined to strangers, priests, healers, and those at very different positions in the hierarchy, between whom elaborate forms of etiquette and deference are often required. It is also different from Wikan's portrayal of paranoid Balinese, for whom the fear of others is always uppermost in their minds.

While the poison of witchcraft may hover in the background, it only becomes a possible diagnosis after someone falls ill or dies, and even then only when the illness fails to respond to different kinds of treatment and if the symptoms are diffuse and ill defined (Howe 1984). People involved in conflict with others never enter their enemies' houses, accept food from them, or speak to them. If they do not fall ill, witchcraft is not mentioned. Witchcraft may be an ever present possibility, but fear of it is held in check, sometimes even effaced, by the many exigencies of ordinary, everyday living, and by the normal precautions that common sense dictates. The point is that while the services provided by officials, priests and healers are often essential, encounters with them need not be overly troublesome as long as one is punctilious. It is second nature to Balinese to humble themselves and avoid any show of arrogance when interacting with such people.

There is also great variation concerning which places are considered to be dangerous. Graveyards, banyan trees, crossroads and village boundaries are usually seen as areas of spirit concentration, but in some cases entire villages are thought to be especially fraught with danger for the unwary. One evening, while living in Corong, I was asked if I was going to watch the shadow theatre in Ketiman, a nearby village. If I did, a friend warned, 'Don't eat there, eat here before you go!'. When I naively asked him if the food there was not very good, he said that this was not the problem. 'The people in Ketiman are bad; the place is broken apart. It's not safe to eat there as you might get hit by "black magic"; don't buy anything there in case you get hit'. I was told it was safe to drink from an as-yet-unopened bottle, but that I should not eat snacks and should take my own cigarettes. Another friend said that he too would never eat anything there: 'It might not be the merchant who sells you the food, but the person you are sitting next to who puts something into it'. 'Why would anyone do this to me?' I asked. 'Because maybe they are trying out their power.' 'And why in Ketiman?' 'Because it's a small village, and the people have narrow thoughts. They only think of eating and gambling, and they fill their spare time by practising sorcery against each other. They are at each other's throats and like to poison each other, and test their skills against one another.' Someone else said that because they were lazy and had nothing better to do, witchcraft was their *obby* (hobby).

Many gentry in Corong sneer at the all-commoner village of Ketiman, saying the villagers are unbelievably *kasar*, use very coarse language, and are stupid to boot. For example, there are several shared bathing places in the valley that separates Corong from Ketiman. One is a cave, difficult of access and considered magically charged (*tenget*), but where the water is said to have health giving properties. In the cave water is channelled through pipes so that a shower can be taken by candlelight. I was told that those in a state of pollution (*sebel*) should not bathe there, on pain of being bitten by the snake which lives in the pipe. It was asserted that people from Ketiman were so dimwitted that they did not know whether they were polluted or not, and hence were regularly bitten. Others repeated the same injunctions about Ketiman, and sometimes extended the list to include other villages. Yet when I visited these villages, usually to watch cockfights, I often found people from Corong buying food. Was it safe to do so? 'Yes, so long as you trust the seller.' It is interesting that it is phrased in this way since it implies, other things being equal, that much of the time trust overcomes suspicion.

In the evenings cockfighting was the main topic of conversation in my house in Corong, at least among the men who liked to mull over the day's events. Witchcraft was rarely mentioned. At a friend's house, however, all we ever seemed to talk about were macabre stories about people being bewitched and sorcerised. This atmosphere of suspicion may relate to the fact that he lived in a badly lit house where the black night seemed impenetrable, that he had spent time in Lombok, the island immediately east of Bali thought to be saturated with black magic, and that he lived across the road from a retired senior policeman who had a reputation as a regular practitioner of black magic. At my local coffee stall, by contrast, talk about witchcraft among the mixed group of young men who gathered there in the evenings was usually light hearted and irreverent. It was often directed specifically at me, perhaps to scare me or test my gullibility. Perhaps, having not personally witnessed anything dramatic themselves, they were uncertain whether witches existed, and wished to voice their doubt.

These coffee stall discussions always opened with the stock phrase 'Have you ever seen a witch?' (*taen tepukin léyak?*). I responded by asking for details about witches, like 'What do they like to eat?' 'They like what ordinary people detest – excrement, babies and human flesh. They always do their work at night, and appear in various guises. They are present in the house of someone dying, waiting for them to die or hastening their death. They can fly, emit fireballs and shoot these through the air. Ghosts (*tonya*) are almost as bad and inhabit the crossroads, dark places and big trees, and pounce on passers by. Spirits of the uncremated dead hover around the graveyard and in the general vicinity, howling, crying and attacking the unwary.' On such occasions young men tried to show bravado by saying that if they encountered a witch at night they would kick it up the backside, or set fire to it. Others dared me to accompany them to the graveyard at midnight. If I agreed I was taken by the arm and walked twenty yards down the road, only for my partner to burst out laughing and turn back.

At other times someone would tell me I was sitting next to a witch, but it was ignoring me because it did not find me 'tasty'. In this kind of company it is common for Balinese to tell strange or dramatic stories in the hope of getting others to believe them, only to burst out laughing with '*uluk-uluk*' ('Ah, got you there! It was a joke'). This banter may be a means of alleviating fear, but it could equally suggest that anxiety is neither deep seated nor pervasive. Either way, different Balinese believe quite different things, and will almost certainly change their views as they mature. What frightens a child may be dismissed as childish by an adult; what was once a preoccupation may later become an object of indifference. As people grow older they often take a less literal perspective. Several friends asserted that witches cannot change form, that it is the spell that distorts the observer's perception. Some people believe witches are real, some talk as if they are symbolic – are symbolic witches as frightening as real ones? – and some did not believe in them at all.

Avoiding witches, dealing with witches

This section looks at two forms of sorcery, poison and the magical use of bodily exuviae; and at defences against witches and sorcery. Wikan stresses the importance of the magical use that Balinese can make of another's hair and other bodily exuviae to cause harm, although she provides few actual cases. In the villages I am familiar with this form of sorcery created little concern. In both Pujung and Corong people regularly have their hair cut by barbers who set up their stalls in the market or elsewhere. Others have it done at home or next door by friends or neighbours, leaving the cut hair on the ground to be swept up later. I always cut my nails in the open, as did most of my friends. Nobody ever warned me that it was foolhardy to leave them on the floor for others to pick up.

This lack of concern contrasted with warnings about poisoned food, for one of the fears that looms large in the popular imagination is the possibility of being poisoned. To 'poison' someone (*nyetik*) requires the insertion of a magically powerful object (*papasangan*) into the body of the victim. The object is made dangerous by pronouncing a spell over it which must include the name of the intended victim so that it is not harmful to others. The most common means of poisoning someone is to insert the object in food or drink. Balinese regularly eat snacks and take drinks outside the home, and such occasions are consequently potentially hazardous.

Most villagers showed little concern over what might be in their food when eating at home, at their friends' houses, or at stalls where they regularly took meals. They conscientiously rake through their rice, but whether to detect poison or to prevent their teeth being damaged by stones I am not sure. They rarely treated other food in this way. On the other hand, several people regularly looked closely at their glass of coffee, and it is conceivable they were inspecting it for poison. One old man told me that you should always put your hand over the top of the glass for a few seconds. If no condensation appears on your palm, then it is best to throw it away. I have never seen anybody actually do this. In private friends told me that you were not completely safe even at your local stall, so you should always check to see who is there before you eat. You might be among friends, but everyone has enemies, and so you must weigh up the situation. Such verbal cautioning rarely had a behavioural analogue, however, and most of my friends never seemed to show concern about the snacks they ate at coffee stalls. Sorcery of this kind tends to be an *ex post facto* explanation of illness. People suffering from long debilitating illnesses often search their memories for occasions when they ate in someone else's house or in another village, and attribute the attack to this foolish negligence.

Two omissions in Wikan's analysis are the lack of any account of the resources Balinese use to repel attacks, and any reference to the fact that witches are not themselves invincible. According to Wikan, the only source of help Balinese have recourse to is their healers, without whom they 'would feel (indeed, be) entirely powerless and vulnerable' (1990: 84). According to her own testimony, however, people are often afraid of their healers. Some of my male friends told me that counterattack is the best form of defence. Should you meet a witch disguised as an animal the best thing to do is hit it with stones or a stick, and that might be sufficient to get rid of it. Hildred Geertz reproduces a Balinese painting in which a demon who is attacking a farmer is itself being beaten by several other peasants with their farm implements, and another in which a man confronts a woman in witch form – when she does not reply to his questions he jumps on her back and starts hitting her (1995a: 66, 91). In the latter case Geertz surmises, from the evidence available in the painting, that the witch may be a Brahmana priest. If a witch is wounded in such an attack it is imperative for the witch to approach the assailant the next day to request something personal – a cigarette, a piece of clothing or some food. If it cannot get this its wound will fester and the witch will die. It is, however, a bad policy to refuse the request since *karma pala* – the consequences of action – will intervene and you will suffer for contributing to a death. It is much better to surrender the item on condition that the witch does not disturb you again.

The story of the witch Basur (Hooykaas 1978) is illuminating in this regard. Basur wants to marry his son, Tigaron, to Sukanti, but because he is ugly she refuses, and gets her father to marry her off to another man. Tigaron is very upset and beseeches his father to intervene. Basur goes to the graveyard and calls on Durga – the powerful deity who controls the 'death' temple – to assist him. With her blessing he is able to change into the witch Rangda (Belo 1949) and make Sukanti sick. Sukanti's father summons a healer to help him. The healer appears to think the matter is not serious – he prepares some medicine and Sukanti quickly recovers. The healer explains that a sorcerer has been the cause of the girl's sickness, and points Basur out as the culprit. Basur in turn pleads with the healer not to kill him, and all the healer does is scold him and tell him to find another girl for Tigaron.

I was told that some Balinese are stronger than others because their blood is 'hot' (*panes*), or that they have 'hot' hands, and as a result witches are afraid of them. Some men say of themselves that they are too strong and tough to be struck by witchcraft (Ruddick 1986: 148). Those who are themselves *anak sakti* possess further means to ward off attacks. They can tell at a glance whether there is anything wrong with their food, and they can distinguish a real animal from a witch in animal form. They know spells which immobilise a witch by rooting it to the spot, and can force the witch to reveal their name, the result being that the witch thus becomes powerless. Even though witches may disguise themselves as dogs, dogs can warn that witches are around. Being like witches, dogs can see them and hence bark at them (Wiener 1995: 293).

One important defence against supernatural attack is to live a moral, upstanding life. Despite the powers of witches it is difficult to 'hit' someone with witchcraft if that person gives no cause. Honest, generous and tolerant people, described as *polos*, are believed to have strong bodies and souls because they are protected by their ancestors. If one is 'hit', part of the problem is that this protection has already been withdrawn (Wiener 1995: 287). Those who are mean, arrogant and aggressive, on the other hand, lay themselves open to attack by others, not only because they make many enemies but because their stock of power is diminished by the *kasar* way they behave.

Emotional disturbance, illness and laughter

The weaker a person is, the more likely they are to be attacked by witches, sorcerers and spirits. Weakness may be a function of age, conscious state, gender or general disposition. Just as sorcery induces illness and confusion, so these states can also open a person to attack. Every fifteen days, on the day called Kajeng Kliwon, malevolent spirits are thought to be particularly active, especially at dusk. Babies are frequently woken up at this time, since they are more vulnerable to attack while asleep.

A significant behavioural consequence results from these ideas of susceptibility. To remain healthy, Balinese generally strive to maintain emotional equilibrium by avoiding shock, unpleasantness and confrontation. This characterisation must be qualified, however, because in modern Bali many young men drink alcohol, are hot tempered, and like to fight, and in some contexts direct and candid speech is welcomed. Nevertheless, because strong emotions are contagious, others admonish their friends and kin to laugh and be happy, so that they are not themselves rendered vulnerable to attack by the sadness which the troubles of others generate. To put on a 'bright face', to laugh and ignore distress is a defence mechanism which not only protects a person, but also safeguards those close to them.

Wikan (1990) analyses the connections between sorcery, emotional disturbance and the role of laughter in some detail, but there are two issues she does not address. The first is that there are many forms of response to emotional disturbance, illness and physical violence. During fieldwork I have observed several extremely serious incidents between close kin, often resulting in blows and occasionally in injury requiring long hospitalisation. In none of the situations I witnessed was sorcery mentioned, and nor – in any serious sense – were the combatants enjoined to laugh. Laughter as a form of healing is much more appropriate when it relates to an individual's personal grief, and of little use when the situation involves the complex entanglements of close kin in enduring relationships.

Indigenous explanations for extreme forms of violence and personal turmoil usually devolve both on the well known structural problems that exist between co-resident kin and affines, who ideally should cooperate but whose interests often diverge, and on the ancestors and spirits that are frequently believed, through a spirit-medium's revelation, to foment such trouble. Ancestral wrath is visited on families for a variety of reasons, often manifesting itself in quarrelling and fighting between members of the afflicted family, and sometimes in their illness or even death. Balinese may also explain violent behaviour in terms of spirit invasion. The class of spirits known as *buta-kala* is said to cause hatred, jealousy, anger, confusion and fear. Balinese possessed by these spirits behave abnormally, and to keep spirit invasion to a minimum offerings are provided for them at regular intervals and at particular locations (see Chapter 4).

Responses to interpersonal violence are also varied. A family might go to a medium to determine the ultimate cause of the problem, but merely knowing this cause and thus placating ancestors and spirits through appropriate ritual is not usually sufficient to solve social problems, because words have been uttered and blows have been exchanged. Serious disturbances usually lead to a change in existing arrangements – husband and wife may divorce, mothers in law may insist that their 'insubordinate' daughters in law toe the line, brothers may separate their living accommodation and disentangle their material interests so that they no longer need to cooperate (Howe 1989a). An additional response to events of this kind, also often seen in relation to those who have suffered a severe shock, fainted, had an accident or fall, or who feel generally very run down and exhausted, is to perform a small ritual called *ngulapin*. This 'recalls' the soul which has temporarily left the body, and restores the components of one's body to their correct relationships.

Illness may also be conceived of as a 'natural' event, and treated with a wide variety of herbal remedies and concoctions. A large range of indigenous tonics (*jamu*) is readily available; and a particular class of healer (*balian*) specialises in herbal medicines, many of them based on restoring balance to a body that has become too 'hot' (*panes*) or too 'cold' (*nyem*). Market days often see a travelling salesman setting out his weird and wonderful collection of ointments, medicines and aphrodisiacs, made by soaking bones, teeth, skins and other parts of animals in water or oil. They are said to cure or prevent anything from backache and impotence to rashes and deformities. These days, however, the first response of many who fall ill is to go to a western trained doctor rather than to a *balian*.

Balinese often respond to illness by returning to their natal village, for that is where they are safe, where their kin can protect them, and where a cure is most likely to be effected. Most Balinese I know extol the virtues and curative properties of their village's springwater and the rice grown on village land. Several people told me how they were cured once they had come home. One young man who worked as a tour operator in Denpasar came down with acute stomach pains. After several fruitless visits to doctors, he became very weak and returned home. His family took him to a temple considered magically potent, and there asked for a blessing (*nunas ica*) from the god. After several days of drinking Corong water he began to feel much better. Another told me he too used to live in Denpasar where he had a floundering trucking business. He became very ill, and it was not until he returned to Corong and took traditional medicine and drank the local water that he recovered.

The second of Wikan's omissions is a wider understanding of the role of laughter, even though she includes a penetrating analysis into the subject. I was frequently admonished by friends to laugh and joke more, and told not to ask too many serious questions because they gave everyone a headache. Laughter helps to keep grief private, so that it does not upset others, and it is a means of dissipating grief in a safe and controlled manner. When I did begin to laugh more, friends would often remark, quite ingenuously, 'Oh, look, he can laugh', or 'Oh, you know how to laugh then'. I think the subject can be probed a little deeper, albeit speculatively. Wikan rarely attempts to see what light an analysis of laughter can shed on political relations. Injunctions to put on a bright face or laugh in the face of suffering could encourage the acceptance of loss without complaint because it is thought to be caused by invisible forces – angry ancestors, capricious spirits or evil witches – outside a person's personal control, rather than by socially unequal relationships.

Significantly, Wikan fails to note that a linguistic representation of laughter sees it as a gift from god. The common word for laughter is *kedék*, but there is also a high Balinese term, *ica*, whose constellation of meanings – laughter, gift, blessing – is instructive. Balinese receive gifts and blessings (*ica*) of various kinds from their deities and political overlords. *Ica* come in many forms – the bestowal of *sakti* which empowers the recipient, the gift of a miraculous cure, a magically powerful object such as an unusual stone, amulet, dagger or palmleaf text, the gifts of land and food which a lord provides for subordinates, or the blessings associated with holy water. A young man in Pujung, ill for many months, took himself to the graveyard to die, but he heard a voice in the sky ordering him to go to the 'death' temple. There he conducted an all night vigil and was cured by a gift (*ica*) from god. A priest in Pujung had a source of holy water in his family temple. In the past it had been necessary to replenish it periodically. After leading a devout life, however, no matter how much the water was used it now never diminished – this was an example of *ica*. The original inhabitants of Pujung possessed a gun which was said to be a gift (*ica*) from the gods. It had miraculous powers such that, for example, it only needed to be pointed at birds and they would fall out of the sky. It became a sacred heirloom of one of the village's temples, and now is only brought out and fired during the annual temple ceremony. A final example concerns a high caste friend in Corong who was plagued by misfortune in his business dealings. He was convinced that the cause was sins from a previous life which had not yet been expunged. He took to praying in his houseyard temple every night, and one evening an ancestor spoke to him. It told him that his grandmother had failed to carry out a vow. He must therefore take certain offerings to a village temple. When he did, part of the money that was a constituent of the offering disappeared and in its place he found fine strands of gold. This gold, he said, was a gift (*ica*) which could be used as medicine and to repel witchcraft.

Ica is the word most commonly used to describe such blessings and gifts. Those who request holy water, beseech god for a blessing, or beg a boon from a lord, all engage in *nunas ica*. *Ica* is also the high Balinese word for 'laughter', or 'smiling with favour'. To *nunas ica* is thus to beg for a favour, grace, or a gift, and to be smiled on, and this all carries the implication that the gift is bestowed on an inferior by a superior (van Eck 1876: 8; Hunter 1988: 330). The verb form of *ica* is *icén* and means to give, and the common phrase *icén-nunas* (*baang-idih* in low Balinese) means something like 'allow me to beg for this'. If this is something substantial then the receiver is placed in the donor's debt and becomes his client and follower.

These phrases are very commonly used in ordinary conversation in contemporary Bali when someone requests something from someone else, though today, outside of religious uses, they most often concern small and trivial things – cigarettes, use of a tool, some bamboo, a few coconuts. If someone asks how much was paid for the coconuts, the frequent reply is '*sing, baang-idih*' – 'no, I asked for them', and in such cases debt is not a serious issue. Another meaning of the term *nunas* is 'to eat', particularly in relation to rice, itself mythically seen as the source of life since originally rice was a gift from the gods. The phrase '*titiang kaicén nunas*', which is a common way of saying 'I eat', literally means something like 'I am given to eat' (Eiseman 1990, vol. 2: 138–9). As Eiseman points out, the idea here is 'that a person of low caste possesses something – even food – only by favour of high castes' (138). Once I asked an old high caste man in Corong why his family owned no rice land. He replied '*ten nunas ke puri*', meaning that when his father moved to this village he did not 'beg' the local lord for a grant of land – being reputedly lazy he preferred instead to 'beg a basket of rice' (*nunas nasi asokasi*) each day so that his family could eat.

In pre-colonial Bali everything that was important in life – land, food, security, health – was seen broadly as a gift or blessing from the superior gods, ancestors and lords, a representation which constituted a kind of ideological legitimation of the hierarchy (Howe 1991). Aside from religious contexts, these practices have pretty much disappeared, though they live on as pale reflections in the language of everyday discourse. Even when they buy food at a roadside stall Balinese feel impelled to say something before they start eating. Often it may be '*tiang dumunan?*' – 'I'll start first, okay?', or '*ngajeng*' – 'I'm eating', requiring others to say '*enggih*' – 'Yes, please do', or '*raris*' – 'Go ahead'. Sometimes people even say '*nunas*', as though they were requesting the food. All these usages suggest, however incongruously given that the eatery is a commercial establishment and the food has to be paid for, that in some sense the rice is not really one's own but is being bestowed on one as a gift. In short, everything that is good in some sense symbolically comes from above, from deities, ancestors and lords. In this context lords and high priests do not so much exploit those below them as act as the sources or intermediaries of health, happiness, laughter and life itself.

Conclusion

Geertz and Wikan aim to highlight characteristic features of Balinese interpersonal behaviour, in part by comparing Balinese and Euro-American 'cultures'. Because this involves homogenising both, the method is flawed. It seems less an analytical strategy than a rhetorical and stylistic device. As such the differences 'discovered' are to some extent an artifact of the procedure. Emphasising difference, suppressing similarity and collapsing variation produce a flat and monochrome picture, given apparent significance by its juxtaposition to an unexamined and equally uniform 'us'.

Balinese people, even in one village, cannot be typified in terms of a set of beliefs and practices concerning either the intensity of interaction or its apparent lack, because there is considerable diversity among them. Balinese differ in what they believe and in the conviction with which these beliefs are held. Some consider themselves vulnerable to powerful forces, others possess methods of defence. Balinese may change their views over time as experience and circumstance dictate. Gender, age and status qualify the texture and strain of interaction, but do not determine it. Stage fright, shyness and elaborate etiquette may well characterise the commoner's visit to the high priest's house, but these are absent with neighbours, gambling friends and workmates. For a variety of reasons one must be on one's guard with strangers, healers, employers and officials, but fear is not the only or even dominant emotion typifying these relationships, and among friends and kin trust is at least as significant as suspicion.

However subtle and brilliant her analysis of Balinese interaction, and however delicate her interpretation of their responses to fear, Wikan nevertheless portrays all Balinese as prey to the same set of fears, making similar responses to them. Despite the illuminating insights Geertz achieves, Balinese people end up as ciphers, reflecting nothing more substantial than the symbolic webs of significance they themselves are said to weave.

4 The efficacy of ritual action and the transformation of religion

Introduction

In earlier periods in anthropology, issues concerning ritual action were often characterised as a series of questions about instrumentality and expressivity. Why are beliefs in magical and ritual action generated? What are the ends and purposes of ritual action? What do ritual and magical action symbolically express about social relationships and societal arrangements? Are such practices rational? It used to be the anthropologist who asked these questions – nowadays it is quite often members of the group being studied. They may do so because they are uncertain as to whether they should carry on believing in the efficacy of ritual action, and are unsure whether the resources of time, money, labour and materials consumed in ritual are necessary or simply wasted. They may need to decide which among competing religious systems they should give allegiance to, given that one system demands ritual action while another denounces it. They may question whether an emphasis on ritual deflects attention away from a different meaning of religion, a different attitude to divinity, or a different kind of religious experience.

Many Balinese today are engaged in debates of this kind. Their motivations come from a range of religious concerns. What sort of god do we have? What is the most appropriate way to approach god? Which is more important, ritual action or ethical conduct? Are priests essential mediators or do they exploit people? Is the money, time and labour spent on ritual necessary, or are these expenditures the outcome of a religious system which has become distorted? Why do we do this ritual? These questions show that such religious issues cannot be divorced from political and economic concerns, but they also imply that the religious dimension is of particular importance. In my analysis of the religious landscape of contemporary Bali I try to avoid reductionist explanations which see religious matters in terms of material factors, even though to some extent religious ideologies define patterns of political and economic conflict.

In Bali these religious concerns emerged when colonial officers and Javanese Muslims began to criticise Balinese religion as being hardly a religion at all. Balinese religion, as it existed in the nineteenth and early twentieth centuries, became problematic for the Balinese because others compared it with alien

The efficacy of ritual action and the transformation of religion 57

systems – Christianity and Islam – which were very different and which made Balinese think hard about their own religious practice. Before considering these problems, let us first look at the ethnography of Balinese religious activity.

Balinese religion and ritual

Balinese religious practice at the turn of the twentieth century can best be described as an orthopraxy rather than an orthodoxy (Geertz 1973b: 186), because in general religious action was more about performing ritual and getting it right than about belief in verbal doctrine. As long as the appropriate rituals were carried out on the right days and in the proper way, then the ancestors, divinised through the rituals of cremation, would protect the living, bring them prosperity and make their fields fertile. Such a religion is

> highly localized; it consists of rites relating specific groups of people to one another, to their ancestors, and to their territory. Moreover, it is a customary obligation for the Balinese: participation in its rites is a consequence of membership of a local community as well as membership of a descent group.
> (Picard 1999: 31)

At that time it would have been very difficult to isolate and identify something in Bali called 'Balinese religion', in the sense of a domain of belief and practice separate from other – economic and political – spheres of life, and within which only limited relationships obtained. Contemporary western societies tend to circumscribe religion by conceiving of it as a private matter of individual faith, thus marginalising its influence on secular and public affairs. In Bali 'religious' activity permeated every aspect of communal customary practice. Kinship groups were also temple congregations practising ancestor worship. Subsistence rice production was highly ritualised, with success depending on the blessings of deities and the observance of taboos. Relationships between lords and subjects paralleled those between gods and people. States were not secular political organisations based on a social contract between ruler and ruled, but magico-religious realms underpinned by divine kingship.

I refer to this kind of collective religious practice as *adat*, after the Arabic word first used by Muslims in Indonesia to refer to indigenous customary law as opposed to imported Islamic religious law, broadened by the Dutch to designate the traditional social order of Indonesian societies (Warren 1993: 1). Since that time there has been protracted debate among Balinese, especially among elites, academic intellectuals and urban classes, about the point and efficacy of *adat* ritualism. While most Balinese still continue to perform their ceremonies in broadly 'traditional' fashion, this debate is taking place in an environment of considerable religious diversity engendered by the introduction of a state sponsored religious orthodoxy of a decidedly Hindu kind, together with the import from India of the Hindu devotionalist movements Sri Sathya Sai Baba and the

Hare Krishnas, which emphasise ethical conduct and belief in a unitary god over ritual practice and the worship of ancestors and spirits. This process and its outcomes are discussed further in the next chapter.

Balinese ceremonies are today classified in two ways. One describes the kind of ritual, the other the level at which it is performed. Within the first classification are five classes of ritual (*yadnya*) – those devoted to gods (*dèwa*), human beings (*manusa*), holy persons (*rsi*), malevolent spirits (*buta-kala*), and the souls of the dead (*pitra*). Any temple ceremony is a *dèwa yadnya*, because it concerns worship of the gods which that temple exists to support. All rites of passage – birth, naming, birthdays, puberty, tooth-filing – are *manusa yadnya*. Purification ceremonies are *buta yadnya*. Any particular ceremony may consist of rituals from more than one class. The ordination of a priest requires offerings to ancestors and gods, to *buta-kala* spirits, and offerings for the person becoming a priest.

In regard to the second classification, the level at which rituals are performed, rituals vary in size and complexity. The lowest level (*nista*) is the simplest form of ritual, with few people involved, few offerings, and only small animals – if any – being slaughtered. The intermediate level (*madya*) increases the quantity, quality and range of offerings, the number of people involved, and the kinds of animal killed. The highest level (*utama*) sees a further increase in all these inputs, and the addition of subsidiary elements within the ceremony. A tooth-filing performed by a poor family for its children may be attended only by close kin and neighbours, with the minimum of offerings and the slaughter of one pig, a ceremony hardly noticeable by the rest of the village. A rich, high status and powerful household, by contrast, might invite two hundred guests, slaughter ten pigs, seclude the children for three nights, pay for a shadow play open to the public, and prepare sumptuous food and impressive offerings. It will be a very public performance, which the family hopes will be spoken of for months to come. Needless to say, the more elaborate ceremony costs many times more than the simple one.

Ceremonies often have two objectives, one explicit, the other implicit. The explicit aim is the need to obtain the greatest benefit for those performing the ceremony and, in the case of rites of passage and rituals for the dead, for those for whom the ceremony is being held. Since the material offerings are complex and the ritual is about security and prosperity, the important thing is to get it right (Howe 2000). However, status competition is an abiding concern of Balinese, and the implicit objective of many ceremonies is to make a statement about relative prestige by creating a ritual at least as impressive as your rivals'.

Rites of passage (*manusa yadnya*) are very important to Balinese. At birth a child is 'still a god' (*nu dèwa*) because it is a reincarnation of a purified ancestor whose soul now animates the material body of the newborn infant. As such the child may not touch the ground for three Balinese months (105 days), because the earth is considered polluting. Since the process of birth also produces pollution, neither the mother nor the baby may enter any kind of temple, the mother for 42 days and the baby for 105 days. During these three months therefore the child must be carried everywhere. At the end of this period the rite of *nelubulanin* is performed, during which the child is ceremoniously lowered to the ground for the first time. In the associated ceremony of *nyambutin* the soul is officially welcomed into the body. In the final act of *nelubulanin* the ritual *matataban* is performed, in which the parents assist the child by wafting the contents of a tray of offerings to sustain their spiritual or immaterial wellbeing. Although now allowed to touch the earth, the child is not permitted to crawl or shuffle on its hands and knees, as this is considered too reminiscent of animal behaviour and thus anathema.

The ceremony of *nyambutin* is repeated at 210 days (one *oton*) and subsequently every *oton* until the child is about six years old. The child is now considered a social agent with the developing capacity to distinguish right from wrong, and thus able to commit breaches of moral and ritual rules. If a child dies after this time, full cremation rights are necessary to detach the child from its commitment to the social world. If a child dies earlier, rites of cremation need not be performed, burial being sufficient for the child's soul to reach heaven directly. After the age of six the child begins to suffer defilement, spoken of in terms such as *sebel, leteh, resem* and *cemer*, used to describe various forms of pollution, filth or dirt, which periodically have to be removed. Consequently at each subsequent *oton* the child wafts the offering called *bia kaon*, which is designed to achieve this cleansing, rather than the *matataban* offering.

For girls the next major ceremony, often omitted by poorer households, is *menék daa* – becoming a marriageable woman – held around or after puberty and before marriage. There is no puberty ceremony for boys, so their next rite of passage – as for girls – is either tooth-filing (*mapandes*) or marriage (*masakapan*). Tooth-filing may be performed at any time before cremation, though most families try to do it before marriage, since delayed tooth-filing is a sign of poverty. While the earlier rituals are usually household affairs with few status overtones, the ceremonies of *menék daa*, marriage and tooth-filing are all very status sensitive, and households try to outdo each other in the ceremonial clothes bought for the children, the size, quantity and quality of offerings, the number and importance of guests invited, and the number of animals slaughtered. I have regularly been asked to photograph not only the ritual proceedings, but also the impressive line of guests' cars parked in the road outside the house.

Tooth-filing is a one day ceremony, though for several weeks leading up to it the household and its neighbours and kin are busy preparing the many offerings and erecting temporary structures. On the morning of the appointed day – decided on the basis of a 'good and bad day' system – many villagers turn up to slaughter pigs, ducks and chickens, prepare a number of large and highly elaborate offerings, carry other offerings to temples around the village, and prepare food for the afternoon guests. The ceremony itself takes place about midday, and may be performed for all the children in the family to save on costs. The children may have been secluded in a room for one or three days, and now emerge in expensive, traditional dress. One by one, or two by two, they ascend the ritually important pavilion in the house compound known as the *balé dangin*, lie down with their heads in the most auspicious direction – towards the central mountains, and have two plugs of sugar cane inserted between their molar teeth, both to prop the mouth open and to produce copious amounts of saliva. Standing at their head, the priest – or it may be a metalsmith – begins to file the top middle six teeth until the points have been removed so that they form an even and straight line. The idea is that human beings must be differentiated from animals. By filing down the points of the canine teeth (*caling* or 'fangs'), a symbolic connection is made with the removal of the coarse, selfish and socially disruptive dispositions such as greed, lust, jealousy and anger (the *sad ripu* or 'six enemies', Eiseman 1990, Vol 1: 108–14), seen as characteristic of animals. The filing also has an aesthetic value, since those Balinese who have not had their teeth filed are considered less attractive. Between marriage and death there are no important rituals unless the person becomes a priest or shadow puppeteer, or assumes another religious office.

The rituals of death and cremation are the affair of the local community (*banjar*), though the household of the deceased takes the lead in making the decisions as to when and what kind of cremation is to be held. When someone dies their body is taken home, where it lies for three days to allow villagers to pay their respects. Some villagers stay in the house overnight, the men playing cards, the women preparing offerings, to support the bereaved family and to keep evil spirits at bay by producing a lively and noisy atmosphere. The body is then washed, wrapped in white cloth and a bamboo casing, and buried in the graveyard in a sombre ceremony towards the end of the day. Ideally the body should lie in the earth until the flesh has decomposed and only the bones remain. This process returns to the earth the material that made up the fleshly body which had itself been sustained by food – rice – grown in the earth. This leaves the soul, symbolically represented by the permanence of the bones, to be returned to the ancestors, whence it came, through the fires of cremation (Warren 1993; Howe 2004).

Cremation (*ngabén*) is a very costly business, and families may wait years before cremating a relative, though those who can afford to do so may cremate immediately, even without burial, as a demonstration of piety – or, as others might see it, as a show of wealth. Because of their augmented purity, certain categories of people, such as priests, should not be put under the ground at all, and thus have to be burned straightaway.

The long sequence of events that make up a cremation, while bewildering on first acquaintance, is reasonably straightforward. If the deceased has been buried for a while the remains are disinterred, though in the simplest ceremonies just a portion of earth from the grave is collected. These remains are taken home where, with other materials, they are fashioned into a bodylike form. On the day of the cremation this effigy is transported in a long and boisterous procession to the graveyard, whereupon it is cremated.

Cremations are costly affairs for a number of reasons. Though the members of the *banjar* are obliged to make a contribution – rice, coconuts, bamboo and the like – most of the expenses fall on the deceased's family. The whole *banjar*, as many as a hundred households, has to help in the preparations, and thus be fed and plied with coffee, snacks and cigarettes. There are many offerings to prepare and various structures to be built. Two of these structures are the *badé*, a pagoda-like tower with an odd number of receding roofs – the number being an indication of status, in which the body or its remains is carried to the graveyard, and the *patulangan*, a sarcophagus in the shape of a real or mythical animal, in which the deceased is actually cremated. Both of these structures can either be very large and elaborate or quite small and simple. Cremation is followed by further rites at intervals sometimes stretching years into the future, all designed to make sure the deceased finds its final resting place with the ancestors, from where it will reincarnate. In this sense death is not an event but a long drawn out process which provides the time and space for social rearrangements to take place, and for the living slowly to come to terms with their loss.

Cremation lends itself best to the gambits of status competition. Any cremation, whether cheap or expensive, simple or complex, achieves the desired ritual end if performed correctly. But it also affords an opportunity to engage in status assertion by, for example, building a cremation tower with more roofs than is usually acknowledged as appropriate for the deceased's status group, or a sarcophagus usually reserved for a superior group. Such projects are risky, since they may arouse the disapproval of the *banjar* and result in the structures being intentionally damaged and even the corpse being abused (Connor 1979; Howe 2001, Chs 3–5). The attempt to enhance status through overly extravagant ritual activity may also have a deleterious influence on the fate of the soul. In a village in east Bali, on the night after the burning, family members were woken by strange sounds. When they investigated they saw the 'departed relative, his mouth stuffed with the elaborate offerings, moaning that he was too heavy … to enter heaven' (Poffenberger and Zurbuchen 1980: 123–5).

Life cycle ceremonies are just one part of Balinese ritual activity. A typical household is a member of perhaps ten temple congregations, some of which may be miles from its home village. Each of these temples has a yearly festival, lasting between one and nine days, which the household has to participate in and prepare offerings for. There is also an endless round of calendrical ceremonies which fall on particular days of the month and on new and full moon days. There are up to ten such rituals in any 35-day month. Most of these rituals are completed early in the morning by laying offerings in the houseyard temple, in other buildings in the compound, and in the street. Many are small and require few offerings, but some are considerably more complex, and many offerings have to be prepared. Additionally, any building – domestic, temple or otherwise – has to be ritually activated, 'brought to life', before it can be used (Howe 1983). Finally there is a new year's ceremony (*nyepi*) every solar year, and the major festivals of Galungan and Kuningan every 210 days (Eiseman 1990, Vol. 1).

No group of people would countenance the vast amounts of time, labour and materials involved if these rituals were not perceived as having many and significant benefits. The most important is the protection and safety of people and possessions guaranteed by ancestors and spirits pleased by this extraordinary devotion. Another is the sheer enjoyment people obtain from large scale communal ritual practice. Major temple festivals, particularly those which last nine days, are eagerly anticipated events as they regularly involve drama performances, gamelan music, temple dances, shadow plays, the *barong* dance, the attendance of gods from other villages which arrive in impressive processions, cockfighting, and much else. These are times when people parade their best clothes, show off their ability to make and carry tall offerings, indulge their sensual appetites through gambling, eating and flirting with the opposite sex, and sustain their spiritual wellbeing through receiving holy water blessed by the temple deities. The whole village becomes transformed during the festivities, as merchants descend on the local area from surrounding districts and create a bustling night market. One of the greatest pleasures for Balinese is to participate in an atmosphere they call *ramé* – crowded, noisy and lively. Temple festivals, markets and cockfights are the epitome of this excitement.

A third benefit is that collective ritual endeavour binds a community together in a series of exchanges producing a solidarity – albeit one sometimes fractured by conflict – that is highly valued and jealously guarded. It is impossible to mount such extravaganzas as tooth-filing, marriage and cremation without considerable assistance from others. It is the convivial sociality of these collective enterprises which makes ceremonial activity thoroughly enjoyable. All of this has to be reciprocated, and Balinese make precise calculations of what comes in and what goes out.

Much of what lies at the heart of Balinese social and cultural life depends on ritual action. As well as the status implications of ritual performance, the significance of ritual lies in the fact that it underpins basic cultural understandings of the nature of human–supernatural relationships. Invisible deities, ancestors and spirits are principal actors on the Balinese stage, and their interventions constitute many of the most important events in the lives of Balinese Hindus. Eliciting their help and avoiding their sanctions are what engender health and prosperity, and the only way the proper relationship between Balinese and their ancestors can be preserved is by frequent and substantial material offerings. Few Balinese go through life without finding out at first hand that laxity in the performance of ritual leads to very unhappy outcomes. Constant ritual performance might sometimes be felt as a burden, but it appears to be a necessary one.

There is another side to this. Households may go into debt or sell land or other possessions in a bid to participate in ritual at an acceptable level. If a household cannot compete adequately its members will suffer from an emotion known as *jengah*, a corrosive mixture of shame and anger which spurs them to do better next time. If, out of religious conviction or poverty, a household tries to economise too much on the expenses of ritual activity, it may be branded as mean, uncaring and aloof – serious accusations in a society which values collective endeavour and conformity. Finally, while the event may be enjoyable – even the preliminary work sessions – the period leading up to a major ritual can become quite tense as copious offerings have to be made, much has to be purchased, nervous reliance has to be placed on others, and anxiety contained as to whether the right people will turn up at the appointed times to help with all the work. While anthropologists have spent inordinate amounts of time detailing and interpreting actual ritual events, they have rarely documented the before and after of such events. The overall economy of ritual action is surely an issue worthy of more sustained research.

A new Balinese religion

There has probably always been some dissatisfaction about this burden of ritual, especially for poorer Balinese. During the economic depression of the period spanning colonialism, the war and its revolutionary aftermath, many found it impossible to meet the costs of cremating deceased relatives, and thus had to confront the illness and strife caused by the anger of the neglected and unpurified souls of the dead which, until they have been cremated, may cause havoc. Even in times of economic growth – such as that created by the tourist boom – poorer households can still face problems because richer ones continually ratchet up what they are willing to invest in ritual, thus leaving their poorer neighbours behind. As a consequence some Balinese have questioned not just the costs of ritual activity, but also its very basis.

The arguments about the efficacy of ritual, which began in earnest in the 1920s, are part of a wider debate concerning nothing less than the structure and organisation of Balinese society. The late nineteenth and early twentieth centuries witnessed the emergence of a worldwide Islamic reform movement which has influenced Islam in Indonesia, the formation of numerous political parties, proto-nationalist and cultural movements, trade unions, and religious organisations right across Indonesia, and unrest and rebellion in both rural and urban areas of Java and Sumatra. One result of this quickening social change, what Shiraishi (1990) has called 'an age in motion', was that religious identities and religious systems began to assume more politicised and oppositional forms (Ricklefs 1981). In the social and political ferment of the early twentieth century, a group of commoner Balinese intellectuals working as teachers, civil servants and other officials in the north Balinese town of Singaraja, the headquarters of the colonial regime, began to think hard about their religion and attempted to construct it in a new way. Their thinking and motives were influenced by several factors – their desire to make sense of their own situation in a rapidly changing world, criticisms by Dutch colonial officials and Muslim scholars concerning the content and status of Balinese religion, the need to counteract the growing threat posed by Muslim and Christian proselytising, and their admiration for western notions of democracy and equality, acquired in part through education in Dutch schools in Bali, Java or Holland.

Working with a nineteenth century evolutionist view of religion, outsiders derided Balinese religion, branding it as backward and primitive. Balinese were labelled polytheistic, people who indiscriminately worshipped stones, trees and a vast array of local spirits, and possessed neither a holy book nor a high god. To many Muslims Balinese religion was hardly a religion at all, and was certainly unlike Islam. Balinese found it very difficult to answer these denunciations, which sensitised some to what they themselves began to construe as deficiencies in their own religion. Their project of reinterpretation was thus an attempt to rework their religion into something resembling a freestanding system of doctrine and practice which could be explained to others, both insiders and outsiders. The Sanskrit word *agama* was adopted by Balinese leaders in an effort to elevate this modified religion to an equal status with Islam and Christianity, already so described as *agama Islam* and *agama Kristen*, and so help block attempts at conversion.

Part of this effort at constructing a Balinese religion in a more universally acceptable form involved an argument between high and low castes, gentry and commoners, concerning the link between religion and the hierarchical caste system. Influenced by ideologies of merit and wisdom, commoners challenged gentry hegemony by claiming that status should be based on education and achievement rather than on birth and ascription. In the debate between these two groups in the 1920s, carried out in periodicals, two rather different versions of Balinese religion emerged. Gentry contended that the traditional social order – hierarchy, ritual, priests, customary behaviour, what Balinese had come to refer to as *adat* – was inextricably linked with religion, and thus could not be separated from it. Commoners, by contrast, wanted to strengthen *agama* – 'religion' – by expunging from *adat* what was both unfair and an obstacle to progress, which in practice meant the caste system. Gentry promoted a form of Hinduism seen as specifically Balinese, tied to the hierarchical order, and with its origins in the Javanese empire of Majapahit, portrayed as the source of aristocratic court culture. No doubt one reason for maintaining this position was that the privileges they obtained from their high caste status continued to be justified and legitimated through being linked to customary religious and ritual practices focused on ancestors, themselves differentiated by origin and rank. Commoners insisted that their religion was properly Hindu, that it originated in India, and that it should be separated from caste.

Because these early debates were conducted in Malay rather than Balinese, and thus potentially had a wide circulation outside Bali, they were considered part of broader nationalistic and anti-colonial movements of protest, which the Dutch found it expedient to defuse. This they did either by exiling dissidents and trouble-makers, or by channelling their efforts into safer and less controversial projects, such as the study and recording of popular culture and religious traditions (Vickers 1989: 152–3). The die had been cast, however, and when the arguments resurfaced after World War II they were even more vital, because the broader context had placed Balinese religion in a very difficult position.

After independence in 1950 the issue of just what kind of religion the Balinese practised became very controversial. The constitution of the new republic was, and still is, based on the *Pancasila*, or 'five principles', the first of which is belief in one god – the other four are nationalism, humanitarianism, democracy and consent, and social justice. The state is neither secular nor Islamic, but is founded on broad religious values. The Ministry of Religion, headquartered in Jakarta and staffed mostly by Muslims, insisted that only those religions (*agama*) which were monotheistic, possessed a holy book and a prophet, and were not restricted to a single ethnic group, were truly universal religions and thus eligible for state support and protection. Initially this limited the field of acceptable religions to Islam, Catholicism, Protestantism and Buddhism, and omitted Balinese religion, which was classified as 'tribal' and thus not an *agama*. The Balinese were said to be *belum beragama*, 'not yet to have a religion', an idea which exposes the thinking behind state policy about religion which placed Balinese religion in a backward stage of development. Furthermore, since it was the duty of members of state-sponsored religions to convert those who were *belum beragama*, though illegal for members of 'tribal' religions to do likewise, the situation was potentially disastrous for the Balinese, who would quickly become targets for Muslim and Christian proselytisation (Swellengrebel 1960: 72; Picard 1999).

During this period reformist organisations, instituted to advocate the Balinese case, argued that Balinese religion was a variant of Indian Hinduism. To consolidate this claim Balinese intellectuals went to study in Indian universities, and Indian scholars were invited to Bali (Bakker 1993: 2–3). Promises were made to rationalise Balinese religion by simplifying and standardising rituals, stressing doctrine and theology, bringing to greater prominence a previously rather shadowy high god (Sanghyang Widi), and by translating Indian religious texts into Indonesian – almost identical to Malay and the official language of the Republic of Indonesia. In the face of insistent pressure from Balinese intellectuals and religious officials, President Sukarno, whose mother was Balinese and who holidayed in Bali, accepted that, despite its seeming polytheism, Balinese religion was in reality monotheistic and that, in the *Bhagavadgita* and other Indian texts, it possessed a sacred literature.

As a result this modified religion, named *agama Hindu Bali*, gained official recognition in 1958, and an official religious organisation, the *Parisada Hindu Dharma Bali*, was set up in 1959 to supervise its development. A few years later, under pressure from the Ministry of Religion to universalise the religion so that it should not be associated with one ethnic group, its name was changed to *agama Hindu*, and the *Parisada* was renamed *Parisada Hindu Dharma Indonesia*. This allowed Indonesians outside Bali to join *agama Hindu*, and many from Java, Kalimantan, Sulawesi and other islands have since done so, preferring Hinduism to Islam. In little more than thirty years Balinese religion was transformed, at least in theory, from local ritual practice to an *agama* with transnational potential. To begin with it was little more than a religion in name only, and much remained to be decided. What were its finer details of doctrine and practice to be? How was the new religion's relation to *adat* to be construed, and how would it be promulgated?

These matters will be taken up in the next chapter, where I document the process of establishing *agama Hindu* in Bali. One of the most interesting aspects of this reorganisation was how the institutionalisation of the new religion opened up space for the unexpected introduction of other forms of Indian religious traditions into the island. While the state sought to impose a religious orthodoxy in Bali from the top down, in part to dampen religious and political conflict, the unintended outcome was an explosion of new and diverse religious thinking and activity, largely initiated at grassroots level.

Reforming ritual

Beginning in the 1920s and emerging from the debates concerning the structure of Balinese society, various efforts have been made by Balinese reformers to simplify ritual practices, especially cremation (Connor 1996). Combining concern for the plight of the poor with an agenda for egalitarian reforms of hierarchy, privilege and power, these reformers championed rationalised and less expensive ceremonies. In the beginning these reforms were limited, geographically restricted, and dependent on cooperation between priests, villagers and progressive village leaders. It was only in the early 1960s that significant and widespread reforms took place, reforms which were a response both to the economic hardship of the times and to the promises made to simplify and standardise ritual as part of the programme for the new *agama Hindu*.

The trigger for these reforms was the performance of a gigantic purification ritual at Bali's 'mother' temple, *pura* Besakih, on the slopes of Mount Agung, a ritual supposedly held only once every hundred years. Before the ceremony could be performed it was decreed that the whole island had to be purified by the cremation of all buried corpses. Since poverty and political turmoil had prevented many families conducting these ceremonies for their relatives for several decades, there was a very large backlog of corpses waiting to be cremated. For many this sudden expense posed an insurmountable economic burden. Religious officials of the Parisada and other organisations began to search for ways to reform prevailing practices, principally by promoting certain religious texts, up to that time rarely consulted, which advocated cheaper and simpler ceremonies. There was considerable resistance to this by many high priests, who saw their authority as spiritual guides being undermined. The fact that cheaper ceremonies also meant smaller remuneration for priests was probably not without significance (Connor 1996: 196). Nonetheless, the reforms were eagerly accepted by many, and less expensive ceremonies began to be performed.

In addition to these cheaper individual ceremonies involving minimal offerings, other reforms introduced collective cremations in which a group of families co-ordinated their activities and shared a number of important offerings and the services of a priest. The success of this form depends on the kind of collectivity involved. If the individual households coming together share the same status title, and are thus equal in rank, the collective cremation poses fewer problems than if the collectivity is composed of people of different hierarchical rank. In the latter case, as Connor (1996) argues, there are numerous difficulties. If one cremation tower (*badé*) is used for all the corpses or their effigies, instead of one tower for each corpse, how are they to be arranged in the tower? The fluid and contested nature of hierarchical status in any village, one of whose prime indicators is alignment on a vertical axis, makes it virtually impossible to obtain agreement about which of the deceased should be at the top and which at the bottom. Decisions as to which offerings to use, which priest should officiate, which temples should supply the holy water, all raise similarly difficult problems. A more recent innovation has been the introduction of streamlined cremations which compress several phases of the rite, which are otherwise spaced over twelve days, into a twenty-four hour period. Requiring less preparation, fewer material resources and less labour, they are consequently less costly. In contemporary Bali many of these reforms are now common practice.

Reforms of ritual practice are in part underpinned by new interpretations.

Cheaper ceremonies are validated by the argument that the efficacy of a rite remains constant irrespective of the material level at which it is performed. Only a minimum of offerings is necessary to perform the ceremony properly, so the destruction of the offerings and the paraphernalia used in more lavish ceremonies may be condemned as an irrational waste of money which disproportionately penalises the poor. In a combination of local versions of Indian karmic theory and western ideas about merit, the fate of the soul is argued to depend on the quality of the person's actions during life, and thus cannot be affected by ceremonial activity after death however much money is spent.

While these views help legitimate cheaper ceremonies, and an ethicised rather than a ritual approach to religion, they only do so up to a point. When Balinese can spend more on ritual, they often do. The rationale for this apparent extravagance comes both from the desire not to be outdone in status competition, and also because most Balinese believe that offerings are not an optional extra but an absolute requirement for success. In regard to status rivalry, precisely because collective cremations give the appearance of flattening status differentials, those who can afford to cremate individually – which has clear status overtones – often opt to do so, with the result that the introduction of collective ceremonies ironically provides further opportunities to display differences. In regard to the purpose of offerings, for many Balinese these are not merely symbolic, but actually nourish the soul of the person undergoing the rite. In cremations, for example, complex offerings constitute the 'provisions' for the deceased to help them negotiate successfully the long and dangerous journey in the afterlife before they reach their destination. Offerings also demonstrate the intensity and centrality of the association between the living and the ancestors. Without them ancestors may become angry and take supernatural revenge.

Attempts to restrain ritual consumption through simplified ceremonies is problematic in other ways. If offerings are essential to wellbeing, cutting down on them leads to accusations of an uncaring attitude to one's ancestors and children. In the ceremonial sphere social approval depends on visible demonstration of substantial ritual activity. The substitution of an ethical orientation to religion in place of a ritual one, entailing fewer offerings, poses problems of impression management.

Simple ceremonies may also give rise to difficult social relationships. Since the reciprocal exchange of unpaid labour during ceremonies constitutes a cornerstone of harmonious community relations, the pressure to provide labour for others – and to ask for it for oneself – is very great. The performance of important ceremonies for which little or no outside help is requested looks suspiciously like an attempt to extricate oneself from such obligations, and unleashes the strongest contempt. Villagers who remain aloof from and rarely participate in the daily affairs of the village and the rituals of its members become a focus for gossip, and may eventually have their own cremations badly disrupted. Finally, ceremonies are more likely to be thought of as successful if they are *ramé*, lively, crowded and bustling, which is only guaranteed if the ritual is relatively lavish and hence requires a lot of assistance.

As already mentioned, ceremonies can be performed at different social levels – low, medium and high. In the past the primary significance of this classification was that households were expected to conduct their rituals at a level commensurate with their caste rank. Those of higher status are therefore both privileged and obliged to perform ceremonies in a more elaborate manner than those of lower status. Reformers have had something to say about this issue too. In an effort to ameliorate conditions of poverty, they suggested that the level at which rituals are performed should be related less to caste status and more to wealth (Connor 1996: 187). Such a reform can have unexpected consequences, since it encourages aggressive status drives in which newly affluent commoners attempt to convert wealth into cultural capital by staging expensive rituals and using offerings and equipment usually reserved for higher status groups. This may in turn lead to conflict with those groups who perceive the status differential between themselves and those below them being whittled away, and who consequently take retaliatory action (Howe 2001: 36–42).

In contemporary Bali the discrepancy between what a household does in the ritual sphere and what is expected of it is closely monitored. Complaints may be made to village leaders (Poffenberger and Zurbuchen 1980: 125). Villagers may remonstrate with officials if a household oversteps conventional practice in the amounts and quality of the comestibles – coffee, cigarettes, food – served to villagers who help with preparations. Some village associations have even instituted regulations stipulating what and how much it is permissible to serve on such occasions, and there may be village guidelines for the appropriate number of guests to be entertained (Warren 1993: 157). This is important because these goods account for a significant proportion of the overall costs. Such restraints on spending may be seen as harsh by affluent villagers who want to be generous to those who assist at their rituals. If they are prevented by strict village codes from being as generous as they would like, they can paradoxically find themselves on the receiving end of others' accusations of being tight-fisted. Sometimes accusations of meanness are merited – *yén suba sugih, sing nyak maliat tuun* ('now they are rich they ignore the poor') is a stinging rebuke to those who fail to redistribute their wealth in lavish feasts or in other ways. Some families may have to invite guests from other villages where no such restrictions apply, and are therefore forced to default on their reciprocal obligations. Democratic injunctions which invoke the same limits for everyone in a village may contradict others which specify a link between scale of ceremony and wealth or status.

There are clearly contradictory forces in operation. On the one hand is a drive to simplify, standardise and rationalise many ceremonies, especially cremation, with a view to controlling costs, thus allowing poor Balinese to participate fully in ritual life, and to bring Balinese Hinduism into some conformity with world religions. On the other hand is the strength and resilience of the status hierarchy, which motivates people to maintain difference with others through elaborate and increasingly costly ceremonies financed through rising income from the expanding economy. Similarly, new ethical interpretations of religion rub against the grain of traditional ritual interpretations. While the former emphasise behaviour and conduct in life and disparage belief in the magical benefits of ritual, the ritual orientation does the opposite. While the new ethics attempts to restrain the consumption of elaborate offerings by deeming them unnecessary, most Balinese continue to believe that substantial offerings are a prerequisite for successful ritual outcomes. The social relations of exchange, so powerful in a village, make simplified rituals difficult to maintain. Decisions on exactly how to mount a major ceremony are therefore fraught with risk and anxiety (Howe 2000). A lavish ritual may enhance a household's prestige and please the ancestors, but if the mark is overstepped villagers may become offended and disrupt proceedings. On the other hand a low-level performance may be in tune with the new religion and its ethical emphasis, but it may be interpreted by others as a cynical ploy to spend less money rendered acceptable by being dressed up in a new religious idiom.

Animal sacrifice

All major ceremonies, and most small household rituals, require offerings of meat and blood to spirits and deities of various kinds – ancestral spirits, houseyard guardian spirits and malevolent spirits. For most ceremonies, whether directed at ancestors and deities or at low spirits, chicken, duck and pig are usually sufficient. In the major purification rites – part of the class of rites known as *caru* – dedicated to *buta-kala* spirits, dog, goat, cow and water buffalo become necessary (Stuart-Fox 2002: 155–8). The greater the misfortune, crime or disaster, and thus the impurity and disorder created, the more elaborate the ritual, and the bigger the animals needed. As far as purified ancestors and deities are concerned, offerings – which include music and dance – are presented to please the gods and to demonstrate devotion and obedience, so that ancestors continue to provide benevolent protection. In such offerings, where food is the major component, it is believed that the deity consumes the immaterial essence (*sari*). What is left behind (*lungsuran*) may be taken home and consumed by the household so as not to be wasted.

Some purification ceremonies are either periodic or event-specific in nature. An example of a periodic ceremony is the annual *caru* performed at the village crossroads at dusk on the last day of the solar year, the day which precedes the first day of the new year on which the ritual of *nyepi* ('to make silent') is carried out (Eiseman 1990, Vol. 1: 226–49). An example of an event-specific rite is a *caru* performed at the site of a serious theft or accident. *Caru* are also a component ritual in other ceremonies such as temple festivals and life crisis rites, where they are staged in order to purify the locale of, and the participants in, the main ceremony before it actually begins. Whatever the context of such ceremonies the point remains the same – to reorder the world so that things are in their rightful place.

In order to understand why animal sacrifice is necessary this concept of 'being in the rightful place' needs to be explained. Balinese cosmology pictures the world (*buwana agung* or 'great world') as highly structured. Purer things should be physically above relatively less pure things, low caste people should position themselves below those of superior rank, purer spaces such as temples should be higher than mundane spaces such as roads, shops and living quarters (Covarrubias 1937: 266). In many purification rituals a cosmological scheme known as the *nawa sangga* (both words mean 'nine' – see Fig. 1.1) is used to set out offerings. The ritual offerings, representing the world and its entire contents, are arranged on the ground in the form of a mandala, according to the eight compass points around the centre or 'navel' (*puseh*), a structure which provides a spatial metaphor of the Balinese universe. Each peripheral point is associated with a god, the demonic aspect of a god, a colour, a number, a metal, a tree, and a body organ. The centre, representing Siwa, constitutes unity or totality (Stuart-Fox 2002: 213). This scheme is replicated for the human body (*buwana alit* or 'little world'). One aspect or component of a person is the *dasa bayu* ('the ten energies'), and when someone has fallen, had an accident or been badly startled, and is thus confused or 'mixed up' (*pusing*), a small ritual is performed in which a priest instructs each *bayu* to 'go home' (*mulih*), each time stipulating a particular body organ (liver, spleen, heart, etc) which is the 'seat' of that specific *bayu*. Order is achieved when everything is in its rightful place, but order is always provisional and temporary, and always liable to be disrupted.

In the context of ritual Balinese see the process of order deteriorating into disorder partly in terms of the presence and activity of *buta-kala* spirits. These spirits are said to be everywhere – in nooks and crannies around the house, at crossroads, village boundaries, in trees and ditches. They are also said to be more active at midday, dusk, and on certain days of the month. They thus inhabit boundaries and transitional places and times (Howe 1981, 1984). The most important quality of these spirits is that they are animal-like, in the sense that they are selfish, gluttonous and capricious. They may attack and possess (*kasusupan kala*) anyone, causing people to behave like the spirits – selfishly, aggressively and unthinkingly, as animals do. In drawing a strict boundary between themselves and animals Balinese see certain forms of behaviour – fighting, incest, twin birth, hypogamous sexual relations – as transgressions of this boundary. The purpose of the *caru* purification ritual, whether large or small, is to reclassify that which has become mixed up. This is very clear in the litanies which priests recite at such ritual performances. These recitations enumerate large numbers of spirits, asking them to eat and drink their fill from the offerings provided and, thus satiated and placated, to return to their abodes – their rightful places (Hooykaas 1974: 68–77). Since the spirits are animal-like they need to be given appropriate food – meat and blood. This helps to explain why cockfighting is a religious requirement during temple festivals. While cockfighting and gambling are the great Balinese male pastimes, the blood spilled in the fights also has ritual value – it placates the animal-like spirits which would otherwise interfere with the festival. Because these offerings are for low spirits and placed on the polluting ground, the food that is in them is never taken home to be consumed, but always left on the ground for the dogs and chickens to eat.

Being possessed by a *buta-kala* spirit is seen as a temporary episode, but it is also thought of as the demonic manifestation of a deity which is itself temporarily experiencing strong emotions such as anger. Gods experience anger when they are neglected or insulted, whereupon they are considered to metamorphose into their malevolent aspect, the *buta-kala* spirits, and then cause harm and misfortune. If a Balinese household suffers more than its fair share of illnesses and accidents, representatives of that family may visit a spirit medium to obtain a revelation about the cause, and frequently they are told that their ancestors are angry because they have not conducted this or that ceremony. In this way families are often burdened with extra ritual activity to compensate for past ritual deficiencies. Once the demon is placated and 'returns home', this also involves its reverting to its divine form. Once back in this form the spirit is no longer a hindrance to the ceremony being performed, and can now participate in a constructive way (Stephen 2001, 2002, 2005). In such an interpretation these troublesome spirits are real entities with an independent existence, and consequently must be given offerings of meat, blood and alcohol in order to assuage and change them. In this sense animal sacrifice is a *sine qua non* of Balinese ritual.

There is, however, another kind of interpretation which, though less widespread, is gaining ground among proponents of the new religion of *agama Hindu*, the recently imported devotionalist movements from India which advocate vegetarianism, and more philosophically minded Balinese. In this interpretation *buta-kala* spirits are simply symbols of morally bad behaviour. They do not have an independent existence, but constitute a way of thinking about socially disjunctive conduct, feelings and thoughts. While the representation of internal dispositions as external entities may assist people in understanding what the ritual is about, it is also risky because people may attribute a false reality to these spirits and be deflected from what is really important – monitoring their own behaviour in ethical terms. According to this interpretation the sacrifice of animals is based on a misconception which wrongly privileges the outward and concrete symbol – the spirit – over the inner abstract meaning – animal-like behaviour in humans which has to be suppressed. While proponents of this interpretation accept that one aspect of ritual is to draw attention to the fact that human beings share with animals certain unpleasant dispositions which should be eradicated or at least inhibited, they believe that this recognition can be accomplished more properly through using animal shapes made of rice, or using some part of the animal – a tuft of hair for example, rather than actually killing it. This contradicts the customary view of ritual in which animal flesh and blood is actually consumed by the real demon, not just a symbolic representation of it. In the customary interpretation it is pointless to use a picture of an animal or a tuft of hair, since demons cannot feast on these things.

There is an ambiguity in traditional Balinese thinking about the purpose of offerings, expressed in the phrase *suci baan banten, suci baan kenehé*, which translates as 'pure through offerings, pure through thoughts'. Some Balinese explain this phrase as meaning that a benefit – becoming *suci*, or pure – can be obtained in two different ways, either through material offerings or through purity of thought. This interpretation adds weight to the idea that malevolent spirits are real physical entities which can be placated with offerings of real meat. Another explanation is that offerings are merely outward signs of inner sincerity, and therefore not really necessary. This places the emphasis on an ethical interpretation rather than a ritual one, since it relates to a person's actions and intentions. The ambiguity is further compounded because, according to a widespread Balinese injunction, offerings are only efficacious if they are constructed from materials unsoiled by prior usage, made while one's thoughts are pure and calm, and ungrudgingly given. A similar kind of ambiguity is detectable in the tooth-filing ceremony, in which a *caru* ritual with full meat offerings occurs alongside an expressly symbolic action – the removal of the animal aspect of humans through the filing of teeth.

Militating against more recent and more expressly symbolic interpretations of animal sacrifice is the fact that most rituals would completely change their character and lose much of their social appeal if they were conducted without substantial offerings and without animal flesh and blood. The killing of pigs, chickens and ducks on the day of the ceremony, together with the preparation of huge quantities of rice, vegetables, spices and special dishes, later consumed by workers and guests, makes for a wonderfully convivial atmosphere which is at the heart of Balinese collective village life.

The preceding discussion may give the impression that ritual reforms and the debate over animal sacrifice have occurred within an agonistic framework which pits the ritualism of traditional *adat* religion against the ethical stress of the new religion of *agama Hindu*. While this is correct in one sense, in another it oversimplifies matters. Consider the issue of animal sacrifice in relation to the doctrine of *karma*. Though ideas about *karma* can be found in indigenous Balinese texts, the doctrine has not had much influence among ordinary Balinese until relatively recently. With the inception of *agama Hindu*, doctrines such as *karma*, *dharma*, and other Indian ideas have become part of the school curriculum in religion; many young people have become acquainted with them and have begun to use them in their everyday lives. Some Balinese now argue that killing animals for food or enjoyment – in cockfights for example – brings bad *karma*, and therefore should not be done. I have been told by adherents of Sathya Sai Baba, most of whom are vegetarians, that meateaters gradually take on the characteristics of the animals they consume, so those who eat too much chicken start to speak nonsense and those who eat too much pork become fat and lazy. These new karmic ideas are also used to denounce the killing of animals for ritual purposes. However, the tables are easily turned, and the advocates of *adat* ritualism enlist the same doctrine to argue that, because the killing is done for proper ritual purposes and constitutes an offering to deities and spirits, the sacrificer does not accumulate bad *karma*. On the contrary, it is the sacrificed animal which becomes sacred and privileged, accrues merit, and thus improves its *karma*, enabling it to be reincarnated as a higher form of life. In this way, some of the new doctrines of *agama Hindu* may be used to support the ritual traditions of *adat* religion.

Why do we do this ritual?

In recent decades many Balinese, particularly the young, have begun to question not just the efficacy of ritual but also its point and purpose, even to the extent of wondering whether ritual is detrimental to their interests. There are many reasons for perpetuating ritual – the enjoyment it brings, the pressure of social expectations, the need to please the ancestors so they release their blessings and protection, and the role ceremonial spectacle has in attracting tourists. But there are also factors discouraging ritual. The rest of this chapter looks at the practical issues, and the next chapter the political and religious ones.

On the practical side, some people are concerned about the effect that lengthy ritual procedures have on their jobs in the modern economy. Employers, especially if they are in the tourist sector and thus often not Balinese, are not always sympathetic when Balinese ask for time off to attend a family ceremony. Frequently employees must trade the loss of a day or more's wages in order to fulfil social obligations. More ominously, some employers have become explicit about their irritation concerning this issue, and are inclined to hire migrant labour since it is more 'reliable'. This concern about job security reinforces the drive toward simpler and less time-consuming rituals among Balinese, but also exacerbates already hostile ethnic relations between Balinese and migrant workers.

Another problem is that ritual does not seem to address the difficulties that young people face in their everyday lives in contemporary Bali. In the past most Balinese found work in traditional occupations in their villages of birth, as farmers, smiths, builders, healers, priests and puppeteers, but in today's vastly diversified economy their horizons have widened considerably. As a result of high levels of education, regularly up to fifteen years of age and often to eighteen and beyond, many young Balinese have expectations of employment far exceeding those of previous generations. As a result many traditional occupations, including farming, have become less attractive; since much agricultural land has been converted to other uses, work in agriculture may no longer be available. Given the high population growth, the problem now is that there are not enough jobs in the economy to satisfy rising aspirations, a situation made worse by recent events such as the Bali bomb, whose dramatic effect on tourism put thousands of people out of work. The young unemployed male is an ever-present sight in village Bali. Such people may always have been a feature of village life, but they were usually able to find some work. Now, however, they are more visible, and are thought of as a distinct category. I have spoken to many young men caught in this trap who are angry, either because they do not have the connections or the bribe money to secure government jobs, or because their parents are unable or unwilling to provide the finance for further education which they confidently suppose will help them find work. Many cope well enough by doing odd jobs around the village, some subsist on parental help, and some devote themselves to gambling. The gambling set often comprises high caste young men who for reasons of status consider menial jobs inappropriate. Although this lifestyle, which is sometimes accompanied by heavy drinking, conforms to a traditional high caste avoidance of unskilled manual labour, today it provokes accusations from commoners that such gentry are idle layabouts and parasites. Left with nothing to do, young people wonder what benefit their rituals have for them on a personal level. Ceremonies are supposed to bring prosperity, long life and health, but while they may be healthy they do not feel very prosperous. Many young men remark that while they enjoy participating in ceremonies, they find the expense a burden, especially if they are married, and cannot always see what advantage they derive from them. 'Why do we do this ritual?' they ask. 'What is the point of it?'

It is impossible to withdraw from ceremonial activity without incurring severe social costs. One way out of the predicament is to join a new religious movement, of which there are several kinds. What many of these movements have in common is the promise of a more direct relationship with a divinity or a supernatural force which will assist in solving real world difficulties. Balinese *adat* ritualism is particularly good for villagers' spiritual health and wellbeing, and for the fertility of fields, but less useful for ameliorating the problems faced by young people in modern day Bali.

There is one set of new movements which the state insists cannot be given the status of 'religion' (*agama*). These are instead known as *aliran kepercayaan* ('streams of belief', Ind.). In Bali there may be as many as twenty-five such movements, some very local, some having branches all over the island. Officially the difference between these movements and *agama* (state-recognised religions) is that while *agama* possesses a set of universal teachings revealed by god, a holy book, a prophet and a holy place, *aliran kepercayaan* are locally valid beliefs in a powerful mystical force. In order to demonstrate they are neither deviant from *agama Hindu* nor subversive of the state ideology of *Pancasila*, *aliran kepercayaan* are constrained to advertise themselves as movements in pursuit of 'spirituality' (*kerohanian*, Ind.), because this concept is at the heart of *agama Hindu*. In practice these movements are usually based on the Indonesian martial arts of self-defence, allied to the development of 'supernatural inner power' (*sakti* in Balinese, or *tenaga dalam*, Ind.), a force which is branded as 'irrational' within official religious circles (Howe 2001: 156–61). This force, in the past linked to hierarchical status, now appears to have been democratised by its availability to all through membership in these new movements, observance of their taboos, and performance of their prescribed exercises. When young men join these movements – which does not interfere with their obligations in *adat* religion which they continue to perform – they have the chance of augmenting their 'inner power' (*tenaga dalam*) with a view to enhancing their chances of success in many other areas of life. In joining these movements young men appear to be taking control of rather aimless lives and cutting free of their passive dependence on village ritualism.

A second category of new religions includes the devotional movements of Sathya Sai Baba and Hare Krishna, both imported from India, which are also refused the label *agama*. As with *aliran kepercayaan*, membership of these movements does not entail withdrawal from *adat* religion. However, as we shall see in the following chapter, members claim that devotion to Sai Baba gives them spiritual sustenance and a new kind of religious experience which together provide the inner strength to help them cope with the problems of life in contemporary Bali, benefits which they feel *adat* ritualism does not deliver.

Plate 1 Balinese terraced rice fields

Plate 2 Low-paid female workers sanding and varnishing woodcarvings for the tourist market

Plate 3 Market day in the village of Pujung, northern Gianyar

Plates 77

Plate 4 High-caste men in Corong indulging in the typical early evening pastime of discussing the merits of their fighting cocks

Plate 5 Cockfighting preceding the annual temple ceremony at Samuan Tiga, Gianyar

Plate 6 Seven-roofed cremation tower (*badé*), Ubud village

Plate 7 Last-minute details being added to sarcophagus (*patulangan*) in which a body is cremated – this one is a strange combination of winged pig with fish tail, Peliatan village

Plate 8 Bull sarcophagus for a high-caste Balinese, Ubud village

Plate 9 Doorway to the palace (*puri*) of Cokorda Pemayun, Corong village

Plate 10 Snacking in the late morning at the local coffee shop (*warung*) in Corong village

Plate 11 Welcoming Rangda (the fearsome mask) during an annual temple ceremony in Corong

Plate 12 Stately procession (*mapeed*) of hamlet women to the temple, Corong

Plate 13 Preparation of food for guests and offerings on the morning of a tooth-filing, Corong

Plate 14 Some of the many offerings for the tooth-filing ceremony, Corong

Plate 15 The eleven young men and women about to undertake the tooth-filing ordeal, Corong

Plate 16 Low-caste couple getting married in Pujung village

Plate 17 The proud fathers of the bride and groom

Plate 18 Two couples receiving admonishing advice about marriage from a priest in the temple, Pujung

Plate 19 The Sai Baba temple in Denpasar

Plate 20 The Hare Krishna ashram on the outskirts of Denpasar

Plate 21 A view of some of the shrines at Besakih, Bali's 'mother temple'

Plate 22 Street scene in Kuta, the tourist mecca on Bali's south coast

Plate 23 Garbage disposal scarring Bali's tropical landscape

Plate 24 Western tourists waiting for a ritual in a temple ceremony to begin

5 New religions of Bali
Agama Hindu and Sri Sathya Sai Baba

Introduction

When independence was achieved in 1950 the fledgling Indonesian state faced many challenges. The most pressing was how to create a unitary nation state in the face of the unprecedented cultural, ethnic and religious diversity of the societies which now comprised it, and which threatened to pull it apart. One possible solution was to make Islam the state's official religion, since the majority of its people were Muslims. However, many of the mostly Javanese authors of the constitution and leaders of the revolution were only nominally Muslim. In practice they followed a speculative and philosophical religion, a syncretic blending of both Hindu and Islamic beliefs (Geertz 1960, Ch. 17; Beatty 1999, Ch. 6). They were concerned that an Islamic state would be disruptive to national unity, since it would alienate those of other religious persuasions. An uneasy compromise was reached in which belief in one god – rather than specific belief in Allah – would be the first principle of the national ideology, the *Pancasila*.

This broad religious monotheism advocated a consensus which transcended local ethnic and religious loyalties, and appeased Muslim demands because only those religions similar to Islam would be officially sanctioned. At the same time, however, it created other problems. Most importantly, only those religions – to be called *agama* – which possessed a high god, a holy book, a prophet and were not linked to a single ethnic group, qualified for state support and recognition. This meant, and still means, that the religious traditions of small communities were not considered as *agama*, being termed *belum beragama* ('not yet to have religion'). Such an evolutionary concept of religion clearly implies that societies without *agama* are backward and primitive, and can only be brought into the modern and progressive Indonesian world once they have converted to one of the recognised religions.

Such conversion often entails forced economic, political and cultural change – moving from a nomadic to a sedentary way of life, replacing local political structures with state bureaucratic rule, and modifying ritual practices and consumption patterns to bring them into line with 'superior' Javanese ideas. As Jane Atkinson points out, 'the religious charter of Indonesia is a cultural model for inclusiveness; in a profound way, however, its application is exclusive' (1987: 177). Since 1970

92 *New religions of Bali*

the problems that geographically peripheral Indonesian peoples have had to face from the interventions of colonial rule, missionary activity and the Indonesian state have been a staple research topic for anthropologists (Kipp and Rodgers 1987; Tsing 1993; Schiller 1997; Aragon 2000; Spyer 2000; Schrauwers 2000).

While much of this research literature examines the processes of conversion to Islam, Protestantism and Hinduism from the perspective of so-called pagan communities on Indonesia's periphery, the move to the 'new religions' is not usually seen by the Balinese as conversion at all, but rather as a return to a lost tradition now being rediscovered. Nevertheless, what has resulted in Bali from the interaction between powerful colonial and Indonesian state voices on the one hand and resilient and imaginative local voices on the other is not unlike what is happening in communities on Indonesia's margins. The state religious agencies and the Balinese elites have tried to impose a particular kind of Hinduism on Bali, but the processes they have unleashed have ironically resulted in a shifting religious landscape characterised by constantly evolving, multiple and competing forms of Hinduism.

Agama Hindu

The *Parisada Hindu Dharma Bali* (later the *Parisada Hindu Dharma Indonesia*) was instituted in 1959 to manage the affairs of *agama Hindu*, itself only established a year earlier. Its remit was to coordinate 'the religious activities of Balinese Hindus by regulating, promoting and developing the [new religion] in order to strengthen the awareness of the Hindus in their religious and social life' (Bakker 1993: 230–1). As this remit implies, much work had to be done to bring *agama Hindu* to the mass of ordinary Balinese. The *Parisada* was made up of a council of priests – all Brahmana *pedanda*, a council of experts, and a three-man executive, one of whom – the council president – had also to be a *pedanda*. Branches of the *Parisada* were gradually introduced throughout Bali and in other parts of Indonesia.

Through the 1950s there were discussions as to what the content of this religion would be, and many of these changes now began to be implemented. One of the first was the building of a new temple in Denpasar, rather different in structure from other temples. Its most important and largest shrine, a *padmasana*, was dedicated to Sanghyang Widi, previously a rather remote deity known mostly from esoteric texts and very marginal to village ritual practice, but henceforward to become increasingly central in the new religion. Until that time no other temple in Bali had a shrine specifically devoted to Sanghyang Widi. The new temple was open to all ranks of Balinese, again a new departure, since many other temples are restricted to the descent group which worships its own deified ancestors there.

This new temple demonstrated that Balinese religion is monotheistic and universal. Instead of the temple having an annual festival, services are carried out every new and full moon day and on other holy days, and the presiding *pedanda*, after performing the ritual to make holy water, gives a sermon, yet another innovation and departure from traditional practice. In 1961 the *Parisada* decreed that every temple in Bali should have a *padmasana* shrine to Sanghyang Widi, though I believe that many still do not have one.

Just as important as the principle of monotheism were the doctrines of *agama Hindu*, disseminated through the publication of religious books by the *Parisada*. These books were to be the basis of the school curriculum in religion (Parker 1992a, 1992b). They were written either by a collective (for example, Upadeca 1968), or by single authors (for example, Punyatmadja 1976), and are widely available in shops and market stalls. In the 1980s and 1990s there was an explosion of literature on many aspects of (Indian) Hindu religious beliefs, written either under *Parisada* sponsorship or by other religious scholars. The core of the early books comprised a description of the central tenets of *agama Hindu*, the *panca cradha*. The five tenets are belief in Sanghyang Widi as the one god, belief in the *atman* as the eternal essence of all living beings, belief in *karma* as the consequences of action, belief in *samsara* or reincarnation, and belief in *moksha* or liberation from the cycle of rebirth. These early *agama Hindu* guides stressed the more philosophical and ethical doctrines of Hinduism, and justified them by reference to Indian literary sources. The books also contained standardised prescriptions for the offerings and procedures to be used in many of the rituals.

While some of these *agama Hindu* teachings can be found in Balinese palmleaf texts owned by priests and others, most of them were either unknown to ordinary Balinese or known in a very different way. Original Indian concepts such as *samsara* and *moksha*, for example, are alien to village *adat* religion. While reincarnation is a universal belief in Bali, it is limited to the idea that one is reborn into one's own descent group, ideally as one's great-grandchild, and never into another form of life, as is the case in Indian ideas about *samsara*. Moreover, as Parker notes (1992b: 111), religion is taught in Balinese schools in a very intellectualised manner, with much of the material presented in the form of codifications and lists – types of sacred places, the five techniques of self-control, the seven darknesses or evils, and so forth – none of which has any place in village *adat* religion. The main activity of women and girls, the making and presentation of offerings, barely gets a mention. Another example of the difference between *agama Hindu* and *adat* was the omission from the Upadeca, in its discussion of death rituals, of the crucial Balinese idea that the deceased, through cremation, eventually turn into the ancestral gods (*déwa*) who are worshipped in the temples – presumably to avoid any criticism that the religion is a form of primitive ancestor worship. Ritual also received a new interpretation. Offerings were to be seen as the outward and material signs of inner feelings and convictions. In ritual, it was argued, one can reflect on god with the aid of visible representations which allow one's thoughts to unite with god. The thrust of all these changes is the restructuring of religion, moving its emphasis from ritual to scripture, magical action to ethical injunction, diversity to uniformity, and collective practice to individual faith – a kind of Protestant Hinduism.

The point of *agama Hindu* is not to supplant traditional Balinese ritual practice but to simplify and standardise it, and to provide it with theological substance and philosophical justification, so that ritual ceases to be efficacious on its own and instead becomes symbolic of devotion to, and faith in, god. The fact that there is no word in Balinese for 'faith', the Indonesian term *percaya* (belief, trust, confidence) being used instead, gives an idea of how profound some of these changes are. The establishment of *agama Hindu* has provoked tension between the new religion and *adat*. While *agama Hindu* is not meant to oppose *adat*, since it is designed to underpin it, when the two come into conflict it is *adat* which has to give way (Bakker 1993: 290).

The friction between the two variants of Hinduism stems from differences in religious emphasis and from differences of interest within the Parisada and on the part of Balinese reformers. Three particular examples of this discord are the problems relating to the origins of *agama Hindu*, the *Parisada*'s interpretation of the caste system, and the role of ritual.

In an attempt to convince government officials as well as Muslims that Balinese religion is securely anchored in Hinduism, the *Parisada* had to present *agama Hindu* as a religious tradition which had been brought to Bali from India by holy sages millennia ago, thus emphasising its Indian rather than its Majapahit origins and contradicting Balinese gentry arguments of the 1920s. As well as supporting the Indian origins of Balinese Hinduism, the *Parisada* was also under pressure to maintain the specific Balinese character of the new religion so that the reforms would not sever the connection between the new religion and *adat* practices. Religious authorities have regularly expressed concern that Balinese are not learning the new doctrines quickly enough, since it appears that most continue to perform their rituals without much recourse to scriptures. *Agama Hindu* had to introduce many new concepts and ideas to make it conform to national religious directives, but it also had to demonstrate its ancient pedigree by pointing to its intimate connection with Hinduism. Thus *agama Hindu* is both a recent innovation and represented as the rediscovery of a lost or distorted ancient tradition.

In regard to caste and hierarchy it is not surprising that the *Parisada*, staffed mostly by high castes, argued for the retention of the *catur warna*, the division of the population into four classes, while commoner activists continued to advocate its abolition. In trying to make this doctrine more palatable to ordinary Balinese, the *catur warna* was interpreted less in terms of hierarchical ranking and more in terms of complementary and interdependent functions, having the overall aim of improving the prosperity of all. However, the manner in which this was explained in texts betrayed the hierarchical thinking behind it. The members of each *warna* are said to have specific qualities and talents with which they are born. Thus Brahmana and Satria have the capacities to lead society spiritually and politically respectively 'for the good of all', while Sudra are said to have the characteristics of bodily strength and loyalty, and thus be the agents of prosperity, but only under the guidance and instruction of Brahmana and Satria (Upadeca 1968: 54–5). This interpretation gives prominence to caste-based inborn proclivities, rather than to merit and achievement. It will become clearer in Chapter 6 that the conflict over the existence and meaning of the *catur warna* is deep-seated and enduring.

As we have seen, many reforms centre on simplifying ritual so that it does not disadvantage poorer Balinese and in order to redirect attention from mechanical ritual procedure to spiritual meaning. However, given the collective and highly competitive nature of ritual, this poses the many problems examined in Chapter 4. Balinese cannot simply extricate themselves from the status game without losing face and, to compete, households continually have to invest more resources and find ways of distinguishing themselves from others. While the new religion stresses ethical meanings and simple rituals, Balinese find they are financially able to mount ever more elaborate ceremonies. These cultural imperatives privilege this-worldly objectives over other-worldly ones, a tendency contrary to the spirit of the new religion.

State-imposed orthodoxy and religious innovation

Agama Hindu is the rationalised and theological form of Hinduism created to make Balinese religion acceptable to the state and designed to gain its support and protection. Even though the initiative originally came from the Balinese, the framework within which *agama Hindu* was created and took shape was largely determined by the Indonesian constitution, the Ministry of Religion and the *Parisada*. It is a state-imposed religious orthodoxy which has enabled Balinese to resist a proselytising Islam, and to assuage the sense of inferiority that Balinese intellectuals experienced in an earlier period.

Once religious innovation had started, however, it proved difficult to contain. If *agama Hindu* was now the Balinese version of Indian Hinduism, what was to stop Balinese drawing on other Hindu traditions which might serve quite different purposes? The dialogue between Balinese and Indian Hindus led to the realisation that Hinduism is not in any sense a unitary tradition, but a varied mosaic of different traditions – Brahmanic ritualism, devotionalist movements, sects of world renouncers and much else (Fuller 1992). If *agama Hindu* was introduced from the top by the state and Balinese intellectuals, why could ordinary Balinese not do something similar? Not content to allow the government alone to set the agenda for reform, some Balinese have imported other forms of Hinduism which are more in tune with their particular religious interests and needs. The most significant of these are the devotional movements of Sri Sathya Sai Baba and the Hare Krishnas, and the appearance of Sai Baba and the Hare Krishnas can be seen as the most vital and institutionalised current in a broader river of Balinese Hindu revival. A number of indigenously inspired new religious movements (*aliran kepercayaan*) have also emerged, owing something to both *adat* and *agama Hindu*, and there is increasing interest in Indian holy men such as Swami Sivananda, Swami Vivekananda and Mahatma Gandhi (Jendra 1996, Titib 1994, Wiana 1992, 1995).

The upsurge of religious movements such as Sai Baba represent an unexpected, powerful and imaginative local challenge to national policy concerning what counts as acceptable religion. Rather than the state bending local cultural and religious institutions in its quest for religious and cultural uniformity, a movement such as Sai Baba channels local interests into new forms which energise religious and political change in ways which slip through state control. In its attempts to produce religious orthodoxy and curtail religious diversity with its concomitant political conflict, the Indonesian state has unwittingly created the conditions in which religious innovation has been able to flourish. What began as a struggle to promote a specific version of Balinese Hindu religion has resulted in a new, complex, differentiated religious landscape which has, in turn, proliferated conflicts over the nature of religious truth, the role of high priests, the purpose of ritual, the formation of identities, the link between religion and the state, and much else.

I shall illustrate some of these issues by examining the Sai Baba movement; to avoid confusion I use the phrase 'Sai Baba' to refer to the movement, and 'Baba' to refer to its founder. For a description of the much smaller and less important Hare Krishnas, see Howe (2001).

Sri Sathya Sai Baba and Balinese Adat Religion

Born in 1926 in the village of Puttaparthi in the Indian state of Andhra Pradesh, Sri Sathya Sai Baba is an Indian 'god-man'. As a child he is said to have performed small miracles, but came to wider prominence when as a young man he proclaimed himself to be the reincarnation of a nineteenth century saint Shirdi Sai Baba, at which time he took his new name, thus linking himself to a famous holy lineage. After this proclamation his miracles became more dramatic and increased in frequency, and he began to attract a large following of devotees. In 1950 he built an ashram at Puttaparthi which has since grown very large. It includes an arena where he preaches and performs miracles, a hospital, conference rooms, and extensive accommodation for the thousands who come from all over the world to visit the ashram.

In 1963, after an illness which was supposedly self-induced and self-cured, he proclaimed himself to be all the gods and goddesses of the Indian pantheon, and to be the god of all religions. Baba's charismatic appeal rests largely on the notion that he is the manifestation of the universal god who has the power to work miracles, cure illnesses and resurrect the dead. His principal and simple message is that there is only one religion, the religion of love; only one caste, that of humanity; and only one language, that of the heart (Klass 1991: 103). While remaining Hindu in spirit, Baba's is a universal theology preaching an inclusive doctrine of love, compassion and individual spiritual development. Baba's broadly egalitarian message encourages a deeply personal, direct and highly emotional relationship between Baba and each devotee, and eschews priestly mediation and ritual. For Balinese this doctrine is very different from both the caste-based, scribal, priestly and ritual traditions of Balinese *adat*, and the philosophically-based, abstruse and unemotional doctrines of *agama Hindu*. Not surprisingly, those Balinese who experience existing religious traditions as deficient or disadvantageous find in the Sai Baba movement an exciting and congenial home, especially since Baba does not preach conversion but instead encourages devotees to maintain their allegiance to other religions, so that these may be brought back into the fold of 'true' religion from which they have deviated.

Sai Baba worship began in Java in 1981 and was rapidly introduced into Bali, where there are now about 12,000 members. Meetings were initially held in members' houses in Denpasar, but in 1984 a permanent site was obtained on which a large pavilion has now been built. At the front are portraits of Baba surrounded by pictures of other Hindu deities and garlands of flowers. There is also a richly upholstered chair which, though apparently empty, is conceived as being occupied by Baba. During the singing of *bhajan* (devotional songs) musicians and lay leaders sit at the front while the mass of devotees sit cross-legged behind them, men on the right and women and children on the left. Another small pavilion contains a room housing recording equipment, stores of books, cassette tapes and pamphlets for sale. There is also a small shrine for the worship of Balinese gods located to the side of the main pavilion, and ceremonies are held there every new and full moon. The centre in Denpasar is the largest in Bali, but there are many smaller ones dotted around the island.

Sai Baba worship is organised very differently from local traditions of Balinese Hinduism. Most Balinese are members of several temple congregations. Their names are listed on a register, they all make equal contributions to the upkeep of the temple and its ceremonies, and fines are levied for infraction of the rules. It is a highly structured organisation, often with a written constitution detailing the obligations and privileges of members. The Sai Baba movement has no register of members, devotees attend or not as they see fit, expenses are met entirely by voluntary and often anonymous donations, and rich members often pay large bills out of their own pockets.

While a Balinese temple congregation has no extracurricular activities and exists only to support the gods of that temple, Sai Baba centres, both in India and Bali, have three broad programmes of activity – the development of devotees' spirituality, religious education, and service to the community. Centres organise free classes in religious education open to anybody, in which more expert members explain and clarify the teachings of Baba, with special emphasis on how these teachings help members to understand the spiritual significance behind traditional rituals. The stress is on the religious truths which only Baba, as god, can reveal. It is not so much that Balinese priests are accused of telling religious untruths, but rather that in their obsession with ritual, these truths have been lost or distorted. So, for example, Balinese are said to misdirect their energies when they participate in ceremonies and pray to their ancestors and temple deities, because in reality they should be offering devotion to god and striving to develop themselves spiritually in order eventually to unite with him and thus achieve salvation.

Charity work is also a major activity of the centres, because devotion to god can only be achieved by devotion to others who are all in themselves a part of god. 'Love all, serve all' and 'help ever, hurt never' are two of the more important maxims that devotees frequently quote. Members make charitable donations – money, materials, labour – to assist others whether they are followers of Baba or not, and some contribute to good causes and help to clean and renovate hospitals, schools, Balinese temples and other communal facilities. Members also help in the preparations for major temple festivals such as those conducted at Besakih. Sai Baba is thus a very open form of organisation with significant social outreach functions, an aspect which facilitates its integration into mainstream society.

Sai Baba services are strikingly different from Balinese temple ceremonies. They begin promptly at seven in the evening. As devotees arrive they segregate into two sections, men on one side, women and children on the other. They meditate and pray for a few moments. The special *adat* dress compulsory for Balinese temples is virtually never worn, and most male and female devotees wear white shirts and trousers. Apart from some flowers and incense there are no offerings at a service. Priests do not officiate because Baba is the only *guru* ('teacher') and all devotees approach Baba directly. The devotional songs are in Hindi, Tamil or Sanskrit, but books of translations are available. Usually eight *bhajan* are sung at a meeting, and as each finishes an obeisance is made to Baba as god with clasped hands raised above the head. At most *adat* temple ceremonies singing is obligatory but is performed by small groups of men and women; singing is something of a sideshow and not central to what others are doing. At Sai Baba services *bhajan* singing is the centrepiece of the meeting, and allows members to surrender themselves to god by expressing their devotion, love and subordination. Many worshippers emphasise its calming and soothing qualities; others stress the intense emotional experience the singing engenders. A lay official, a lecturer at one of Bali's universities, told me that singing *bhajan* is a method of freeing oneself from sin and a way of achieving liberation (*bebas*, Ind.). When singing many devotees appear utterly absorbed in what they are doing, with their eyes closed and in a semi-trance. The pounding rhythms, simple and hypnotic melodies, and communal nature of the singing facilitate a subordination of the individual to god through a merger of the self into the group.

After the singing a member gives a short talk which is almost always in Indonesian. The subject matter may include an account of the speaker's visit to the ashram in Puttaparthi; a sermon on the merits of discipline, vegetarianism and self-sacrifice; an exegesis of Baba's words; or a personal account of what led someone to become a devotee. The final act is the distribution of sacred ash (*wibuti*, miraculously produced by Baba and shipped all over the world to different centres of worship) and holy water to the congregation. Balinese temple festivals, by contrast, are replete with elaborate offerings. Priests recite prayers and litanies, some in Sanskrit – largely unintelligible to the congregation and often to themselves, and perform complicated ritual actions unheeded by others. Meanwhile the congregation passes the time chatting. Apart from the extensive preparations, lay members really only take part in a temple ceremony at its climax, when they perform acts of obeisance to the assembled temple gods and receive holy water.

It is important to recognise the tremendous emotional devotion to the person of Baba, evident not only during the *bhajan* singing but in devotees' everyday lives. Devotees pray to Baba several times a day to ask for advice and peace of mind, and to surrender themselves to him. Their homes are full of his pictures, and many devotees carry portraits of Baba on their person, in their cars or on their motorbikes. If Baba's miracles are important in attracting new members and convincing them that Baba is a living god, it is this intense personal relationship that sustains them thereafter (Babb 1986). To those who have had a sight of Baba in India, and especially those who have touched him or been spoken to by him, it is the experience of ineffable joy that is truly impressive. Even those – the majority – who have not seen him in the flesh frequently dream of Baba, and express a great longing to see and touch him. In speaking about these experiences, either in private or in the public talks at meetings, devotees are often on the verge of tears.

This intimate and emotional experience in Sai Baba congregations is unlike anything expressed by Balinese towards the gods of their *adat* religion. Balinese gods are ancestors who, through the cumulative processes of cremation and post-cremation rites of purification, gradually become divinised. In this process they progressively lose their individual characteristics and become remote, anonymous, impersonal and conventionalised. During ceremonies prayers to the gods are formulaic, communal and public; they are directed by the temple priest who provides instructions, now to pray to this god, now to that one. Outside of these communal events Balinese rarely pray to their gods.

On the other hand, Balinese ceremonies are not without their own emotional impact. The gods descend to the temple; they are 'embodied' in material objects and carried on the heads of worshippers in processions; they are bathed, fed and entertained; and people can make vows to them. The relationship between gods and congregation is thus not entirely formal, but includes substantive and occasionally intimate elements. After the ceremony Balinese often describe themselves as refreshed, calm and happy, but this is a much less intense experience than the passionate devotion to Baba.

Hierarchy and equality

One reason given by many Balinese for their membership of Sai Baba is that they are dissatisfied with village *adat* religion. When young Balinese pose questions such as what is the purpose of this ritual, or what does an offering mean, they are not always content with the answers received from parents and teachers. Since *adat* stresses ritual action rather than verbal doctrine, priests are also often incapable of supplying the kinds of answers that such questions appear to demand. Responses tend to be of a very conventional kind – 'that's just how it is' , 'this is what we must do', 'to obtain a blessing from the ancestors'. The new devotional forms of religion are more amenable to questions of this sort, relying on an accessible verbal doctrine more psychologically in tune with life in modern Bali. In addition they are far less dependent on ritual, open to all, and the doctrine is taught to anyone who wants to listen.

Not surprisingly, therefore, growing numbers of Balinese have been joining these movements. Devotees accuse *adat* religion of being embedded in an oppressive caste order which emphasises impersonal rituals, expensive offerings and domination by priests, making it exclusive, secretive and inaccessible. Even priests, supposedly knowledgeable in religion, are said to be unhelpful in providing exegeses of the significance behind rituals, however expert they may be in the proper conduct of rites. Brahmana priests are denounced as backward and ignorant, their ritual condemned as automatic and mechanical and thus of having lost sight of the true spiritual aims behind ritual. Though sometimes credited with religious knowledge gleaned from their texts, they are criticised for keeping this knowledge secret, justifying this secrecy by claiming that undisciplined dissemination of sacred knowledge to the ritually unprepared dilutes the power of that knowledge and endangers the recipient.

Since payment is required for their indispensable ritual services, priests are also accused of exploiting their clients, over whom they exercise a degree of social and supernatural control since clients have a hereditary attachment to a priest and may unleash the priest's curse should they detach themselves from him or her. This critique is often framed within an historical argument. Eternal religious truth, brought to Bali by Hindu sages and still to be found in Balinese texts, was once available to all. In the course of time, however, its meanings were overlaid with the dross of ritual and the venal and vested interests of priests and rulers working to bolster their privileges within the caste system. What passes for *adat* religion is thus said to be a deviation from and a degradation of what it once was. Joining Sai Baba provides an opportunity to discover these lost meanings and escape from the control of priests.

This criticism of Bali's hierarchical social order is also based on Sai Baba's – and *agama Hindu*'s – monotheism, and their claim that all Balinese enjoy equal access to god. *Adat* religion, by contrast, has many gods, themselves hierarchically ranked. While descent group members worship their own deified ancestors in their own temples, the worship of ancestors from an inferior group results in being demoted in caste (*nyerod*) to an inferior level. Sai Baba provides a refuge for those who take seriously the unity and transcendence of god. Though devotees are separated from Baba by a gulf, among themselves they are equal, and no intermediary or priest is allowed to intervene. Distinctions of caste within the movement are therefore irrelevant, both doctrinally and organisationally. Critique of hierarchy is reinforced by the movement's stress on individual spiritual development, the high value placed on hard work, the unrestricted dissemination of religious knowledge, and voluntary service to the community, all of which encourage a rejection of ascriptive privilege and the endorsement of merit and achievement.

Such criticisms of ritualised religion are by no means uncommon, and the Sai Baba movements in India (Babb 1986), Trinidad (Klass 1991) and Malaysia (Kent 2004) have been interpreted as responses to a sense of alienation from customary forms of life and Brahmanic ritualism in the context of a modern, rational and urban economy. Babb notes that most Indian devotees of Baba come from the affluent and educated urban middle class. He argues that many are culturally rootless and 'distanced from their tradition by background and education', and that Baba provides an identity which links their nostalgia for that lost tradition with their place in the modern world (1986: 191). For those Balinese who find the archaic ritualism of *adat* embarrassing, the caste system unfair, and the doctrines of *agama Hindu* abstruse, Sai Baba offers a way to re-enchant the world by embodying modern values of achievement, hard work and equality in a genuine Hindu tradition based on loving devotion to a universal and living god.

As we have seen, miracles are an important aspect of Baba's life and of Sai Baba as a movement. I have occasionally been told about very dramatic miracles, such as a spontaneous cure of cancer, though most have related to decidedly mundane events, such as the inexplicable reappearance of a wallet thought to be lost, the avoidance of traffic accidents, a problem-free application for a travel visa or an unexpected windfall of money. But perhaps it is the very triviality of such 'miracles' which demonstrates how the miraculous is part of everyday life, and thus how the mundane and transcendent worlds are not disconnected and separate, but rather fused into one by Baba's permanent presence in devotees' lives. What before were events and happenings of little significance now become signs of Baba's continuous involvement in everyday existence. As Baba assumes a greater prominence for devotees, they claim that their activities become shaped by a higher purpose and meaning.

Many devotees are successful in academic and business life, but the miraculous does not necessarily contradict their modern scientific and economic rationalism. Baba's constant love and protection give strength of purpose and inculcate habits of discipline, hard work and dedication so that worldly success *and* miracles become the by-products and rewards of devotion. As Kent (2000: 12) has pointed out, devotees 'are not required to choose between spirituality and worldliness'. Because Baba's love procures worldly success, the values of the secularised and modern world now receive a higher form of validation. This is further reinforced by the movement's stress on charitable service to the community and its rejection of forms of individual world-renunciation. Spiritual salvation and worldly success are both realised by selfless service to others and devotion to work and duty, reminiscent of the Calvinist Protestant ethic (Weber 1985).

The political uses of religion or the religious uses of politics

Emphasising its challenge to traditional Balinese hierarchy and priestly domination makes the Sai Baba movement look like a religious vehicle for pursuing political ends, even if its membership, in caste terms, has a similar profile to that of the wider population. Though the movement is clearly a reflection of broader social and political conflict, is this all there is to it? Its members may criticise caste inequalities, but the reasons people give for joining the movement in the first place are not usually overtly political. Many said they joined because they experienced or witnessed a miracle cure effected by Baba. Others described how they were leading a dissolute life of drinking, gambling, petty crime and unemployment, and were brought to their senses when introduced to the movement by a friend. Several told me how they had been very depressed, even suicidal, but had their life turned around when attending their first or second *bhajan* session. Several members told me that Baba has helped them control strong feelings of fear, anger, desire and jealousy, and that overcoming these 'internal enemies' (*musuh dalam*, Ind.) was the most important thing in consolidating their devotion. Some told me that Baba directed them to the movement without their conscious knowledge, so that it was not even their decision to join, but rather Baba's. Some joined for no particular reason other than they had come at the invitation of a friend and enjoyed the experience because it was so different from the experience of customary religion.

Younger members especially see the movement as providing some solution to the practical problems of unemployment and directionless lives. By being a constant and protective companion Baba not only helps reshape Balinese lives by infusing them with new meaning and a purpose beyond the mundane, but also instils new habits and lifestyles which make them better prospects in the labour market. It is also worth adding that the movement acts as a kind of surrogate family for those who have fractious relationships with kin, and as an informal job market since more affluent and better connected members appear keen to assist the more disadvantaged.

The reasons for joining Sai Baba are diverse and cannot be reduced to a single political motive. However, once socialised into the movement, having experienced the movement's open attitude to religious knowledge, its leaders' patient willingness to teach and explain, its stress on individual spiritual development, and the equality of believers, a member's past may be reconceptualised as a spiritual quest for meaning or in terms of a denunciation of caste inequalities. Several members told me that they began to see the deficiencies of village religion only after they had joined Sai Baba, in which case their rationalised and politicised perspective may be partly an effect of membership rather than a cause. Once this is recognised it becomes possible to view the movement primarily in religious rather than political terms.

Many long term devotees stressed the ethical values preached by Baba, the doctrine of spiritual development and salvation, and the establishment in society of a higher moral code. Such an orientation includes criticism of the state's political intolerance of religious plurality and the iniquities of the caste system, but what it primarily speaks to is the search for a more satisfying religious life. When Sai Baba first appeared in Indonesia it was thought by state religious officials to be dangerously close to communism, and thus subversive. Because of complaints an investigation of the movement was conducted in 1993, which concluded that its activities contravened the proper arrangements for religious life in Indonesia, generating unrest and disturbing the harmony of the religious community (Supartha 1994: 153). Some of the movement's current lay leaders, mostly commoners with academic and public sector careers, were the original founders of Sai Baba in Bali. In the early 1980s many of them were harassed by the police and questioned about the movement's doctrines. For these men, then as now, the significance of Sai Baba was not that it provided an outlet for political ambition, because the movement was too dangerous for that, but rather that it supplied a new and more satisfying form of religious experience.

In contemporary Bali the movement is now considerably more secure and acceptable than it once was, and several members are eminent Balinese and influential officials in the *Parisada*; even the odd Brahmana high priest has given a talk at the centre in Denpasar. These men have used their positions to argue that Sai Baba is a force for good in Balinese society. They are using existing political channels to further a religious cause, rather than, in what is the more usual tradition among Western scholars, to interpret 'religion as no more than an instrument for achieving political-economic ends' (Hefner 1997: 112; see also Anderson 1977: 21). While devotees' desire for political reform and religious plurality and toleration in Bali is strong, they tend to see political change less as an end in itself and more as a means for securing and extending the influence of the religious truths revealed by Baba.

A new form of religious experience

When attempting to understand the place of Sai Baba in Bali, another reason to emphasise the religious over the political is to look at devotees' discovery of a new and distinct kind of religious experience, not available to them in other forms of Balinese religion. As we have seen, traditional forms of religion in Bali are rather impersonal and mechanically ritualised, temple deities are anonymous and distant, and worship, mediated by priests, does not fully engage the emotions. In contrast, after several visits to the Sai Baba centre, some devotees are overcome with uncontrollable emotion and find themselves crying. Devotees 'love' (*sayang, cinta,* Ind.) Baba, they 'long' and 'yearn' (*rindu,* Ind.) to see or touch him, they dream of him, and Baba becomes the pivot around which their lives revolve. Singing *bhajan* brings some to a high pitch of emotional arousal, for others it helps drown out unpleasant feelings. Meditation is said to calm and cleanse, and to help defeat the 'internal enemies'; vegetarianism and other abstenances improve the body and the mind. As a result, Baba comes to dwell within the devotee, guiding, protecting and soothing. Intense bodily and mental experiences cement the relation between devotee and Baba. Balinese rarely speak in such emotional ways in relation to their traditional or *adat* religion.

The creative manner in which Sai Baba combines the collective with the individual so that each builds on and benefits from the other is striking. *Adat* religion is almost entirely a collective enterprise. It is true that individual Balinese may make personal vows and take on personal ritual commitments for particular reasons, but these are far less important than the collective household, temple and community rituals which comprise the greatest part of *adat* religion. These rituals are of course what make Balinese religion what it is, and what sustains Balinese in strong and cohesive communities. It is not so much religious experience that matters but the way in which ritual action, and the reciprocal obligations this entails, binds people together at the same time as tying them to their gods and ancestors and to their village lands.

This is a tradition which largely discounts the vagaries of an inner religious life and personal religious convictions and beliefs in favour of a more concrete communal harmony forged through collective ritual practice. It does not really matter what anyone thinks, feels or believes, so long as everyone fulfils their ritual and other obligations. Friends have sometimes told me privately that even if they do not believe in life after death, or are sceptical of the ability of the dead to intervene in the lives of the living, or that witches do not exist, they dare not say so too publicly for fear that they will be ostracised and isolated. Individuals cannot simply cease performing rituals dedicated to their ancestors on the basis that they might be a waste of time and money, because this would effectively sever the all-important relationships with their co-villagers. For similar reasons the problems which devotees of Sai Baba experience in their home villages almost always concern how they behave rather than what they believe.

Sai Baba, however, makes inner religious experience a priority. As each person forms his or her dyadic relationship with Baba, the movement can appear to be little more than an aggregate of individuals who share a belief in the divinity of Baba. Each devotee is encouraged to strive for personal spiritual development; there are no obligations to the movement, no dues to be paid, no sanctions for non-attendance and few rules to break. Consequently it is the figure of Baba which holds the members together. Unlike a Balinese temple congregation, the Sai Baba movement does not in any sense constitute a corporate group.

Yet the devotees present at a Sai Baba service clearly do function as a collectivity. New members learn how to behave, and in all likelihood what to experience, by observing and talking to others. They have probably begun to learn something of Sai Baba even before their first meeting, having read a book about Baba or been told of his miracles by existing members. Emotional arousal is given shape and meaning through discussion with other devotees, by attending educational classes and by listening to the sermons, and it is thereby converted into a distinct religious experience. Although some devotees have told me that they sing *bhajan* silently to themselves while at work or at home, the emotional force of singing devotional hymns is dependent on a highly structured and regimented collective performance. Devotees are advised that if they have problems and doubts they should discuss them with other devotees rather than with outsiders, who may lure them into temptation. In these and other respects, individual spiritual development and inner religious experience are achieved and interpreted partly on the basis of collective action.

This kind of religious experience is becoming more widespread within Bali, as *agama Hindu* is also gradually trying to substitute spirituality for potency and belief for ritual. *Agama Hindu*'s emphasis on ethical intention, meaning and doctrine over ritual action requires Balinese priests to play a rather different role. High priests, whether from Brahmana or other groups, have to take exams to demonstrate they are conversant with the new doctrines. Rather than simply performing a ritual they are now being encouraged to play a greater role in people's lives by providing religious instruction and giving sermons at temple ceremonies. Ordinary Hindus are increasingly taking to private prayer and meditation in their own houseyard temples, apparently in an effort to create a closer and more intense personal contact with god.

Potency or spirituality

Supernatural power or potency (*sakti*) was, and in part still is, at the heart of Balinese magico-religious and political practice. It is an indigenous theory of cosmic power which ensures that followers and material benefits accrue to those with a stock of *sakti*. Rulers, as exemplary and silent centres, possessed so much that their mere words were immediately efficacious; clients automatically did what was required of them without coercion. Potency is partly a function of status – the higher one's rank the greater the amount one is born with. Through their immersion in sacred literature and their ritual initiation priests too accumulate *sakti*. *Sakti*, however, can be acquired by anyone – through a gift from god, performing diabolical rituals, by becoming a spirit medium – and therefore can emerge outside the normal channels legitimated by the hierarchy. Ordinary Balinese, like their Javanese counterparts (Keeler 1987; Brenner 1998), may perform ascetic exercises and fasting to augment their stock of potency so that they can ensnare a loved one, pass exams, gain promotion or cure sick children. Once acquired, however, potency is not stable, and may flow away to others. It must therefore be continually cultivated and demonstrated in visible ways by, for example, holding extravagant rituals (Howe 2000). Belief in *sakti* helps to explain why some people are rich and have numerous followers and clients, and is therefore a theory about success in this world.

Religious officials have tried to expunge notions of *sakti* from *agama Hindu*, denouncing its pursuit which they brand as 'irrational'. They portray it as a throwback to times when Balinese believed, and were criticised for believing, that the cosmos was pervaded by a supernatural force which could be tapped by individuals for their private interests. Books published by the *Parisada* rarely mention *sakti*, instead stressing spirituality (*kerohanian*, Ind.), which is a relatively new concept in Bali – there is no Balinese word for it. In this respect *agama Hindu* and Sai Baba converge, since the latter also condemns *sakti* on the grounds that it emphasises self-interest, separates one from god, and brings merely the illusion of happiness. Spirituality, by contrast, comes from surrendering oneself to god, denying oneself the sensuous pleasures of this life, and thus eventually merging with god which brings eternal bliss.

While the concepts of *sakti* and *kerohanian* are quite different they are regularly conflated, because the means of acquiring them are outwardly similar. For example, despite claiming that they are only interested in spiritual development (*kerohanian*), members of Sai Baba are often accused of surreptitiously trying to increase their stock of potency (*sakti*). Vegetarianism, abstention from drinking, gambling and spicy food, private meditation and the recitation of mantra, all enjoined by the movement, are interpreted by opponents as traditional forms of asceticism designed to augment potency. Several devotees have told me that they have a difficult time convincing their village friends they are not learning 'black magic'.

Members of the much smaller Hare Krishna movement, which is illegal but remains in operation (Howe 2001), face the same problems only with greater force, because the injunction to be vegetarian and the proscriptions against alcohol, tobacco, spicy food and sex outside marriage are much stricter. Ironically, the claims by non-members that Hare Krishna devotees seek to increase their potency is a reason members give to explain why the police do not harass them. Devotees attribute this response by the police to a fear that, because the Hare Krishnas may command great *sakti*, it is too dangerous to impose severe penalties. To confirm this fear of *sakti* one devotee gave me examples of the dire fates – illness, bankruptcy, accidents – befalling those who complained to the police about the movement. He hastened to add that this was not because 'we have power', but because 'Krishna protects us'.

The view from the village

Over the last fifteen or twenty years officials of the *Parisada*, priests and other observers have noted an increased enthusiasm for religious worship among all sections of Balinese society. This revived interest in religion has been brought about by the activities of many Balinese in their campaign to get Balinese Hinduism recognised by the state, and by a grassroots reaction to *agama Hindu* and *adat* evidenced by the emergence of many new religious movements. Officials are worried that if people are not given religious guidance they will be led astray and fall into 'deviant' (*sesat*, Ind.) sects which may sow the seeds of community conflict. The accusation of deviation from true religion is used by both devotees and opponents of Sai Baba. It is commonly said by elites that ordinary Balinese are not yet 'resolute' (*mantap*, Ind.) in their new religion, and when confronted with conflicting teachings they waver and become confused. As a consequence priests are now required, in addition to performing their rituals, to provide sound instruction in order to channel this enthusiasm in the right direction.

The new religions may cause problems in some villages, but this seems to arise in part because many ordinary Balinese are not clear about which belief goes with which religion, and which practices are legitimate and which less so. Vegetarianism is a case in point. For members of Sai Baba vegetarianism is enjoined, but for non-members, as we have seen, it is a suspicious practice often interpreted as a means of accumulating potency. Devotees extend the ban to the use of animal meat in religious offerings, an injunction endorsed by *agama Hindu* – here *adat* ritualism comes into conflict with both these new religions. In 1997 an indigenous new religious movement (*aliran kepercayaan*), known as Tuntunan Suci, was investigated by the police after complaints by local villagers that the movement carried out ceremonies which deviated from the teachings of *agama Hindu* in that it forbade the slaughter of animals and the use of eggs to make offerings. Yet, as we have seen, while *adat* religion insists on animal flesh and eggs for offerings, seeing them as essential to placate the spirits, *agama Hindu* argues that sacrificing animals is unnecessary and ethically dubious. The complaint was therefore dismissed because it appeared that the activities were in conformity with *agama Hindu*.

Any new indigenous movements must base themselves on the state philosophy of *Pancasila* in order to be granted a license to operate, and hence must espouse spirituality and are constrained to advertise themselves as branches of *agama Hindu* or at least as springing from the same source as *agama Hindu*. In practice, however, these organisations often emphasise notions of *sakti*, which *agama Hindu* repudiates, and recruit members on the basis that they can help followers increase their inner power quickly. It is no surprise that for some Balinese religion has become a confusing matter.

It is rare for a village to have more than a few individuals or families who belong to the Sai Baba movement. Centres of worship are situated in the main towns and attract devotees from surrounding villages. Given their isolation from likeminded people, devotees often find it hard to maintain their membership in the face of opposition and criticism from suspicious villagers. Because *adat* ritualism is highly communal, everyone carries onerous obligations, and these are monitored so that even one recalcitrant individual can create severe problems. Devotees sometimes come under great pressure from parents and friends to terminate their membership. Sai Baba followers have told me that their refusal on religious grounds to eat meat and slaughter animals has caused friction with close kin who worry that they will leave *adat* religion, a move which would certainly bring about the devotees' social death.

It is worth remembering that membership of Sai Baba carries with it the injunction to continue participation in the local religion, so that its members can be brought back into the fold of 'true' religion. Many Balinese devotees claim that the religious teachings of Sai Baba enhance their understanding of the spiritual purpose of village *adat* rituals, which thereby makes them more, rather than less, diligent practitioners. Sai Baba devotees do not usually take part in the ritual slaughter of animals in their own villages, but do participate in *adat* ceremonies, though praying to Baba rather than to Balinese deities and ancestors. As one friend admitted to me, 'When I pray it's only me that knows to whom I'm praying'.

Religious identity

In the nineteenth century most Balinese probably did not conceive of themselves as a bounded ethnic group differentiated from those living on other islands. There were differences between Hindus (Balinese) and Muslims (other islanders, though some were also Balinese), but there were also multiple Balinese views of, and multiple forms of interaction with, Muslims (Vickers 1987: 35–7, 57–8). All these people shared a regional civilisation in which religious distinctions were much less important than they have since become. It was only in the early decades of the twentieth century, with the appearance of the Islamic reform movement, the communist party and nationalist organisations in Java and Sumatra, that religious identities became more politicised (Ricklefs 1981). During this period Balinese allegiances were for the most part local, based on attachments to village, descent group, local lord, and occupation. Identity was less about being Balinese and more about being a particular kind of Balinese.

When Balinese religion and culture were slandered in the colonial era, the ensuing reforms of religion and ritual, culminating in the establishment of *agama Hindu*, came to act as an internal unifying symbol. Though a recent creation, *agama Hindu* is represented as the recovery of a lost tradition (Hobsbawm and Ranger 1983), and conceived of as the inspiration for Balinese culture and artistic genius. In a Balinese botanical metaphor which connects religion to artistic creations, religion is the root, *adat* is the trunk, and the plastic and performing arts are the leaves and branches (Picard 1999: 17). Within this conceptual framework Balinese Hinduism began to be promoted by state authorities, religious officials and tourist entrepreneurs as the symbol of collective religious unity, and thus as the key marker of Balinese ethnic identity (*kebalian*) (Picard 1990b, 1997). However, since exclusive connections between state sponsored religion (*agama*) and an ethnic group (*suku*) is forbidden in Indonesia, *agama Hindu* had to be universalised within the Republic, thus allowing other Indonesians to join. In fact there are now more members of *agama Hindu* outside Bali than within (Ramstedt 1995: 6), thus rendering its links with a purely Balinese identity problematic. As this new ethnic identity assumed clearer outlines, the varieties of Hinduism on the island (Sai Baba, Hare Krishna) began to multiply, further complicating the association between *agama Hindu* and Balinese identity.

This religious innovation and diversity has had profound effects. In pre-colonial times Balinese religion approximated to what Bourdieu has called a doxa, a universe of undiscussed and undisputed belief and practice (1977: 168). To a large extent Balinese lived their religion rather than reflected upon it. The legitimacy of this religion went largely unquestioned because there was little to challenge it. When outsiders started to make disparaging assessments of Balinese religion, Balinese had few answers and began to question it themselves, generally using alien concepts to do so (Picard 1999). This self-examination set in motion the reforms of the twentieth century, creating competition over what counts as religious truth and heralding the break-up of doxa into orthodoxy – state-sponsored religions, and heterodoxy – deviant movements such as Sai Baba (Bourdieu 1977: 169).

The creation of *agama Hindu* provided a yardstick against which *adat* religion could be measured, and as a result Balinese developed a critical and questioning stance towards religious practice and belief, which has been further intensified by the appearance of devotional forms of Hinduism with which *agama Hindu* can be compared. The presence of distinct forms of Hinduism in the same social arena creates a conceptual distance between believer and belief, because Balinese can no longer think of their practices as axiomatic but must consider what kind of relationship they might have with these different Hinduisms. These variants of Hinduism now appear as 'competing possibles' (Bourdieu 1977: 169), options, though not necessarily mutually exclusive ones, between which Balinese can choose, and for which they require reasons and justifications for the choices they make. Moreover, because *agama Hindu* enabled Balinese to differentiate themselves from Muslims and Christians by defining their ethnic identity in terms of Hinduism, the emergence of new forms of Hinduism has supplied the necessary conditions for competing forms of identity.

For many long-time devotees of Sai Baba, and especially those who have visited India and seen Baba, attachment to him becomes so strong that it encourages the formation of an identity which is removed from concerns that are peculiarly Balinese. The rejection of *adat* practices in favour of a universal message marks out devotees as increasingly committed to a global world. In talks at services members frequently refer to terms such as 'universal', 'the world' and 'global', and hardly ever mention Bali. This new identity is about the individual in his or her specific relationship to the universal god, an identity based on the essential self deep within. Experienced and dedicated devotees frequently speak about improving and developing themselves, monitoring and reforming their behaviour, and policing their thoughts, desires and feelings. This preoccupation implies an internalisation of religion in which the devotee's 'emotions, attitudes and conscience become increasingly pivotal in validating behaviour in a manner which recalls Protestant values' (Kent 2000: 12).

Such an internalisation represents a considerable transformation of the Balinese self as it has been analysed for example by Geertz. In *adat* religion communal harmony is a matter of the performance of divinely sanctioned relations with kin, other Balinese, ancestors and spirits, all conceptualised as interdependent parts of a structured whole. In Geertz's analysis the public outer persona is all important, not the individual's particular personality or biography (Geertz 1973c). Failure to carry out obligations results in supernatural sanctions, pollution or ostracism by the community, and issues of sin, guilt and conscience are generally absent. According to Hardacre, writing about Japanese new religious movements, such a system sees the self as 'under' the control of external powers. Devotion to Baba, however, begins to change the character of the self. The relationships which now matter are those within one's own mind and body, and between oneself and Baba. In this transformed situation the self is 'in' control (Hardacre 1986: 15). Concretely this change manifests itself in how devotees speak about their attempts to control and overcome the 'internal enemies' of anger and jealousy, in private meditation and prayer, in cleansing the mind and body through vegetarianism, and abstention from drugs and illicit sex.

Over time this new religious allegiance progressively takes on a specific shape, moulded by changes in lifestyle and gradually filled with content through participation in charitable events, educational classes, singing *bhajan*, listening to members' talks, and visiting Baba's ashram in India. Focusing on the divine person of Baba enables Balinese devotees to expand their horizon as they come to recognise that they share an essential commonality with fellow devotees from India, Europe and Africa. For many this new self remains partial and elusive, because they never leave Bali, but they appear to experience the change vicariously. This new identity gradually replaces or submerges the 'delusory' Balinese self which used to be socially presented to others (cf. Babb 1986: 191). Meditation, prayer, devotion and singing are the activities which help the devotee to discover, strengthen and develop what they now consider as their once-hidden inner self. By modifying some of the ritual and communal connections with one's fellow Balinese through a quest for personal realisation, members procure the conditions for establishing new spiritual relationships with others from very different cultural backgrounds, Baba acting as the fixed centre drawing them all into a community of equals. Though devotees maintain their involvement in *adat* ritual practices, they apply a changed orientation to them and bring to them a new understanding of what they are doing. Devotees have told me that during temple ceremonies they do not pray to Balinese gods, but to Baba. This separation from other villagers is reinforced by their vegetarianism, abstention from cockfighting, and regular prayer and meditation. Consciousness of these differences renders attachments to local identities – village, status, occupation – less meaningful, and they begin to dissolve into the wider and more encompassing identity that grows from devotion to Baba. As Baba becomes the centre of their lives and as they become conscious that they belong to a worldwide 'imagined community' (Anderson 1991), being Balinese, seeing oneself as Balinese, assumes less significance. The creation of a transnational identity is effected through a conversion of the essential inner self into a public outer self. It is as though the devotee is turned inside out, and many claim they have been changed by Baba in precisely this way.

6 Controversies about Balinese hierarchy

Introduction

This chapter looks at the changing and dynamic nature of caste and hierarchical social relations in modern day Bali by looking at three key issues – competing interpretations of Balinese social structure, wealth and hierarchical status, and commoner kinship associations. I shall demonstrate that despite the relative lack of interest in this area of Balinese social life by other anthropologists, caste and hierarchy remain crucial institutions. Hierarchy in pre-colonial Bali is beyond the scope of this book, and interested readers are encouraged to consult the excellent works of Boon (1977), Geertz (1980), Wiener (1995) and Schulte Nordholt (1996).

The Balinese naming system is central to any social analysis of Balinese life. All Balinese who are members of the three highest categories – Brahmana, Satria and Wésia – are *anak jero* ('insiders') or, occasionally, Triwangsa. They constitute eight to ten per cent of the population, and Geertz refers to them as the 'gentry'. They belong to titled local descent groups, and the group title, indicating relative rank, is an integral part of a person's name. The title of a Brahmana male is *ida bagus* and of a female *ida ayu*. Anyone whose name begins with Ida Bagus or Ida Ayu is therefore a Brahmana. There are many titles in the Satria category – *anak agung, déwa, ngakan, predéwa, sang,* etc. Anyone whose name begins with one of these titles is therefore a member of a local descent group in the Satria *warna*. Anyone whose name incorporates the title *cokorda* is also a Satria, but is usually classed as Satria Dalem. *Cokorda* was often the title of ruling princes, and thus denoted a status superior to those groups classed as unmarked Satria, the term *dalem* indicating a greater degree of 'insiderness', itself a measure of superiority.

All Balinese who are gentry have names consisting of three parts – the title, a birth-order term (of which there are four – *putu, madé, nyoman, ketut* – after which the series repeats itself), and a given personal name. Thus a Brahmana might have the name Ida Bagus Nyoman Oka, where Nyoman indicates that he is the third (or seventh) child to be born and Oka is his personal name, in this case meaning 'son'. The words making up this name translate literally as 'honoured, handsome, third-born son'. Someone born into a local Anak Agung group might be given the name Anak Agung Ketut Alit, in which the terms literally translate as 'person, great, fourth-born, small'. In village life the full name is virtually never used. A young unmarried Brahmana male is addressed as Gus Man (Ida Bagus Nyoman) or Gus Tut (Ida Bagus Ketut). If there are several Brahmana who fit these descriptions, as often happens, the personal name may be used to differentiate them, such as Gus Man Jina. A male Brahmana married with children may be addressed as Gus Aji, the term *aji* meaning 'father', while a female Anak Agung married with children is usually addressed as Gung Biang, *biang* meaning 'mother'. Ideologically these gentry titles mark out their holders as persons of substance, refinement and beauty, and even in some sense as closer to the gods than commoners. The term *ida* is an honorific also used to address gods, *bagus* means 'handsome', and *ayu* means 'beautiful'. The title *anak agung* can be translated as 'big man' or 'great man', while *déwa* can also mean 'god'.

Anak jaba ('outsiders', infrequently referred to by Balinese as Sudra) comprise some ninety per cent of the population. Geertz refers to them as 'commoners'. Their names are simpler but again consist of three parts – a gender marker (I for males and Ni for females), a birth-order term (*wayan, madé, nyoman, ketut*), and a given name. Typical names are I Wayan Minyik and Ni Madé Selem. In the past Balinese commoners used either meaningless words (like *minyik*) or ordinary everyday words (like *selem*, black) as personal names. About forty years ago parents began conferring rather flowery names on their children, such as Juniartha or Suwastawa (shortened to Was), which are either never used or severely abbreviated; they are usually addressed by their birth-order name. Like gentry, commoners typically belong to named descent groups such as Pasek, Kebun Tubuh and Pulosari, but in only one case, that of Pandé (metalsmiths), is the group title incorporated into the names of its members. It was partly this naming system, which appears to anonymise rather than individuate Balinese, which encouraged Geertz to claim that Balinese cultural orders of definition depersonalise the individual.

From one perspective this hierarchy is framed by the *warna* system of Brahmana, Satria, Wésia and Sudra, derived ultimately from the original Indian version but, as Geertz perceptively notes, this system 'is not in itself a cultural device for making status discriminations but for correlating those already made by the title system. It summarises the literally countless fine comparisons implicit in that system in a neat ... separation of sheep from goats, and first-quality sheep from second, second from third' (1973c: 383). This might suggest that relative rank is an important matter all the way through the hierarchy, but the claim is misleading because commoners are rarely exercised by issues of rank amongst themselves. Among the gentry, hierarchy is a highly sensitive matter as Ngakan compete with Déwa, Déwa contest rank with Anak Agung, and Cokorda and Brahmana both claim the top position (Howe 2001, Chs 3–4). Among commoners it would make little sense to ask if Kebun Tubuh is superior or inferior to Pulosari. When the members of a village commoner group, say Pulosari, attempt to improve their rank they do so by claiming they are 'really' gentry, not by claiming they are, say, Pasek. At the upper reaches, among *anak jero*, the hierarchy consists of fine and hotly disputed gradations, while at the lower end *anak jaba* tend to see themselves, and to be seen by others, as roughly equal. In all-commoner villagers strong ideologies of equality exist, and marriages between members of different commoner title groups are frequent and generally unproblematic.

To an outside observer it is well nigh impossible to tell from appearance who is a gentry and who is a commoner. They dress in identical fashion and eat the same foods, and even if the house compounds they live in are known by different names (*gria* for Brahmana, *puri* for very high castes, *jeroan* for lower gentry, *umah* for commoners), they all have similar buildings in them laid out according to the same cosmological principles (see Chapter 1). Furthermore, in contemporary Bali status cannot reliably be equated with wealth. An affluent commoner with a good job or a successful business may live in a large, beautiful and lavishly furnished house, while a Brahmana may be a poor farmer and live in a small dilapidated one. On the other hand, some Balinese believe that visible distinguishing characteristics do exist. Given the titles they enjoy one could forgive gentry for describing themselves as having fine features, light skin, and faces which 'shine', and that their character, deportment and behaviour are refined and graceful. Commoners, by contrast, are described by gentry as having dark skin, coarse features and faces which are dreary and dull. Not surprisingly, commoner men and women only draw attention to these descriptions in order to dispute them.

It is only when one knows a person's name, hears them speak, watches them interact or observes their ceremonies that rank becomes noticeable to outside observers. The Balinese language is itself hierarchical in that, while most words have only one form and are thus insensitive to status, some 1,500 everyday words – the most common nouns, adjectives, verbs, pronouns, negatives – each have two or more lexemes which are hierarchically ranked and thus highly status sensitive. The basic rule is that caste inferiors must use more refined (*alus*) terms when speaking to or about superiors, whereas superiors may use less refined (*kasar*) terms when speaking to or about inferiors. For example, there are at least ten different Balinese verbs which translate 'to eat', the choice of word depending on the relative difference between the speaker and the person – or animal – he is addressing or referring to. Thus a commoner would say that pigs *ngamah* (eat), lower gentry *ngajeng*, and high priests *ngunggahang*, with finer gradations in between. Speaking therefore invariably involves making statements about relative ranking. For this reason Balinese who do not know each other cannot begin to converse until they have ascertained each other's caste rank, which they do by asking the question '*nunas antuk linggih?*' ('where do you sit?', meaning 'what is your rank?'), though this usage appears to be in decline. Once relative position is established they can select the appropriate speech terms without causing offence.

There are many subtleties to all this. Ideally one should linguistically lower and humble oneself and elevate one's interlocutor. Speech patterns should be accompanied by appropriate bodily postures, eye movements, and head and arm gestures. Relative physical head height is important, so that in gatherings of people of different caste rank inferiors should make sure they are not sitting above superiors. In the past infringements of these rules were harshly punished by fines and even debt slavery (Schulte Nordholt 1996: 43). Today the extremes of language use have been largely abandoned because these sanctions can no longer be applied, allowing commoner Balinese to treat gentry with linguistic contempt should they so desire and if they think they can get away with it. At the same time many commoner Balinese extol the beauty and necessity of high Balinese. It is after all the literary language, the language used in prayers to their ancestors, and the language employed in public meetings. Commoners continue to use it because a good command of its intricacies confers prestige, and they are willing to speak it to superiors so long as superiors reciprocate by conferring respect on their inferiors (Howe 2001, Ch. 5).

Stated thus this elaborate linguistic and bodily etiquette suggests interactional formality and rigidity but, as I argued in Chapter 3, in everyday village life, where commoners may live next door to gentry, play together, go to the same school, belong to the same *gamelan* orchestra, and do a great many other things in concert, language use is in practice highly flexible and contextual. Cross-caste friendships can be strong and intimate, in which case many speech rules are put aside and gentry and commoner may use very similar terms when talking to each other. Yet the distinctions of rank, linguistic or otherwise, are never entirely absent, and they are continually applied in new situations. Gentry often complain privately about the inappropriate way their commoner friends speak to them (Howe 2001: 86–7). It is still the case that gentry overwhelmingly marry other gentry and commoners marry other commoners, because cross-caste marriages involve many sensitive status problems. In school teachers often treat high caste children differently from commoner children (Parker 1997).

Many privileges are still linked to rank, which is why hierarchical position remains important and relevant to all Balinese. At its most basic gentry who are poor still have their title, and can thus assert their right to the language of respect from caste inferiors, though this may be grudging or even withheld if the former are dissolute, unsociable, mean-spirited, or do not fully meet their proper obligations to other villagers. Just as importantly, caste rank confers considerable ritual privileges. High castes are buried at the upstream end of the graveyard while commoners are buried at the downstream end. The higher the caste position the more roofs a person is entitled to on their cremation tower, so that while Cokorda often have eleven, Anak Agung nine and other gentry seven, commoners typically have only one. Similarly the form of the sarcophagus in which the body is cremated varies, high castes often using a bull while lower castes use the inferior lion or fish-elephant (*gajah mina*). There are many other forms of ritual paraphernalia to which gentry are entitled which, if employed by commoners, cause offence and precipitate conflict.

Rank also plays a significant role in the economic and political sphere. Many commoners have achieved success in education, business and commerce, and there are many poor and uneducated Brahmana and other gentry, yet high castes disproportionately fill high political office and are either elected or appointed to many of the more important positions in provincial, regional and village government, and in other bureaucratic organisations such as the *Parisada* and the universities (Parker 1992b: 96; Warren 1993: 273). Many of the core line descendants of nineteenth century high caste rulers still also own large tracts of land, the revenues from which are used in business ventures of many kinds (Geertz 1963b). In this sense, as mentioned in Chapter 1, descendants of the pre-colonial and colonial Balinese elite have to some extent maintained themselves as a modern economic and political elite. Despite the continued prominence of gentry in all areas of economic and political life, the comparative success of many commoners means that it is now fairly common to find employment settings – both in bureaucracies and private enterprises – where low castes are in positions of authority over high castes. In such contexts there are no formal rules governing language use, so if Balinese is used rather than status-neutral Indonesian it is not clear who should speak at what level with whom. A member of an Anak Agung group may try to assert his right to hear high Balinese from his work superior who happens to be a commoner, but may have to accept a much lower form because he is, in this context, in a subordinate position. A Brahmana friend of mine in Corong came home every day from his menial job complaining of headaches caused by the coarse words of his commoner boss.

One of the most significant aspects of the title system and of Balinese hierarchy generally is its dynamic nature, but sometimes its detailed workings become obscured by a tendency to see it as a timeless system of standardised categories in which individual character and ability are irrelevant. Geertz has argued, cosmologically speaking, that

> the prestige gradients implicit in the title system ought to be reflected in the actual distribution of wealth, power and esteem in society, and, in fact, be completely coincident with it. The degree to which this coincidence actually obtains is, of course, moderate at best. But, however many exceptions there may be to the rule – Sudras with enormous power, Satrias working as tenant farmers, Brahmans neither esteemed nor estimable – it is the rule and not the exceptions that the Balinese regard as truly illuminating the human condition. The Varna System orders the title system in such a way as to make it possible to view social life under the aspect of a general set of cosmological notions: notions in which the diversity of human talent and the workings of historical process are regarded as superficial phenomena when compared with the location of persons in a system of standardised status categories, as blind to individual character as they are immortal.
>
> (Geertz 1973c: 384)

Though there is a profound truth in what Geertz says, in the sense that the title system does indeed embody a 'general set of cosmological notions' which underpins Balinese ideas about and reactions to the status system, I think he misjudges the way it works in practice. The ideal title system, in which each person has an uncontested right to a specific rank position, is obviously important, but it is important precisely because it provides the framework within which Balinese dispute their actual positions. Geertz goes on to argue that the 'diversity of human talent and the workings of the historical process are regarded as superficial phenomena', but who is it that regards them as superficial?

The problem is that, since the 1920s and possibly earlier, there has been no unanimity about the criteria by which Balinese should be allotted to their hierarchical positions, and therefore no agreement as to what is essential and what is superficial. For some the principal criterion is birth. No matter how dissolute, lazy and ignorant, if a man is a Brahmana he remains a Brahmana and his children are Brahmana. For others life achievement is paramount, so a Sudra occupying a powerful political role might well think he should be a Cokorda. In both cases the distinction between rule and exception is clearly defined, but what counts as rule and what as exception becomes extremely contentious.

Because Geertz assumes that ascription by birth, rather than by merit, is at the heart of the ideal system, and that power, wealth and esteem should ideally correlate with rank, he consigns the existence of a powerful Sudra to the class of exceptions. From the Sudra's perspective, however, he is not an exception – he has the wrong title and thus the wrong position. A dissolute Brahmana may not believe he is an exception because he is a Brahmana by birth, but his commoner neighbour may well think he is because this Brahmana does not behave in a meritorious way. My misgivings about Geertz's analysis are twofold. First, he stresses the rules too much and the exceptions too little, when the focus should properly be on the relationship between them. Second, with its tacit emphasis on birth status Geertz's description tends to endorse a high caste view of the system; his supposedly neutral analysis reproduces the explanation given by rulers and Brahmanas and discounts the views of commoners.

Balinese perceptions of the workings of the hierarchy are highly ambivalent. Caste confers both advantages and disadvantages – one receives deference from inferiors but has to give it to superiors, so hierarchy is experienced simultaneously as both satisfying and oppressive. Many Balinese are unhappy about the hierarchical position they find themselves in, believing that their achievements entitle them to a higher rank, a rank others deny them because they believe that birth is what counts. This ambivalence can lead to problems in the analysis of Balinese hierarchy, but a promising way forward may be to interpret status drives, new religious movements, and commoner challenges to gentry hegemony as disagreements about the essential nature of hierarchy, cosmological ideals and practical realities.

The following sections look at three examples of how the hierarchy works in contemporary Bali – indigenous debate about the essential character of Balinese social organisation, attempts at status mobility and the complex relationship between status and wealth, and large scale commoner mobilisation to contest gentry hegemony by asserting that all Balinese are equal.

Competing interpretations of Balinese social structure

Catur warna (the 'four *warna*', derived from Sanskrit) (Dowson 1972: 71) is a common, though mostly literary, term denoting the division of the population into the four great classes of Brahmana, Satria, Wésia and Sudra. Since colonial times, however, the new word *kasta* has entered both the Indonesian and Balinese languages to describe the hierarchy (*sistim kasta*). Observing the apparent similarity between Balinese social organisation and the caste systems of India, particularly in the light of the presence of the *varna* terms, the worship of Siva by Brahmana priests, the Hindu custom of widow immolation on her husband's funeral pyre (*sati*), and much else, the Dutch assumed that the Indian system had been imported into Bali in its entirety. Differences between the two, of which there were many (Howe 1987), were attributed to the Balinese version having broken down and become confused. The Dutch writers thus referred to the Balinese social order as the *kastenstelsel* (caste system) or *kastenmaatschappij* (caste society) (Lekkerkerker 1926). The terms caste, *kaste* (Dutch) and *kasta* (Indonesian) all derive from the Portuguese word *casta*, meaning tribe, clan or family, a term used by the Portuguese to describe Indian social organisation when they arrived in India in the sixteenth century (Basham 1971: 149).

The introduction of a new word to describe their social hierarchy provided opportunities for Balinese to interpret their social structure in two very different and antagonistic ways. These different explanations have been debated by Balinese intellectuals in academic texts (Santri 1993), in the editorials and letters column of the island's daily newspaper, the *Bali Post*, and by ordinary Balinese as they defend or challenge hierarchy. The crucial issue concerns the purpose of the titles attached to descent groups.

In one interpretation, denoted by the term *kasta*, these groups are arranged in a hierarchical order of superiority and inferiority according to how their lines of descent are related to precolonial ruling dynasties. In this system the eldest son of a king enjoys the same status as his father, but this son's younger male siblings drop a level in status and ideally should move out of the ruling house and establish their own lesser houses owing allegiance to the original house. This principle of 'sinking status' (Geertz and Geertz 1975: 124) repeats itself at all levels, so that the eldest son of the king's eldest son retains the status of the king, but younger sons of younger sons drop even further down the scale. Such an ideology structures the manner in which the Javanese invaders from Majapahit dispersed themselves across Bali and became lords over semi-independent kingdoms, all more or less owing loyalty and deference to the centre.

The first Javanese established themselves in southeast Bali in what is today the regency of Klungkung. From the sixteenth century onwards the ruler of this kingdom – whose title was *déwa agung* – was accredited as the highest status king in Bali. As his younger children and grandchildren moved out of his palace they established subordinate ruling houses in other regions, and their younger brothers and children did the same, until most of Bali was ruled by houses genealogically related to the Déwa Agung. At least this was how its working was later presented. In practice, however, there were a great many discrepancies from the ideal – rebellions, murders, usurpers, incompetent eldest sons. Such aberrations provided reasons for endemic conflict and war between the nine kingdoms of nineteenth century Bali (Geertz 1980; Agung 1988; Vickers 1989). Whatever the truth, lords usually tried to legitimise their rule by having dynastic chronicles (*babad*) composed in which the necessary but often fictitious kin connections to the Déwa

Agung were established. Thus the Déwa Agung was the principal exemplary centre, and as genealogical distance from him increased so status declined. In village Bali this system was in evidence during colonial times. The eldest members of the family I lived with in Corong in 1993 told me their grandfather had the title *cokorda* because he lived in the palace of the ruling prince – the local exemplary centre – but when one of his sons had to leave the palace and build his own house he had to take on the lower title of *ida I déwa*, later changed to *anak agung* when the Dutch rationalised the title system. Since independence and the consequent removal of all traditional political power from the precolonial rulers – even if their descendants have reacquired it through positions in state government – the ideology of 'sinking status' has today lost much of its significance, so when sons move out of high caste houses they retain the same status as their father.

In contemporary Bali, for high castes at least, it is birth into these titled descent groups which matters as far as issues of hierarchy are concerned, since there are many status prerogatives still attaching to gentry titles. As we have seen, these privileges include exclusive rights to certain kinds of ritual, important items of ritual paraphernalia, being addressed in refined language and other forms of deference from commoners, and asymmetrical marriage and food exchanges through which hierarchical social relations are enacted. All these distinctions are justified by *kasta* ideology.

The other interpretation, denoted by the term *warna*, is a rival interpretation of Balinese social structure increasingly employed by commoners to challenge *kasta* ideology. *Warna* ideology denounces ideas of hierarchy based on birth and ascription, being founded on notions of wisdom and achievement. In the *warna* model Balinese should be given titles in accordance with the functions they perform in society, acquired by dint of merit and hard work rather than inherited through birth into a particular descent group. Titles become descriptors, and are not necessarily prestigious in themselves as they are in *kasta* ideology. However, their holders may gain prestige and respect in accordance with how they serve the rest of society by assiduous performance of the duties attached to their occupation. In its most radical form *warna* becomes an egalitarian critique of *kasta*, because in the *warna* theory of social structure anyone can fill any position, and all Balinese become essentially the same kind of people.

Both ideologies – *kasta* and *warna* – interpret Balinese society holistically, in the sense that prosperity depends on the separation and appropriate performance of roles, individual goals are subordinated to collective ones, and specific roles relate to specific titles. The difference between *kasta* and *warna* centres on how and why titles are conferred.

Supporters of *kasta* claim that the four classes of people – Brahman, Satria, Wésia, Sudra – are ideally suited by their ancestry and origins to one of the four important functions – priest, ruler, wealth producer, servant – needed to maintain social and cosmological order. Another Balinese term used to denote the title groups is *soroh* ('type', 'kind'), also used to distinguish different species of animal and different classes of object. Thus *soroh* Brahmana are believed to be essentially different kinds of people from *soroh* Pasek – some Balinese believe this to the extent that cross-caste marriages are believed to result in sterile offspring. An illuminating instance of this idea occurred in Corong when I met a Brahmana who had recently returned to Bali after several years in France because his family wanted him to become a *pedanda*. When asked how long it would take to learn all the complicated prayers and litanies required of such a priest he replied that, as the child of a *pedanda*, he would only need to go through them once and they would be memorised.

Proponents of *warna*, on the other hand, assert that society's functional roles can be performed by anyone with the requisite abilities, and that the possession of such abilities is not related to ancestry. This claim is reinforced by a historical argument concerning the way *warna* supposedly changed into *kasta*. In the ancient past, while the division of the population into the four great classes existed because it was essential for social order, these classes of people were not hierarchically ranked as superior and inferior. Rather, the classification was one of functions, not people, and implied only separation and complementarity. When the Javanese invaders assumed control of Bali, the separation of functions (*catur warna*) was transformed into the separation of titled groups arranged hierarchically (*kasta*), and children began to inherit their fathers' titles even if they failed to perform the functions appropriate to them. It is interesting that this debate within Bali parallels an ongoing academic debate among anthropologists and historians concerning the meaning of *varna* in ancient India (Dumont 1980; Derrett 1976; Quigley 1993).

This explanation of how ancient social structure has been transformed and distorted is part of the more general commoner argument about the way in which priests and high castes have exerted authority over commoners through status sensitive ritual privileges and exclusive control over sacred knowledge, corrupting and degrading what was once an egalitarian society tied to a more ethicised religion. What actually seems to have happened is that Balinese started to follow Dutch terminology, using the term *kasta* to describe the hierarchy and its associated inequalities and thus providing an opportunity for reformist Balinese to appropriate and redefine *warna* in non-hierarchical terms. They then projected this putative form of social organisation back into the past as though it was an ancient tradition, concluding that *warna* should be re-established by abolishing *kasta*.

The favouring of *warna* began in the 1920s in debates between gentry and commoners about religious reform, and was supported in later years by anti-caste ideas brought back from India by Balinese students who studied there. A prominent Balinese intellectual, Gedé Pudja, who had studied Indian philosophy and religion at a university in Banares, argued that in the ancient Indian scriptures it is not birth but way of life which determines which *warna* one should belong to. A remarkable Balinese woman, Ibu Gedong Oka, was fascinated by Gandhi, translated four of his works into Indonesian, and established a Gandhian ashram in south Bali. Pudja, Oka and others argued for the retention of the *catur warna*, because it is a universal pattern of social organisation and necessary for the proper functioning of society. They contended that its ascriptive, hereditary and hierarchical aspects should be abandoned, along with the resulting privileges, because in reality the members of the four *warna* are equal (Bakker 1993: 124–6).

The controversy surrounding these rival interpretations is encountered all over Bali. In Corong, for example, many villagers are mildly disgusted by the dissolute behaviour of unemployed gentry who spend their days drinking and gambling at cards and cockfights, and question why they should defer to someone with the title *ida bagus* who is plainly ignorant of Brahmana learning and skills. While *warna* appears to be a forceful critique of *kasta* ideology, the partisan manner in which its ideas are applied in practice sometimes produces a rather different picture. The *warna* argument is often used by commoners suffering from what sociologists refer to as relative status deprivation. Someone may complain that a person 'is just a room boy working in a hotel, so why should he be a Brahmana?' or believe that 'although I am a commoner, I am a soldier and therefore should be a Satria' (Ramstedt 1995: 13). Here *warna* ideology is used either to problematise the high status of others, or to assert the right to a higher status for oneself – it is hierarchical status that is at issue here, not functional complementarity. What is being questioned is one's position in the hierarchy, not the hierarchy itself.

A more complicated example reveals the subtlety of some arguments. Lower gentry who might not normally countenance the *warna* ideology – because it would render them equal to commoners – can paradoxically find it a useful weapon in attempts to raise their status. Local descent groups with the title *ngakan* are conventionally inferior to most other gentry, and consequently try to raise their status by claiming the title – *déwa* – of the group just above them. Claiming to be Déwa is not difficult – all they have to do is start using the new title in the names they give to their children. Authentic Déwa do not take kindly to this practice, but there is little they can do to stop it. It is only when Ngakan begin to use ritual prerogatives reserved for higher castes – building cremation towers with nine instead of seven roofs, for example – that physical resistance comes into play. To support the practice of name-changing, Ngakan exploit the ambiguity between titles and names. In Corong, Ngakan assert that titles have lost much of the meaning and significance they had in the past, and that what matters now is merit and achievement. They thus claim that titles are now nothing more than personal names, and since names are a matter of individual choice there should be no objection to the names they give their children. *Déwa* is not meant to be a title, they say, simply a personal name. By using a *warna* argument, Balinese who change their names can appear to conform to an increasingly dominant meritocratic ideology at the same time as surreptitiously enhancing their status. Other villagers are not taken in by this sophistry, but this does not prevent the strategy being a useful first step in a group's ambitions to improve its rank position.

At a general level *warna* ideology is opposed to *kasta*, and is used by genuine social reformers to denounce hierarchy and its privileges. In many other contexts, however, diluted versions of it can be deployed which obliquely endorse hierarchical relations. For many ordinary Balinese, hierarchy itself does not seem to be the issue. They are more concerned with the way in which circumstances conspire to allocate people to the wrong positions in that hierarchy. In many instances the manner in which *warna* ideology is used tends to work towards preserving hierarchy rather than subverting it.

Wealth and hierarchical status

The relationship between hierarchical status and wealth is interesting because although wealth is often seen by others as the trigger for a particular group to attempt to raise its status, it is almost never the reason given by that group itself. When enough members of a descent group achieve a certain level of wealth and success relative to others in the local area, they often attempt to raise the status of their own group by claiming it should occupy a higher position in the hierarchy than the one it presently enjoys. As Geertz argued, this suggests a close correspondence between status and wealth, those groups with the greatest power and wealth ideally being at the top of the hierarchy and those with the least at the bottom. In this sense hierarchy can be seen as a form of economic stratification, which is how some anthropologists have explained the caste systems of India. An important feature of such a materialist approach is that the Hindu cultural theory of purity and pollution, on which the hierarchical separation of castes is said to be based, readily mystifies economic and political exploitation (Meillassoux 1973; Mencher 1974).

One difficulty encountered by this theory concerns what Bailey (1957), otherwise impressed by the correlation between status and wealth in the middle of the Indian caste hierarchy, calls the 'peculiar rigidities' existing at the extremes of the system. Brahmin priests, who might be poor, were still at the top of the hierarchy, while Untouchables, who might be rich, were securely anchored at the bottom. Here status and wealth emphatically do not coincide. Louis Dumont (1980), far from considering these apparent discrepancies as peculiarities of caste, sees them as crucial and defining of the whole system. For him hierarchy is a religious rather than an economic institution, which is why Brahmin priests – fulfilling a religious function and therefore the purest – are at the apex however rich or poor they may be. Untouchables, whose occupations deal with death (leatherworkers and butchers) and bodily excretions (washermen and sweepers) are at the bottom, however rich or poor they are, because they constantly absorb the pollution from higher castes, who thus remain relatively pure. Those castes in the Kshatriya *varna* rank second because they are secular earthly rulers whose function is to maintain social order so the Brahmins can perform the rituals which keep the cosmos going. Castes in the Vaishya category, the wealth creators, come lower still. In Dumont's model the religious function ranks above the political, which in turn ranks above the economic. It is religious purity which determines hierarchical rank, and is independent of wealth or political power.

Dumont's theory appears to be a good explanation. More recent research, however, has shown that Brahmins who are not priests often rank higher than those who are, that some priestly Brahmins are almost 'untouchable' because they receive gifts which pollute them (Parry 1980; Fuller 1984; Raheja 1988), and that the king, who has a magico-ritual function, may outrank a priest who is reduced to a mere ritual technician (Dirks 1987; Galey 1989; Quigley 1993). If the king replaces the Brahmin priest at the top of the hierarchy, the link between wealth and power re-enters the picture.

How does the Balinese situation help us with this conundrum? In precolonial Bali mobility up and down the hierarchy was probably greater than during the colonial period, when the Dutch, failing to understand the complexity of the system, mistook its dynamism for confusion and set about reconstituting it in such a way that every Balinese was allocated a fixed position within it. They hoped this would put an end to complaints about relative rank, but all it did was to foster claims to higher rank by those who had lost out in the reorganisation. These claims usually received adverse adjudications in the courts, and mobility became increasingly restricted. After World War II and the Dutch withdrawal, however, opportunities opened up again and some commoner groups began to reassert dormant claims to gentry status. This was made possible in part by the creation of bogus genealogical histories in which a descent line was traced back to a superior and illustrious origin, thus providing written evidence to support claims of higher status. Boon (1977: 167) describes how impoverished high castes in eastern Bali 'discreetly sent scouts to other districts to contact status seekers. Genealogies were then prepared in the form of sacred *prasasti* manuscripts; the palm leaves were stored in a smutty hearth for ageing and later sold to the appropriate commoners when they journeyed east seeking an elevated source.'

A manuscript attesting to superior origins provides no certainty of success, because any attempt by a local descent group to raise its status has major implications for other groups in the village. If a commoner group claims that it is really Déwa and – as often happens – there are other Déwa in the same village, the upstart group must claim equality with this Déwa group and superiority over groups it used to be equal to. To make the claim stick, other things have to be changed in addition to the adoption of a gentry title – rededication of family temples, new ritual practices, new terms of address and reference. This can only be successful if other villagers are willing to recognise the changes as appropriate, and agree to alter existing forms of interaction. Whereas previously the new Déwa had to use deferential language towards existing Déwa, now they must convince them to converse at the same level, which means authentic Déwa accepting less refined language. Whereas the new Déwa previously engaged at the same level with other commoners, they now expect linguistic and other forms of deference from them, and they can now use ritual procedures and equipment previously denied to commoners. In order to change its status, a group's attributes have to be validated by necessary changes in exchange and interactional patterns (cf. Parry 1979: 92). These changes are extremely contentious and smack of arrogance (*sombong*) a disposition which Balinese loathe. In those cases I have experienced in detail (Howe 2001: 33–57) other village groups strenuously resist such changes because they compromise their own status. Unless the claims can be substantiated, conflict – sometimes of a violent nature – is unavoidable. Other villagers may stop speaking to the new Déwa, refuse to assist in their ceremonies, and disrupt their cremations.

It is very hard to have claims to elevated status ratified and accepted by other villagers. The possession of a genealogical history is helpful, but since it is well known that these documents can be fabricated for a price their authenticity is easily questioned. Another method is to obtain ancestral approval of the claim. This is usually secured from a spirit medium, through whom the ancestral deities reveal their wishes. Though Balinese believe that the ancestors are never wrong, it is common knowledge that spirit mediums may be charlatans who can be manipulated, and even when they are being honest ancestral revelations are often ambiguous and confusing, thus allowing quite different interpretations. As a result many such claims remain unconcluded, and claimants and their neighbours may live in a state of uneasy tension for years, punctuated by occasional bouts of conflict.

Though wealth does not appear to play an important role in status mobility, it is often believed to be a driving factor in claims to higher status. In my experience the status-seeking group never publicly uses their current wealth and success as a means of authenticating their claim, even though others might think this is the underlying reason. Referring to a group of Ngakan in the village of Corong who had been styling themselves as superior Déwa for some years, a high caste friend who had no personal axe to grind remarked to me 'They are rich, they have nice homes, many live in Denpasar and own cars, they are well educated and have good jobs, and they have just built an imposing family temple – if they have all this they will want to change their title'. Barth (1993: 233) quotes a Balinese from north Bali making the same point: 'Balinese always want to improve their level. First they want more money, so as to become rich. Second, they want to better their position in their office, so they can become chief of department. Third, they want to better their education so that they can become graduate [sic] from secondary school ... If they have all this, then also they want to become triwangsa!' Boon (1977: 167), too, argues in a similar vein when he notes that within 'a set of houseyards the wealthier family heads sometimes spearhead upward mobility, and they oblige their lower, less presumptuous kin to affirm the claims'.

The implication is that while wealth – in a broad sense – seems to trigger a status drive, it cannot publicly be used to justify it. The group pursuing elevated status is never likely to acknowledge wealth as the reason, because to do so would automatically render the claim inauthentic – it would provoke the retort that 'you are only doing it because you are rich, and that is not a good reason'. Others point to wealth as the reason for a status drive merely to cast doubt on the propriety of the claim. In reality claims to higher status can only be ratified through authentic cultural means – ancestral revelation, genealogical histories, consensus.

Sometimes, however, it is the exception that proves the rule. In the early 1970s a group of related commoner households on the small island of Nusa Penida, off the south-east coast of Bali, became members of a large and prestigious Déwa descent group resident in Corong some forty miles away (Howe 2001: 50–6). After a series of illnesses, conflicts and ritual disasters in their home village, they sought the cause for their misfortune from spirit mediums, some of whom revealed they were not really commoners at all and were therefore worshipping at the wrong ancestral shrines. Similar events were occurring among the group of Déwa in Corong, who sought guidance from the deity of their origin temple. Speaking through the temple priest the deity revealed that the root of their troubles was that the ancestors wanted them to reclaim a group of their members who, in the distant past, had been expelled from a neighbouring village. As the result of further revelations and coincidences, representatives of the Déwa from Corong 'found' their 'lost' kin on Nusa Penida, and after discussions and tests the ancestral deities welcomed the Nusa Penida commoners as true members of the Déwa group. Following these dramatic developments the new Déwa have been reluctant to alter their forms of interaction with their neighbours in Nusa Penida. They have not attempted to elicit deference, and have not used their new title in their names. The reason they give for this reluctance is that they are poor, uneducated farmers. Here it is lack of wealth which inhibits the display of new status privileges.

A way forward in the status–wealth debate is suggested by Boon, who argues that the title system is

> a native theory of prestige, senseless if it merely mirrors the pragmatics of individual interests in areas of economics or political power ... If the titles simply offered a redundant index of political power, they would ring hollow. It is the guaranteed lag in the hoped-for congruence of prestige and power that animates social life ... every Balinese has self-interested reason to suspect that his title is too low and another's is too high.
>
> (Boon 1977: 184)

Boon believes that the title system establishes 'the cultural problem of pragmatically earned versus divinely endowed status'. This suggests that there is no fixed relationship between status and wealth, but rather that the relationship is contingent, unstable and contextual. If Balinese are poor but high status they deem wealth to be culturally irrelevant, since to do otherwise would be counter-productive. However, if they are low status but rich, wealth becomes relevant because it appears to reveal a gap between present and hoped-for status, and thus acts as the trigger for upward movement. Though there are advantages in the idea that there is no fixed relation between status and wealth, because wealth seems to be an important determinant of status only when one possesses it, it is not an entirely satisfactory formulation. It does not, for example, deal with the issue of Balinese aspiring to superior positions but being reticent to use their wealth as the justification because they know that such a justification would be unacceptable to others.

The situation is further complicated because there is also a cultural relationship between wealth and status. In Bali, as in Java (Keeler 1987, Brenner 1998), traditional ideologies suggest that wealth should follow from power – the supernatural potency (*sakti*) that people of high status are born with. Power should not follow from wealth. According to this theory potency is the magnet which attracts wealth, valuables, followers and women to the one who possesses it (Anderson 1972). It is manifested in the ability to get others to do ones bidding without physical coercion, and by behaviour which is *alus* – refined, composed and elegant. Those who lack potency, typically ordinary commoners, have to work hard to accomplish anything. The pursuit of wealth through trade and business is considered by high castes to be *kasar* – coarse and unrefined – and betokens a lack of potency.

Commoner aspirations to higher status based on the accumulation of this kind of wealth are seen by gentry not just as an unwelcome intrusion by the *nouveau riche*, but more significantly as a challenge to high caste ideologies of power, a challenge which suggests that wealth may be obtained independently of status and potency.

One way of analysing the multifaceted relationship between status and wealth is to argue that a new prestige system is developing. This is a result of the growth and diversification of the Balinese economy in the last fifty years, which has provided many people with opportunities to become wealthy through a host of new occupations and new forms of business and commerce. Affluent commoners have begun to construe their continued deference to impoverished and uneducated gentry as feudal (*feodal*, Ind.) and old-fashioned (*kolot*, Ind.). Because dominant high caste ideologies invoking potency and the value of birth do not recognise the legitimacy of wealth derived in this manner, those aspiring to upward mobility still feel the need to convert it into culturally appropriate forms – lavish ceremonies, new family temples, and the invocation of more illustrious ancestral origins.

The new system maintains a tense and competitive relationship with the traditional title system. As we saw in Chapter 4, mid-twentieth century reforms of ritual allowed the level at which a household could perform its ceremonies, until then dependent purely on hierarchical status, to be related to its wealth. Since this reform legitimately allows a rich commoner household to perform its ceremonies at the same level as a gentry household, new wealth and traditional status become linked, and the notion that the two may be congruent becomes a cultural possibility that commoners are increasingly exploiting. The fact that many high caste Balinese have taken advantage of opportunities in the expanding economy has strengthened the hand of commoners seeking to break old connections between wealth and status, and replace them with new ones.

Geertz argues that the distribution of wealth, power and esteem in Balinese society should ideally be coincident with the prestige gradients of the title system. This conclusion is too simple. The relationship between wealth and status has never been straightforward, depending on the nature of the wealth, the sources it is derived from, and the cultural values which give it meaning. As political and economic conditions within Bali have changed, so too have the complex connections between wealth and status.

In precolonial times wealth was understood to flow from potency, itself largely a function of hierarchical status. Developments in postcolonial Bali introduced the idea that wealth can be accumulated independently of potency and status, so that wealth on its own became the basis of a separate and emerging prestige system. It is the manner in which Balinese creatively use and manipulate these competing prestige systems, and the ideologies which underpin them, which generates some of the complexity and variety of modern Balinese culture.

Challenging the elite: commoner kinship associations

We have looked at some of the processes which help explain the resilience of hierarchical social relations in contemporary Bali; this section explores some of the ways in which the hierarchy itself is being attacked by commoners, using an ideology of the equality of all Balinese. This challenge has been mounted by commoners mobilising on a large scale in kinship associations known as *warga*.

Warga are associations formed from numerous local descent groups whose members all share the same title, and therefore putatively descent from the same distant ancestor. High caste *warga* such as Warga Brahmana Siwa have existed since the late nineteenth century, probably because such gentry groups have been more able to form regional networks and alliances than have commoners (Geertz and Geertz 1975; Rubinstein 1995). A significant feature of twentieth century Bali, especially since the 1950s, has been the development and growing influence of commoner *warga*, such as Warga Pasek, formed from the many local Pasek descent groups and formally established in 1952, and the Warga Pandé, the organisation of Pandé groups, formally established in 1975 though in existence informally since the 1930s. The most important characteristic of these commoner *warga* is that they attempt to establish equality with gentry groups through the politics of religion rather than in economic terms.

In order to join a *warga*, individual households and local descent groups have to determine their descent origins (*kawitan*), since this indicates which *warga* they can apply to for membership. In the early part of the twentieth century many commoner descent groups were organised on a village basis, and did not possess or acknowledge a title. These groups worshipped in temples called *dadia* or *panti*, membership being based on shared descent from a local ancestor going back no more than about four or five generations and after whom the group was named. In the 1950s and early 1960s, for a variety of reasons (Howe 2002: 118–19), many Balinese needed to determine their deeper origins, and thus what their descent title should be. To do this they turned to traditional experts in genealogical history, such as the Déwa Agung of Klungkung who, being the descendant of the highest ranking king of precolonial Bali, had great knowledge of the stories relating to the dispersal of Balinese families across the island to events in the past (Vickers 1989: 166). The Déwa Agung and his priests explained descent origins to petitioners, and provided advice and information about temple festivals and other ritual matters. Armed with this information a local descent group could request membership of the larger *warga* descent association sharing its title. In the context of the intense political and economic conflict following the birth of the Indonesian state (Robinson 1995), the growth in the membership of commoner *warga* facilitated their use 'as political networks to support the various [political] parties, and as religious networks to be mobilised in arguments for the rationalisation of Balinese religion, particularly where that rationalisation involved challenging the central role of *brahmana* priests in ritual' (Vickers 1989: 164–5).

Another way of establishing 'true' origins was – and still is – through spirit mediums, who provided revelations from gods and ancestors about why a local household or descent group was experiencing excessive misfortune and illness among its members. Sometimes, as we saw in the Nusa Penida example, mediums explain the cause of misfortune as stemming either from 'forgetting the ancestors' (Stuart-Fox 2002: 112–13) or worshipping at the 'wrong' temple shrines. The remedy may be the rehabilitation of a neglected temple, through which the group renews worship of its ancestors (Stuart-Fox 2002: 113). It may involve 'the forging of a new relationship with a more inclusive descent group or *warga*' whose ancestors are found also to be the ancestors of the joining group, and whose temples must therefore now be supported by the newcomers. Their new standing may require the adoption of a title – such as *pasek* – which was not used previously, or a change of title given that the previous one was incorrect. Joining a *warga* or changing *warga* affiliation does not cause problems as long as it only involves commoner *warga*, since such a change has few implications for hierarchical status. Commoner *warga* often practise an open-door policy, welcoming new members as long as they can provide evidence of shared origins from recognised authorities, and leaving any mistakes to be rectified later by ancestral intervention.

Even before modern commoner *warga* evolved, many Pandé groups refused to use the services of Brahmana *pedanda* priests – including the holy water they prepare which is considered by most other Balinese as indispensable for the completion of their rituals – because their origin myths and genealogical chronicles forbade it. Even if high castes do not accept their argument, many Pandé groups have traditionally claimed equality with or independence from the Brahmana, on the basis that they have older origins and that their power is greater than that of the *pedanda* priests (Eiseman 1990, Vol.1: 76–81). Many Pandé groups ordain and use their own priests, *sri empu*, to officiate at their ceremonies (Pitana 1999; Guermonprez 1987).

The initial modest aim of associations such as Warga Pasek was similar to that of Warga Pandé – to be independent of *pedanda* by ordaining their own priests and having them officiate at their own rituals. It was only in the late 1960s that Pasek leaders began to speak explicitly of these commoner priests being equivalent in status to *pedanda*, and wanting them to officiate at major public ceremonies alongside *pedanda* (Pitana 1999: 193–4). These ceremonies, like the once-a-century Ekadasa Rudra performed at the Besakih temple complex on the slopes of Mount Agung (Stuart-Fox 2002), involve Balinese from all groups and people come from all over the island. In the past they were conducted by *pedanda* priests with the assistance of certain specified commoner priests who, being subordinate, had to sit at a lower level. Recent claims to equality between Brahmana and Pasek priests have been strenuously resisted by high castes and *pedanda*, even though the *Parisada Hindu Darma Indonesia*, the government body in charge of the affairs of the Hindu community, decreed in 1968 that 'all Hindus are entitled to undergo the "twice-born" ritual in order to become priests [of the purest category] and all [such] priests are equal in status' (Pitana 1999: 183).

Since their appearance in the middle of the last century commoner *warga* have greatly increased in size. Warga Pasek, the largest association with members from all over the island, numbers its membership in the hundreds of thousands. This gives Warga Pasek formidable strength in its fight for equality with the gentry and high priesthood. The province of Bali is divided into eight regencies (*kabupaten*), each divided into several districts (*kecamatan*); one of the aims of Warga Pasek is to establish a Pasek priest in every district, so that all its members can use these priests instead of *pedanda*. To achieve this they must identify candidates for the priesthood who will go through the required training before taking exams and undergoing the purification rituals to turn them into the 'twice-born' priests formally recognised by the *Parisada*, and formally equal to *pedanda*.

The ideology of equality which drives Pasek ambitions is documented in their genealogical charter, the *Babad Pasek*, of which there are several versions (Pitana 1997). Alongside the history of their descent origins from holy sages in ancient times, and ultimately from the god Sang Hyang Pasupati (Brahma in other versions), the Babad contains instructions (*bisama*) which itemise Pasek rights and duties. Pasek groups are strongly advised against the use of holy water made by other priests, including *pedanda*, and enjoined to use only holy water prepared by Pasek priests in Pasek temples. The Babad promulgates the idea that Pasek people constitute a large extended family who are all, in ideological terms, genealogically no further distant from each other than second cousins (*mindon*), thus implying unity and equality, with no one being higher or lower than anyone else. According to their genealogical charter Pasek have the right, indeed the duty, to become twice-born priests (*pandita dwijati*) of equivalent status to *pedanda*. The Babad also states that the Pasek have privileges. Pasek priests, for example, are entitled to a sarcophagus similar to that used by *pedanda* when they die, and those Pasek who reach a high position in society can claim a cremation tower with nine roofs, conventionally reserved only for high ranking Satria castes.

The *Babad Pasek*, and similar documents of other commoner *warga*, claim to document group origins going back to antiquity, but they were in fact written in the nineteenth and twentieth centuries. In the nineteenth century, rulers instructed their court priests to write dynastic chronicles linking them to Majapahit ancestors in order to buttress royal authority, and Brahmanas wrote theirs with a view to placing themselves above the nobility (Rubinstein 1991). Commoners, depicted in these legends as rustic bumpkins with coarse features and comical behaviour, began to write their own genealogical histories as a challenge to high caste hegemony. Groups of Pandé (metalsmiths), for example, compiled theirs (*Babad Pandé*) to claim that their ancestors were equal in status to those of Brahmana. During the colonial period much of this endeavour came to a stop, but there was a resurgence of commoner genealogical writing in the 1950s as they began to reassert their claims to equality with high castes (Vickers 1989: 65–71, 164–5).

The claim by commoner clans for equality with Brahmana has been aided by developments within the Indonesian state. *Pancasila*, as the basis for the Indonesian constitution, proclaims all citizens of the republic to be equal. This creed is voiced by Balinese commoners as *manusa pada* ('all people are equal'). Because the *Parisada* is the government agency which validates Pasek priests by providing certificates of authorisation, giving them formal recognition equivalent to *pedanda*, it cannot disassociate itself from these procedures without appearing to contradict state ideology. The fact that the ruling council of the *Parisada* has a preponderance of Brahmana members makes things doubly difficult for them.

Documenting the rise of *warga* associations Pitana, himself a leading Pasek activist, provides many examples of commoner *warga* contesting the right of *pedanda* to be the principal priests officiating at major ceremonies (1997, 1999). These are major events requiring huge preparation and lasting several weeks, and are managed by a committee of officials and priests which determines how many and which kinds of priest are to officiate. If only *pedanda* are appointed, commoner *warga* representatives mount protests and ask why their priests have not also been appointed. More often than not justifications for the non-appointment of commoner priests involve arguments about the 'traditional' pre-eminence of the *pedanda*, and depend on the fact that commoner priests have not previously officiated on an equal basis. Such explanations are unacceptable to commoner activists, yet the protests are often unsuccessful because *pedanda* are unwilling to preside on an equal basis with commoner priests, and because high castes refuse to pray in a temple where low caste priests officiate for fear of being polluted. Sometimes compromises are reached. *Pedanda* may refuse to sit on the same high platform as commoner priests, but reluctantly agree that commoner priests may officiate on their own platforms built at the same height, though these are often placed in inferior directions. It may be decided that this ceremony should go on as planned with only *pedanda* officiating, but that at future ceremonies priests of different kinds will officiate together.

Many decisive changes have taken place in recent years, and it has become increasingly problematic for *pedanda*, the *Parisada* and high castes to exclude commoner priests and to deny them equality – the commoners have too much power to be ignored, and too many ideological resources at their command. But the commoner *warga* do not have things all their own way. Significant numbers of commoners do not join *warga*, preferring to support and be guided by their Brahmana high priests. Commoner *warga* face several problems in encouraging Balinese to join their associations. Despite accusations of avarice and exploitation sometimes lodged against high priests, many Balinese are devoted to the *pedanda* whose services they use and to whom they may turn for advice on a wide range of issues. There is often a hereditary relationship between generations of priests from a Brahmana household and generations of clients traditionally linked to it, similar to the way a congregation supports a temple. In return for priestly services, clients owe allegiance, loyalty and deference, and assistance at the priest's rituals and other projects. This relationship can be very close and intimate, and is not terminated lightly. If a *pedanda* has proved reliable and conscientious it is disloyal to switch allegiance to an untried commoner priest. Moreover, the correct performance of household and temple ceremonies is of crucial importance to the safety and prosperity of villagers, and a controversial change of priest may jeopardise that safety.

Another difficulty is that village solidarity and harmony, on which Balinese place a high premium, may suffer badly if one faction changes to a *sri empu* priest while other villagers continue to use their *pedanda*. Pitana (1997: 298–307) describes several such cases, some of which erupted into violence. Finally, though *warga* elites are explicitly engaged in a battle for equality with the high priesthood and other gentry, it does not necessarily mean that other commoners see this as an important issue. In the all-commoner village of Pujung in northern Gianyar the mostly Pasek villagers decided not to join Warga Pasek for several reasons – it would be divisive; they already live by ideologies of equality among themselves; they possess their own 'invisible *pedanda*' (*pedanda niskala*) who has always looked after them; and they are not greatly bothered by caste inequality since it is irrelevant to their conditions of their lives (Howe 2002).

Conclusion

This chapter has looked at several processes connected with Balinese hierarchy and challenges to it, and it has been useful to treat these processes as analytically separate so as to avoid confusion. In practice, however, Balinese pursue their private and group ambitions by astute use of whatever economic, political and cultural resources they have at their disposal, leading to unpredictable outcomes. The all-commoner village of Pujung exhibits very strong ideologies of communal equality which are routinely and publicly displayed, yet there is an undercurrent of status assertion by a number of the village's wealthy and powerful households who point to a village origin myth which credits the village founders with a high status title. These core villagers see themselves as 'higher than' and 'above' others, in some sense the local version of what in caste villages would be the *anak jero* (insiders) or gentry. These core villagers prefer to marry first cousins rather than second cousins, to perform the life crisis rites for their children in impressive fashion, and to make supra-village marriage alliances, all of which are typical gentry practices. On the other hand, this particular group of households also seriously entertained the possibility of joining the equality-seeking Warga Pasek movement, and one of its leading lights was invited to become a Pasek priest. To that end they convinced many ordinary villagers, who previously did not acknowledge a title or even know that they had one, that they were members of Pasek descent groups.

In cases like this it is clear that Balinese rarely sign up exclusively either to hierarchy or to equality. Social life is driven by rights, obligations and ambitions, and the contingent nature of unpredictable events. Balinese find themselves in constantly changing situations in which ideologies and social strategies can be regularly reshaped and modified to fit personal and group ends.

7 Tourism, culture and identity

Introduction

Until recently anthropologists treated tourism as a nuisance to be avoided rather than as an object of study in its own right. They conducted their fieldwork in areas well away from centres of tourist concentration, perhaps in the hope of experiencing a less contaminated section of society, as if tourists only made a difference where they were physically present. Even when tourists were present in large numbers, and tourism began to be studied, it still tended to be conceptualised as an isolated phenomenon, an add-on or afterthought to the real business of describing an indigenous culture. Tourism was something that had an impact, but only on the surface of the host society, so it remained marginal, and for the most part could be safely ignored. Tourism was seen as a temporary and artificial meeting of very different – even incompatible – groups of people which could only give rise to artificial outcomes and bastardised, commodified cultures, fit only to be exposed and condemned (Wood 1997: 2–3). Faced with these assumptions it was difficult to describe tourism other than in terms of cost-benefit analysis – asking whether tourism was good or bad for the host society.

Recently, as tourism has become the largest industry in the world (Garrison 1989: 4), this anthropological reticence has gone. Pierre van den Berghe (1980) has argued that tourism penetrates to the heart of the host society. It does not merely modify existing ethnic relations within a social domain; it constitutes a new set. Michel Picard (1996) contends that the idea of tourism as an external force impacting on a host society is misconceived, and that instead we should view it as an integral component of that society. The 'tourist gaze' (Urry 1990) may look benign, but has profound effects, often of a highly political nature (Richter 1989). This new outlook on tourism should not occasion surprise, since national governments see tourism as a major component in their development strategies. By building museums and cultural theme parks (Adams 1995; Pemberton 1994: 152–60) and by designating specific cultural practices from different areas of Indonesia as cultural 'peaks' (Adams 1997), the Indonesian state markets cultures, identifies cultural objects for tourist attention, and encourages the modification of cultural and ethnic performances to fit in with tourist desires and needs. At the same time, the state appropriates these diverse cultural glories as manifestations of a fabricated Indonesian national culture. The state's tourism policy not only gathers revenue but also effects social change as host societies use tourism as a resource in their own political struggles with government bureaucracies and neighbouring ethnic groups. A few examples will give some idea of the degree of penetration into the host society that tourism effects, and the kinds of responses it triggers.

The Toraja people live in the uplands of south Sulawesi in Indonesia. Their claim to tourist fame lies in their architecturally impressive and beautiful houses (Waterson 1990), the effigies of aristocratic ancestors (*tau tau*) installed in niches in the large volcanic boulders, in the limestone cliffs dramatically overlooking their rice fields (Volkman 1990), and in their vibrant ritual life. Toraja Land was colonised by the Dutch in 1906 – the same time as south Bali – who allowed the Dutch Reformed Mission to convert the Toraja to Christianity. An important aspect of this missionary activity was the separation of religion – to be called *aluk* – on the one hand and custom – to be called *adat* – on the other, dividing what had been a seamless unity. This unity comprised religious belief in ancestors and spirits, the ritual slaughter of buffalo – in which the distribution of meat enacted a fluid hierarchy of aristocrats, commoners and slaves, the politics and economics of competitive display, and much else. After this conceptual division the Mission continued to permit the slaughter of buffalo (custom), but forbade meat to be used as offerings to the ancestors (religion), since the latter interfered with conversion to Christianity. The Mission thus tried to regulate what the natives could think by allowing rituals to flourish, but not the beliefs on which they were based. Custom and ritual were secularised, while religion – Christianity – became a separate domain divorced from custom. After 1965 there was a great deal of out-migration, especially of commoners and poorer people looking for jobs in the emerging cities of south Sulawesi, Kalimantan, and other islands. When these migrants returned, many invested their new wealth in big feasts, and thus challenged and undermined traditional status boundaries. This created 'ritual inflation' as resident aristocrats sought to preserve status differences by slaughtering buffalo in ever greater quantities. At the same time an expedient alliance between elites and some modernist youth began to claim that their ritual feasts were no longer authentic, and more devout Christians condemned what to them were the base motives driving these feasts (Volkman 1985, 1987).

It was precisely in the midst of these indigenous debates and struggles that tourism began. By the 1970s some 10,000 tourists were visiting Toraja Land each year, attracted by the prospect of experiencing an 'exotic', stone age culture untouched by modernisation, and a world away from the commercialisation of Bali. Many tourists came to see the great feasts, but what they were presented with as authentic and traditional were actually the Christianised versions. While Christian Toraja have attempted to modify their rituals so that they are modern, rational and modest in scale, they find that success in entrancing the tourists entails the re-creation of the appearance of the old. As one fieldworker remarked, tourists are unlikely to visit Toraja Land on the promise of witnessing 'authentic Dutch Calvinist' rituals (Volkman 1987: 166).

Tourism has also helped bring about a partial collapse of indigenous status distinctions and fostered the creation of a single Torajan ethnic identity which has superseded the former local and differentiated identities (Volkman 1990). The typical Toraja noble house appears on currency notes, t-shirts and jewellery, and in countless brochures. The form of the house remains the same, but displaced from its original context it loses much of its meaning. The different qualities, decorative features and dimensions of Toraja houses were part of an intricate status hierarchy. Once the house was decontextualised for tourist purposes, a process aided by tourist representatives encouraging poor and low status Torajans to imitate the houses of wealthy nobles, tourists were presented with a single type of house, apparently emblematic of Toraja culture, and thus encouraged to see Toraja society as undifferentiated.

The national government depicts the glories of Toraja society as cultural 'peaks' which contribute to the promotion of Indonesian culture and ethnic brotherhood – the Indonesian director general of tourism even declared Toraja Land the 'touristic *primadonna* of South Sulawesi' (Adams 1997: 159). Many Toraja are only too glad to latch on to economic benefits of this celebration of their society. This favoured status, however, has had the unintended consequence of aggravating already difficult ethnic relations between the Toraja and the Muslim Buginese and Makassarese who live on the coastal plains, and who are largely bypassed by tourists. Stung into action by the success of their northern neighbours, the latter have attempted to carve out a tourist niche for themselves. Many of the guides who escort tourists around Toraja Land are not in fact Torajans, but Buginese and Chinese-Indonesians who have benefited from the tour guide schools in the southern city of Ujung Pandang, a centre to which Torajans have limited access.

Tourists can only get to Toraja Land via the airport at Ujung Pandang, and flights are scheduled so that tourists are forced to stay in the city for two days. A cultural theme park has been developed at Taman Budaya Sulawesi, seven miles south of Ujung Pandang. It stands on a site which witnessed one of the last battles between the Dutch and the Makassarese 350 years ago, and features traditional architecture and cultural displays of the main ethnic groups of south Sulawesi. The creation of these and other tourist attractions outside Toraja Land is resented by Torajans, who feel that their recent tourist success hardly balances the uneven access to resources which has characterised Toraja–Buginese ethnic relations over much of their history (Adams 1997). On the other hand, Muslim Bugis and Makassarese, the major populations of Ujung Pandang, have deliberately used Torajan house designs and motifs to provide a facelift for the city to make it more attractive to tourists. The airport, new hotels and other buildings have been constructed to look like great Torajan houses. One might expect that this flagrant appropriation of another group's cultural treasures would lead to an increase in ethnic tension, but Adams (1998: 343) reports that because the city now provides work for Torajan builders and looks more familiar to them, they actually feel safer and more comfortable visiting Ujung Pandang than they used to.

Tourism cannot be seen as having a merely tangential influence on the host society. It creates changes which go to the core of a society while constituting new ethnic relations between neighbouring groups and with the encompassing state. Tourists are unwitting actors in these cultural and political struggles. They do not realise that when a guide takes a group of tourists to visit a noble Torajan in his 'traditional' house, his pleasure at receiving them has mostly to do with one-upmanship in local status rivalries (Adams 1995: 148); that when they are shown around a 'traditional' village it has been purpose-built, the villagers actually living in cheaper and far less impressive Buginese-style houses in the back streets (Volkman 1990); or that when two hundred tourists came to see a cremation in central Bali in 1993 it was probably their presence which prevented an outbreak of violence (Howe 2001: 73). State authorities, tourist agencies, guides, and the hosts themselves change, manipulate and adapt local cultural resources to accommodate tourist desires, needs and expectations, often by emphasising tradition, 'age-old' custom and the exotic. Tourists may not know much about the host society, but for tourism to be successful the hosts must educate themselves about the tourists in order to present themselves and their society as attractive tourist objects. Although the Dutch used their superior powers to enforce and direct change while tourists instigate unintentional change, some of the outcomes are remarkably similar.

The problem of tourism in Bali

The paradox of tourism in Bali is that, as ever more tourists arrive, the anguished cries of alarm predicting that tourism will cause the disintegration of Balinese culture are counterbalanced by the optimistic claim that this culture is so resilient and flexible that it will continue to survive largely unimpaired. Since tourism began in 1914 every generation of observers has raised the same concern. Even allowing for the fact that the various promoters of tourism have a strong economic incentive for providing a rosy picture of tourism's effects, it is still difficult to see how such different prognostications can be understood.

As Michel Picard, on whose highly perceptive analysis much of the following discussion is based, points out, it is the initial question, rather than the answers, which is of most interest (1996: 93). Though the forecasts differ radically, the question remains the same – is Balinese culture 'able or not to withstand the impact of tourism?' What is interesting about this question is that it invariably poses the problem as one of costs and benefits. Tourism brings economic benefits but entails socio-cultural costs. These costs derive from the potential for radical cultural change driven by the needs and expectations of the tourists rather than those of the host society. When the issue is conceptualised in this way it is not surprising that observers emphasise either the benefits or the costs, and come to wildly different conclusions. Moreover, as the problem of tourism became more acute with the onset of mass tourism from 1970 onwards, the question turned to one of sustainable development – how can the economic revenues be maximised and the socio-cultural costs minimised, so that the overall beneficial effects of tourism are optimised over the long term? Though the issue changed, its terms of reference remained stubbornly the same.

Aside from the highly problematical equation between economic benefits and cultural costs, which the tourism industry 'solves' by the dubious method of trying to quantify the costs in order to determine which side of the equation is the greater, tourism agencies also had to decide *how much* of Balinese culture tourists should have access to. An early formulation sought to organise tourist activity in such a way as to keep the socio-cultural costs low by maintaining a suitable distance between tourists and the host society. Interchange between them would be reduced and the destabilising effects of tourism could be minimised – hence the building of hotel complexes in sparsely populated areas, allowing tourists into the cultural heartland of central Bali only for brief and controlled excursions.

This view of tourism placed too much emphasis on tourists' non-cultural leisure activities and impersonal consumption, which reduced Balinese to the status of passive onlookers and generated little revenue for local people. Since it was generally agreed that Balinese culture was the main tourist attraction, and that Balinese people should derive a return for the cultural services they provided, how could tourism survive if tourists and Balinese were kept apart? In response to this dilemma a new formula for tourism, which Picard and others have called cultural tourism, was developed by the World Tourism Organisation in the early 1980s. Its main rhetorical flourish was that cultural tourism is mutually beneficial to both tourists and hosts. The idea embedded in cultural tourism is that tourists should be allowed much greater access to Balinese culture. The idea is that their attention and interest stimulates Balinese pride in their cultural performances and allows Balinese to affirm their identity. Meanwhile, tourist money can be used to sustain and invigorate dance, drama and the arts in exchange for which tourists enjoy an authentic cultural experience. While this looks like a virtuous circle, its success was thought to be conditional on Balinese artists creating for their own socio-religious purposes. If they created cultural productions specifically for tourists, there would be enormous potential for crass commercialisation (Picard 1996: 100–9).

This view of tourism was energetically advanced by the anthropologist Philip McKean (1973), who argued that while Balinese are culturally rich but economically poor, tourists are economically rich but culturally poor, and therefore a fruitful exchange can occur in which Balinese cultural values are exchanged for western economic values. Moreover, in this exchange the Balinese continue to do what they have always done – perform for their gods and ancestors, only now they do it for the tourists too. Since there is no significant change in their cultural productions there should be no contamination, and everyone should benefit. This argument suggests that Balinese are capable of distinguishing between performances for themselves and their gods and those staged specifically for tourists, that they know the boundary between what they can sell to tourists and what they must safeguard from commercial exploitation, and so avoid the problems of the commodification of culture.

During the early 1970s this doctrine of cultural tourism was embraced not only by the foreign tourism industry but also by the Balinese provincial government. Balinese commentators, journalists and academics – the urban intelligentsia – were much more ambivalent. They acknowledged the need for the revenues, but likened mass tourism to a tidal wave, an infectious disease, a kind of rape which would subvert their treasured values (Picard 1996: 121).

While foreign investors saw a virtuous circle in which tourist dollars and Balinese culture mutually benefited each other, many Balinese predicted the opposite – tourist dollars would debase culture. To ameliorate these worries, local government authorities issued advice, instructions and directives on how to make cultural tourism work. These mostly took the form of trying to further Balinese awareness of the philosophical principles underlying their religious practices. Thus armed and strengthened they would be able to make the appropriate decisions about which aspects of culture could be put to the service of tourism without polluting and corrupting their core religious and artistic values. If the Balinese could distinguish what belongs to the sphere of tourism and what to the domain of culture, then their culture would not turn into a 'touristic culture', a culture largely based on touristic values. As far as the local authorities were concerned this could be accomplished by the simple expedient of devoting some part of tourist revenues to cultivating the arts and ceremonies.

In the event there was little agreement among Balinese as to what should be exploited as a tourist object and what should not. Even on a superficial level it quickly became apparent that much in the Balinese presentation of cultural performances had to be changed if the tourists were to be entertained, and some of these changes meant that drawing the boundary between culture and tourism was not going to be easy. Balinese dance and drama are extremely complicated, last a long time, use difficult languages, and have narrative structures very different from those of western drama (de Zoete and Spies 1938; Picard 1996: 134–51). They often accompany a ceremony and are held in a temple rather than on a purpose-built stage for a paying audience. In order to make such performances even partially accessible to tourists they have to be radically modified and adapted, and this has led to new forms of dance and new combinations of motifs from different dances, not all of which have been to the liking of Balinese. Many dances performed for a specifically tourist audience are abstracted from their original contexts to become short solo performances. Ritual – to please the gods – is turned into art – to entertain the audience. One such is the famous *légong* dance, which has become a favourite of the Balinese. However, when the Bali Beach Hotel used the *péndét* – a dance in homage to the gods when they descend into their temple shrines – as a welcome for their tourist audience it brought condemnation from religious authorities, who were concerned that this use of the dance appeared to treat tourists as if they were gods, and was thus tantamount to a desecration of an important ritual dance.

Classifying Balinese dance performances

One of the problems faced by Balinese was how to separate religious practice from artistic performance. Many dance and drama performances are offerings to gods, and thus performed inside temples, but it was impractical and potentially defiling and disruptive to allow tourists indiscriminate access to the inner temple sanctuaries. During ceremonies Balinese must abide by a series of injunctions and prohibitions before entering a temple. They must be appropriately dressed, bathed and purified, and of calm demeanour – menstruating women are barred entry. It is not easy to know whether tourists are equally punctilious. In order to decide which dances could be performed for tourists, Balinese authorities convened a conference of Balinese academics in 1971 charged with the task of deciding which dances are sacred and which are profane. But this essentially Christian conceptual opposition is untranslatable into either Balinese or Indonesian, and even though the participants resorted to using the neologisms *sakral* (Ind.) and *provan* (Ind.), they found it impossible to make sense of the terms, let alone apply them with any consistency, even ending up with a category of 'sacred and profane dances' as if there was little difference between the terms. It is worth quoting Picard at length.

> Such is the 'challenge' that tourism has thrown up to the Balinese. Not only are they called upon to slice into the living flesh of their culture, to perform a new, unknown incision, to draw a 'boundary' (*batas*) where they knew only a continuum, but also, to make things worse, they are obliged to think in a borrowed terminology that visibly makes no sense to them. In their perplexity, they see no other recourse than to look for rescue in the language of their former colonisers. And so they are reduced to searching within a foreign mode of thought for the concepts that are supposed to help them protect the most inalienable of their cultural values from the threat wrought by the presence of foreign tourists in their country.
> (Picard 1996: 153)

Since the use of these alien terms produced an impasse, members of the conference tried to resolve the issue by using terms which they did understand – *agama* (religion) and *adat* (custom). But this distinction is also relatively new to Balinese (Chapters 2 and 5) and not well understood by the mass of people. Western classifications – religion, politics, economics – were meaningless to Balinese. In the early decades of the twentieth century, in response to denunciations by both Dutch colonisers and Javanese Muslims that Balinese religion was hardly a religion at all, and as part of struggle between aristocrats and commoners concerning the caste system, Balinese began to reframe their 'religion' (*agama*) as a domain of thought and action separate from custom (*adat*) which therefore became secularised. By using these terms they could try to decide what was in the realm of *agama*, leaving the rest to be thought of as *adat* and thus as mere custom or 'art'. The importance of such a distinction results from the fact that religion is now seen as the foundation of Balinese cultural identity, so that if a boundary can be drawn around it, this will protect their highest values.

One consequence of the seminar was a classification of Balinese dances into three categories. One was 'sacred, religious dances' (*wali*), which includes those performed in the inner sanctuary of a temple and always in association with a ceremony. A second category (*bebali*) includes those dances performed in the outer courtyard of a temple, also in conjunction with a ceremony. The third category (*balih-balihan*, from the root *balih* meaning 'to watch') includes everything else, and designates performances for pure entertainment which are not associated with a ceremony (Picard 1990a). The second category was an entirely new idea, not understood by villagers and dancers, and it was dropped a few years later. More significantly, the classification of dances in this general way conflicted with the great diversity of local village custom, so that while one village conceived of a dance as *wali*, another classified it as *bebali*. Moreover, while the authorities tried to prevent performances in the first category being used as entertainment for tourists, a survey conducted by Udayana University in Denpasar revealed that while dancers in general deplored the commercialisation of dance, they wanted to promote cultural tourism by staging the most authentic Balinese dances specially for the tourists – the dances in the *wali* category. This demonstrates not just the confusion generated by a classificatory scheme based on alien categories, but also the disagreements and struggles going on among Balinese between those wishing to prevent the profanation of Balinese culture by turning it into spectacle for tourists and those who want to use this cultural heritage to strengthen Balinese identity by stimulating tourism (Picard 1996: 155–8).

Balinese identity

In Chapter 5 I argued that the introduction of Hindu devotional movements such as Sai Baba created conditions for new forms of identity to emerge, forms which were not based on attachments to local institutions and thus transcended, or existed alongside, a specifically Balinese ethnic identity (*kebalian* or 'Balineseness'). This ethnic identity was itself a fairly recent phenomenon, one of the consequences of the processes which led to the creation of the state-supported new religion of *agama Hindu* in the first half of the twentieth century.

Though a recent invention, *agama Hindu* was presented as the rediscovery of an ancient tradition which had become distorted by Brahmanical ritualism and hierarchical institutions purportedly introduced into Bali by the Majapahit invaders from Java. It was shaped to look like a free-standing system of religious and ethical doctrine which, by investing ritual with meaning, could act as the underpinnings of village *adat* religion. Through *agama Hindu* Balinese religion achieved equivalent status to Islam and Christianity, and as such was given higher status than the diversity of local village practices. In the nineteenth century there had been little discernible boundary between religious activities and other aspects of Balinese life; once *agama Hindu* was institutionalised as a conceptually demarcated domain of belief and practice, what was not specifically religious (*agama*) could be consigned to *adat*, that seen as relatively secularised.

Because this new religion of *agama Hindu* was designed to be embraced by all Balinese Hindus, and because it was presented as a venerable tradition, it assumed an elevated status as the source of Balinese culture – *agama* as the root, *adat* as the trunk, and the arts (*seni*) the branches and leaves. Consequently, the renovated religion began to function as a symbol of ethnic and religious unity around which a more global and less parochial notion of Balinese identity (*kebalian*) could form.

In the midst of these processes, from the 1950s to the 1980s, tourism was rapidly becoming the most important sector of the economy, with virtually every Balinese individual affected by it. As we have seen, tourism shaped how Balinese think about their society and culture, though much of this intellectual endeavour has been carried out using the concepts, ideas and languages of other societies. *Adat* is an Arabic word first used in the Indies to denote traditional customary law as opposed to imported Islamic law, then generalised by the Dutch to refer to the whole set of indigenous traditional institutions. Prior to this codification of culture Balinese had many context-specific terms denoting particular aspects of customary practice which the Dutch gathered together under the umbrella term of *adat* (Warren 1993: 3–5). In the struggle between gentry and commoners over caste and the reform of religion, customary practice (*adat*), which had previously encompassed ritual and ancestor worship, became opposed to *agama*, itself a Sanskrit term. As Balinese authorities and the intelligentsia began to grapple with the dilemmas and contradictions thrown up by the colonial policy of *Baliseering* (Balinisation) and by tourism, they had to resort to Indonesian words (*budaya, seni*) and Dutch words (*cultuur, kunst*) for 'culture' and 'art' because Balinese had none of its own (Picard 1999). They strove to classify this 'culture' with the assistance of yet more foreign terms, such as sacred (*sakral*) and profane (*provan*).

Ironic consequences of these processes of change include the 'traditionalisation' of Balinese society, the idea of Balinese culture as a heritage passed on from the ancestors to contemporary generations, and a Balinese validation of the tourist conception of Bali as an unchanging society. As Picard notes,

> it is only once after it had been enlisted as a capital, available for profitable transactions, that the Balinese started regarding their culture as a heritage to be carefully preserved and nurtured. Consequently ... the supposed indivisible and harmonious unity of agama, adat and seni [art] ... far from expressing the primordial essence of their identity, is the outcome of a process of semantic borrowing and of conceptual adjustment which the Balinese had to make, as a result of the recent opening up of their social space to the outside world – via the colonisation, the Indonesianisation and the touristification of their island.
> (Picard 1990b: 24)

To put things in stark terms, tourism has been instrumental in effecting large-scale social change which has resulted in a series of interconnected and paradoxical outcomes – the formation of a new sense of Balinese identity based on a religious culture conceived of as ancient, a new notion of culture seen as a heritage from the past which can be exploited as a capital resource to attract tourists, and the idea that – notwithstanding the changes brought about by tourism – the Balinese are retaining their culture despite increasing exposure to western modernity.

Balinese identity, founded on Balinese religion and affirmed by tourist fascination with Balinese culture, may be a source of pride to Balinese people, but in the context of the Indonesian state it can become a threat to national integration. To understand this threat we need to look at the development of Indonesian national culture.

Indonesian national culture

Ever since independence in 1950 the Indonesian state has endeavoured to create a national unity out of the disparate cultures, religions and ethnic groups of the archipelago. In Chapter 5 I briefly discussed the place of religion in this enterprise; here I focus on the role of ethnicity and culture. A significant feature of the state's attempt to forge unity out of diversity – *bhinneka tunggal ika*, 'unity in diversity', is the Indonesian national motto – has been its manipulation of local cultures to adapt them to the requirements of nation-building and the construction of a national culture (Foulcher 1990; Yampolsky 1995).

Some progress towards national unity as a counterweight to local ethnic loyalties was made before independence by adopting the Malay language, henceforth to be called Bahasa Indonesia, as the national language of administration, commerce, education and the media. After independence President Sukarno used a variety of strategies to build nationalism – military might to crush regional rebellions and secessionist movements (Kahin 1952), confrontations with neighbouring powers to generate national solidarity, the rapid extension of a school system with a centrally-controlled curriculum and a uniform structure, language of tuition, and school dress all over Indonesia (Leigh 1991), the invocation of new national ideologies (such as *Pancasila*) and an emphasis on pan-Indonesian values to instil a sense of common purpose and unity beneath surface differences (Bowen 1986, Bourchier 1997), and the gradual substitution of functional groups in place of ethnic-based political parties in order to strengthen economic and occupational allegiances across cultural boundaries (Suryadinata 1989).

Sukarno also began the process, continued by Suharto after 1967, of incorporating the multitude of 'tribal' groups, known as *suku-suku terasing* (Ind., literally 'foreign' or 'stranger' groups) into the national fold. The phrase *suku-suku terasing* denotes forest dwellers, nomadic hunter-gatherers and other small-scale societies who live in remote or mountainous regions and are not adherents of one of the religions recognised by the state. The label also carries connotations of social isolation and distance from mainstream Indonesian culture. Depicting them as backward, primitive and uncivilised, the state wanted to make them conform to its definitions of a modern, economically productive and respectable lifestyle. Integration was forced by attempts to extinguish ethnic loyalties through a process of cultural homogenisation. 'Pagan' religions were prohibited and people were coerced into converting to one of the state religions, local forms of dress, bodily decoration and dietary habits were denigrated, groups following nomadic and dispersed patterns of residence were herded into neat and tidy nucleated villages and provided with houses of a standard type, and they have been incorporated into the structures of provincial administration (Tsing 1993; Persoon 1998).

When General Suharto assumed the presidency in 1967, after the slaughter of alleged communists in the previous two years, he too was faced with threats to national unity. Communism had been obliterated, but because many Muslim groups had cooperated with the army in the killings they now expected to be rewarded with a much greater say in state political and religious affairs (Boland

1982: 135–56). However, since Suharto and many of his supporters were exponents of Javanese mystical practices (*kebatinan*), which were anathema to many Muslims, he had no intention of allowing Islam a greater role in state politics. In this new context Indonesian cultural diversity, previously seen as a problem for national integration, was now seen as a useful counterbalance to renewed demands for an Islamic state (Schefold 1998: 273). The tremendous diversity of Indonesia's cultural arts, styles of architecture, rituals, and dramatic performances could be used to promote tourism, and thereby enrich the state's coffers. However, such a policy also had a significant disadvantage, since a more positive attitude to local cultures and tribal groups was likely to invigorate local ethnic loyalties and weaken attachments to the new state. As state policymakers conceived it, the problem was how to celebrate cultural diversity at the same time as preventing centrifugal political mobilisation around symbols of ethnic identity. The ingenious solution was to create and promote *regional* cultural and artistic forms at the expense of *ethnic* ones (Sellato 1995; Picard 1997).

Territorially, Indonesia is divided into twenty-six provinces (*daerah*, Ind.) most of which include numerous ethnic groups. The policy of the New Order state in regard to the promotion of cultural diversity was 'to control the political content of performances, to control their moral content, and to upgrade their artistic quality' (Yampolsky 1995: 710). Customary dances, songs, rituals, myths and the plastic arts were changed and modified by the state's local representatives. Performances were abbreviated, raised wooden stages replaced the earthen floor, rough, crude and licentious elements – sexual play, alcoholic drink, rowdiness, rude jokes – were reduced or removed altogether, new elements were added to provide entertaining distractions, elements from one culture were introduced to pep up the rituals of another, and everything was cleaned up to be more respectable, civilised and in keeping with modern times (Acciaioli 1985; Taylor 1994). In addition, the state initiated a programme of provincial festivals in which these hybrids and wholly new performances are put on, established colleges and schools for the performing arts where students learn their own 'cultural traditions' and experiment with them, and promoted regional artistic competitions (Yamashita 2003: 46–52; Hough 1999; Sutton 1995).

The state presents these new and composite forms as authentic Indonesian cultural expressions representative of an entire region (*daerah*). For example, the Toraja noble house is presented as a cultural 'peak' of the south Sulawesi region rather than of the Toraja ethnic group, and thus as a manifestation of Indonesian culture. These regional 'cultures' are in fact inventions which, stripped of much that made them locally meaningful, have been turned into anodyne forms of aesthetic display. Thus while the state appears to be celebrating the authentic cultural richness of Indonesia, it is in fact creating a homogenous national culture by standardising the cultural diversity of the regions. The various cultural performances of the regions are construed as different manifestations of an underlying Indonesian culture and personality. Through this enterprise the state at one stroke depoliticises ritual performance by turning it into 'art', creates 'attractive' and 'exotic' cultural objects for tourist consumption, dampens ethnic resistance to the state by dissolving local diversity into regional homogeneity, yet can still claim to be promoting and safeguarding Indonesia's rich cultural tapestry.

This artificial culture that is called 'Balinese' by tourist operators, state authorities and those in the Balinese 'arts industry' is not so much the culture of the ethnic group of the Balinese people, but a manufactured 'regional culture' which, together with other 'regional cultures', provides cultural objects and performances that enhance Indonesia's national culture. To a large extent these regional cultures are narrowly defined as the visual arts – dance, architecture, plastic arts, and are quite different from the anthropological notion of culture as a complex whole of custom, morals, law, belief and associated practices. These cultural arts have the advantage that they can be easily abstracted from the context that gives them their meaning in an ethnic culture, and can be publicly deployed as representations of national culture.

Balinese houses, temples and other traditional buildings are constructed according to a great many rules (Howe 1983), but it is a simple matter to decorate and embellish modern functional buildings with the same abundance of ornate motifs and sculptures that adorn traditional buildings. Thus in Bali government offices, hotels, art shops, and restaurants are all marked by a fantastic profusion of ornamental detail which displays 'a concoction of styles that astonishes admirers of traditional Balinese architecture' (Picard, 1996: 175), and which has come to be known as 'Bali style'. Picard explains that this 'monumental ornamentalism', imitated elsewhere in Indonesia, is seen in Jakarta as 'traditional Balinese architecture' and even, by extension, as a style which represents 'traditional Indonesian architecture'. However, the 'Bali' being referred to here signifies not Balinese ethnic culture, but state-authorised artificial culture. Rather than the national culture being derived from regional cultures, the regional cultures are construed as subordinate parts of the national culture. It becomes legitimate, even normal, to transfer aspects of a regional culture to another province, so for example French architects used the 'Bali' style as a source of inspiration for their design of the new airport in Jakarta (Picard 1996: 175), just as Buginese used the form of the noble Toraja house to design buildings in Ujung Pandang.

Another striking example of cultural piracy concerns the *sendratari* dance-drama, also known as the Ramayana ballet, and the annual Bali Arts Festival. This dance was originally created in Java in the early 1960s to give a flavour of Javanese dance styles which is accessible to a foreign audience; in order to achieve this it departs considerably from normal Javanese conventions. The dance was then imported into Bali and, with new choreography and set to a well-known Balinese legend, it became an instant hit with the Balinese. It soon became the centrepiece of the Bali Arts Festival, the epitome of cultural tourism. The festival was the brainchild of the island's governor, designed as a showcase for Balinese cultural arts both to foster Balinese culture and to develop tourism. It takes place at a large purpose-built open-air complex in Denpasar, with associated events all over the island. It has been approved by the state, and has on occasion been opened by the President of the Republic; it therefore presents 'Balinese culture' in its state-legitimised form (Picard 1996: 168).

The festival presents this culture not to tourists, however, who rarely attend, but to thousands of Balinese who, while being entertained, are also taught what their culture now is. The festival comprises performances of many kinds, from traditional genres to new styles that have been created in academies and colleges for the performing arts by specialised and professional performers and teachers. The fact that the *sendratari* has become the highlight of the festival is revealing of how Balinese culture has become confused, perhaps even fused, with tourist culture. Although the *sendratari* was created in Java for a foreign audience, the organisers of the Bali Arts Festival have declared that the Festival's 'priority objective is the development of traditional Balinese art under the form of a presentation of the Sendratari Ramayana' (Picard 1996: 169). Moreover, officials of the festival and the arts academy have recommended that *sendratari* be popularised in the villages as a way of conserving Balinese cultural values. The irony goes even further, because in a study conducted by an Indonesian academic in 1985 on the damaging effects of the commercialisation of Balinese culture by tourism, the author concluded that 'the integrity of the Sendratari Ramayana is endangered by its presentation to tourists' (quoted in Picard: 1996: 170). The *sendratari* is not limited to Java and Bali – similarly named dances exist in other regions, for example Sunda in west Java. While it is decreed that the different forms must be accessible to all Indonesians, they must also be 'typical' of the regions in which they are performed. Thus *sendratari* is at the same time an 'authentic' part of Balinese culture and an 'authentic' part of Indonesian national culture.

Rather than Balinese ethnic culture driving tourism, which is supposed to nurture and preserve that culture intact, tourism steers the course that this culture now takes, so that what was ethnic culture is becoming a tourist culture in which dance genres, architectural styles and temple rituals are so many brand images used to market Bali as a tourist haven. The original formulation of cultural tourism, to exploit tourism in order to develop Bali, has changed to one in which Bali is exploited in order to develop tourism. The equation of economic values against cultural values, once thought to be balanced and mutually beneficial, has foundered on the rock of profit – for the state, for provincial authorities, and for the foreigners who invest heavily in the hotels, golf courses, and other developments which increasingly scar the island. And all this is justified by ordinary Balinese as well as members of the tourism industry, by the questionable idea that Balinese culture is so resilient that it selects only what it can adapt and change to conform to Balinese values. It is fitting to allow Michel Picard, who has done so much to illuminate the complex and murky highways and byways of the relationship between Balinese culture and tourism, to have the final word:

> It seems to me that one can speak of a *touristic culture* at that point when the Balinese come to confuse these two uses of their culture, *when that by which the tourists identify them becomes that by which they identify themselves.*
>
> (Picard 1996: 197, his emphasis)

Into the future

When the Bali nightclub bomb exploded in 2002, it not only scarred the families of those who were killed, but also brought to the brink of ruin a great many other Balinese whose livelihood depended on tourism. This included not just those who were directly employed in the tourist industry, in hotels, restaurants and leisure activities, but thousands of others who were indirectly linked to the tourist economy – farmers, shop assistants, taxi drivers, construction workers, employees in the garment industry, hawkers and carvers. Within two months of the explosion, occupancy rates in many hotels had gone from their usual figure of over 70 per cent to under 10 per cent, and it took over a year for them to begin to approach their previous levels. This recovery in numbers disguises the fact that tourists going to Bali in 2004 were spending less time in Bali and less money, so that the economic effects are still keenly felt.

The dire economic consequences of the terrorist attack appear to have drowned out the voices calling for a change in how Balinese organise tourism. Shortly after the bomb many Balinese voiced their concern that it was the materialistic motives underlying tourism and the delinquent behaviour of tourists which brought the disaster (see Chapter 1), and that if tourism was ever to flourish again on the island it had to be of a different kind, one much more in tune with Balinese values. The economic imperatives of empty hotels, bankrupt businesses and high unemployment, however, and the knowledge that many young tourists were unlikely to return to Bali if they could not enjoy the nightclubs, bars, restaurants and discotheques crucial to the economy of Kuta and Legian, have severely constrained opportunities for change. Despite the commemorative monument built on the site of the destroyed Sari Club, it seems that Kuta is being recreated in its old image. Paddy's bar, which the second bomb destroyed, has reopened near its old site, and there has been significant development in Legian where, as the holiday rhetoric has it, the 'drinking, dancing and loud music only gets going at midnight and goes on till dawn'.

Developments in Indonesian politics have exacerbated the situation. With the fall of Suharto and the inauguration of democratic party politics has come new legislation providing for partial regional autonomy. In relation to Bali this means that the eight regencies which comprise the island are now free to make many of their own decisions about economic development, whereas before such decisions were the prerogative of the central state and the Governor of Bali, who tended to confine most tourist development in just two of regencies in the south of the island, Badung and Gianyar. As a consequence of those earlier centralist policies the other six regencies suffered relative underdevelopment, poverty, and out-migration of people seeking work in the tourist centres. In the past this caused resentment and a desire to secure some of the spoils of tourism for the neglected regions. With autonomy these regions have devised ambitious development plans to rectify the imbalance, but with scant regard for the adverse environmental damage. These plans include a spectacular sky-lift from the north coast to the mountains, further golf courses, and even the possibility of a Formula 1 race track. Whether these plans ever come to fruition is questionable, but it seems sad that, feeling unable to compete on a cultural level with the dance, music, drama and the plastic arts of south Bali, the northern Balinese believe that the only way to attract tourists is to exploit their natural resources by building novel – and specifically non-Balinese – entertainments.

Just as important as cultural degradation is the distinct probability of resource destruction. Tourism makes extravagant uses of land and water. It is not simply the foreign tourist, who typically uses as much water per day as a Balinese family of five, who is responsible for the looming water and land crisis, it is also the influx of newcomers, especially from Java, which significantly adds to the pressure on resources. Agricultural land is rapidly being converted for all manner of new uses – hotels, shops, houses, garages, factories, government buildings, and the high prices paid for this land only encourage Balinese to sell. The increasing volume of traffic continually outstrips the ability of the roads to carry it, and rubbish is simply being dumped in deep ravines.

Given these circumstances it is very difficult to see how Balinese can reassert the idealism of tourism for Bali, even if this remains the guise under which tourism continues to prosper. The economic forces now shaping the island continue to exploit Bali for tourism and, three years after the Bali bomb, the processes propelling the international touristification of Bali seem more entrenched than ever.

References

Abbreviations used
BKI *Bijdragen tot de Taal-, Land- en Volkenkunde* (Journal of the Humanities and Social Sciences of Southeast Asia and Oceania)
JRAI *The Journal of the Royal Anthropological Institute* (incorporating *Man*)
RIMA *Review of Indonesian and Malaysian Affairs*

Acciaioli, G. (1985) 'Culture as art: from practice to spectacle in Indonesia', *Canberra Anthropology*, 8, 148–72.
Adas, M. (1981) 'From avoidance to confrontation: peasant resistance in precolonial and colonial Southeast Asia', *Comparative Studies in Society and History*, 23, 217–47.
Adams, K.M. (1995) 'Making-up the Toraja? The appropriation of tourism, anthropology, and museums for politics in upland Sulawesi, Indonesia', *Ethnology*, 34, 143–53.
—— (1997) 'Touting touristic "primadonas": tourism, ethnicity, and national integration in Sulawesi, Indonesia', in Picard, M. and Wood, R.E. (eds), *Tourism, Ethnicity and the State in Asian and Pacific Societies*, Honolulu: University of Hawai'i Press.
—— (1998) 'More than an ethnic marker: Toraja art as identity negotiator', *American Ethnologist*, 25, 327–51.
Agung, I.A.A.G. (1988) *Bali pada Abad XIX*, Yogyakarta: Gajah Mada Press.
Anderson, B.R.O'G. (1972) 'The idea of power in Javanese culture', in Holt, C. (ed.), *Culture and Politics in Indonesia*, Ithaca: Cornell University Press. Reprinted in *Language and Power: Exploring Political Cultures in Indonesia*, Ithaca: Cornell University Press.
—— (1977) 'Religion and politics in Indonesia since independence', in Anderson, B., Nakamura, M. and Slamet, M. (eds), *Religion and Social Ethos in Indonesia*, Clayton, Australia: Centre of Southeast Asian Studies, Monash University.
—— (1991) *Imagined Communities: Reflections on the origin and spread of nationalism*, (revised and extended edition, originally published in 1983), London: Verso/New Left Books.
Appadurai, A. (1990) 'Topographies of the self: praise and emotion in Hindu India', in Lutz, C. and Abu-Lughod, L. (eds), *Language and the Politics of Emotion*, Cambridge: Cambridge University Press.
Aragon, L. (2000) *Fields of the Lord: Animism, Christian minorities and state development in Indonesia*, Honolulu: University of Hawai'i Press.
—— (2001) 'Communal violence in Poso, central Sulawesi: where people eat fish and fish eat people', *Indonesia*, 72, 45–80.

Atkinson, J.M. (1987) 'Religions in dialogue: the construction of an Indonesian minority religion', in Kipp, R.S. and Rodgers, S. (eds), *Indonesian Religions in Transition*, Tucson: University of Arizona Press.
—— (1989) *The Art and Politics of Wana Shamanship*, Berkeley: University of California Press.
Babb, L. (1986) *Redemptive Encounters: Three modern styles in the Hindu tradition*, Berkeley: University of California Press.
Bagus, I.G.N. (1969) *Pertantangan Kasta dalam bentuk baru pada Masjarakat Bali*, Denpasar: Universitas Udayana.
—— (1975) 'Surya kanta: a kewangsan movement of the jaba caste in Bali', *Masyarakat Indonesia*, 2, 153–62.
Baum, V. (1937) *A Tale from Bali*, London: Geoffrey Bles.
Bailey, F. (1957) *Caste and the Economic Frontier*, Manchester: Manchester University Press.
Bakker, F.L. (1993) *The Struggle of the Hindu Balinese Intellectuals: Developments in modern Hindu thinking in independent Indonesia*, Amsterdam: VU University Press.
Barth, F. (1993) *Balinese Worlds*, Chicago: Chicago University Press.
Basham, A.L. (1971; originally published in 1954) *The Wonder that was India*, London: Fontana/Collins.
Bateson, G. (1970a) 'An old temple and a new myth', in Belo, J. (ed), *Traditional Balinese Culture*, New York: Columbia University Press.
—— (1970b) 'Bali: the value system of a steady state', in Belo, J. (ed), *Traditional Balinese Culture*, New York: Columbia University Press.
Bateson, G. and Mead, M. (1942) *Balinese Character: A photographic analysis*, New York: New York Academy of Sciences.
Beatty, A. (1999) *Varieties of Javanese Religion: An anthropological account*, Cambridge: Cambridge University Press.
Belo, J. (1949) *Bali: Rangda and Barong*, Seattle: University of Washington Press.
Boland, B.J. (1982) *The Struggle of Islam in Modern Indonesia*, The Hague: Martinus Nijhoff.
Boon, J. (1977) *The Anthropological Romance of Bali, 1597–1972*. Cambridge: Cambridge University Press.
Bourchier, D. (1997) 'Totalitarianism and the "national personality": recent controversy about the philosophical basis of the Indonesian state', in Schiller, J. and Martin-Schiller, B. (eds), *Imagining Indonesia: cultural politics and political culture*, Athens, Ohio: Ohio University Centre for International Studies.
Bourdieu, P. (1977) *Outline of a Theory of Practice*, Cambridge: Cambridge University Press.
Bowen, J. (1986) 'On the political construction of tradition: gotong-royong in Indonesia', *Journal of Asian Studies*, 45, 545–61.
Brenner, S.A. (1998) *The Domestication of Desire: Women, wealth and modernity in Java*, Princeton: Princeton University Press.
Budiman, A. (ed.) (1990) *State and Civil Society in Indonesia*, Monash University: Centre of Southeast Asian Studies.
Carrier, J. (1992) 'Occidentalism: the world turned upside down', *American Ethnologist*, 19, 195–212.
Connor, L. (1979) 'Corpse abuse and trance in Bali: the cultural mediation of aggression', *Mankind*, 12, 104–18.

—— (1982) 'In darkness and light: a study of peasant intellectuals in Bali', unpublished thesis, University of Sydney.

—— (1996) 'Contestation and transformation of Balinese ritual: the case of ngabén ngirit', in Vickers, A. (ed.), *Being Modern in Bali: image and change*, New Haven: Yale University Southeast Asia Studies.

Couteau, J. (2003) 'After the Kuta bombing: in search of the Balinese "soul"', *Antropologi Indonesia*, 70, 41–59.

Covarrubias, M. (1937) *Island of Bali*, London: Cassell.

Crapanzano, V. (1986) 'Hermes' dilemma: the masking of subversion in ethnographic description', in Clifford, J. and Marcus, G. (eds), *Writing Culture, the Poetics and Politics of Ethnography*, Berkeley: University of California Press.

Cribb, R. (ed.) (1990) *The Indonesian Killings, 1965–1966: studies from Java and Bali*, Monash University: Centre for Southeast Asian Studies.

Crouch, H. (1988; originally published in 1978) *The Army and Politics in Indonesia*, Ithaca: Cornell University Press.

Darling, D. (2003) 'Talking about animal sacrifice', *Latitudes*, 24, 52–7.

de Heusch, L. (1997) 'The symbolic mechanism of sacred kingship: rediscovering Frazer', *JRAI*, 3, 213–32.

de Kat Angelino, P. (1920) 'De robans en parekans op Bali', *Koloniaal Tijdschrift*, 10, 590–608.

de Zoete, B. and Spies, W. (1938) *Dance and Drama in Bali*, London: Faber and Faber.

Derrett, J.D.M. (1976) 'Rajadharma', *Journal of Asian Studies*, 35, 597–609.

Dirks, N.B. (1987) *The Hollow Crown: Ethnohistory of an Indian kingdom*, Cambridge: Cambridge University Press.

Dowson, J. (1972) *A Classical Dictionary of Hindu Mythology*, London: Routledge and Kegan Paul.

Dumont, L. (1980) *Homo Hierarchicus: the caste system and its implications*, Chicago: Chicago University Press.

Eiseman, F.B. (1990). *Bali: Sekala and Niskala* (2 vols), Berkeley: Periplus Editions.

Errington, S. (1989) *Meaning and Power in a Southeast Asian Realm*, Princeton: Princeton University Press.

Fabian, J. (1983) *Time and the Other: How anthropology makes its object*, New York: Columbia University Press.

Feith, H. (1962) *The Decline of Constitutional Democracy in Indonesia*, Ithaca: Cornell University Press.

—— (1963) 'Indonesia's political symbols and their wielders', *World Politics*, 16, 79–97.

Foulcher, K. (1990) 'The construction of an Indonesian national culture: patterns of hegemony and resistance', in Budiman, A. (ed.), *State and Society in Indonesia*, Monash University: Centre of Southeast Asian Studies.

Fuller, C.J. (1984) *Servants of the Goddess: The priests of a south Indian temple*, Cambridge: Cambridge University Press.

—— (1992) *The Camphor Flame: Popular Hinduism and society in India*, Princeton: Princeton University Press.

Galey, J.C. (1989) 'Reconsidering kingship in India: an ethnological perspective', *History and Anthropology*, 4, 123–87.

Garrison, L. (1989) 'Tourism – wave of the future? *World Development* (UNDP), 2, 4–6.

Geertz, C. (1959) 'Form and variation in Balinese village structure', *American Anthropologist*, 61, 991–1012.

—— (1960) *The Religion of Java*, Chicago: Chicago University Press.

References

Geertz, C. (1963a) *Agricultural Involution: The processes of ecological change in Indonesia*, Berkeley: University of California Press.
—— (1963b) *Peddlers and Princes: Social development and economic change in two Indonesian towns*, Chicago: Chicago University Press.
—— (1973a) *The Interpretation of Cultures: Selected essays*, New York: Basic Books. British edition: Hutchinson of London, 1975.
—— (1973b, first published in 1964) '"Internal conversion" in contemporary Bali', in *The Interpretation of Cultures*.
—— (1973c, first published in 1966) 'Person, time and conduct in Bali', in *The Interpretation of Cultures*.
—— (1973d, first published in 1972) 'Deep play, notes on the Balinese cockfight', in *The Interpretation of Cultures*.
—— (1980) *Negara, The Theatre State in Nineteenth-Century Bali*, Princeton: Princeton University Press.
Geertz, C. and Geertz, H. (1975) *Kinship in Bali*, Chicago: Chicago University Press.
Geertz, H. (1995a) *Images of Power: Balinese paintings made for Gregory Bateson and Margaret Mead,* Honolulu: University of Hawaii Press.
Geertz, H. (1995b) 'Sorcery and social change in Bali: the sakti conjecture', paper presented at the Bali in the Late Twentieth Century conference, Sydney University, July 1995.
Gombrich, R. and Obeyesekere, G. (1988) *Buddhism Transformed: Religious change in Sri Lanka*, Princeton: Princeton University Press.
Grader, C.J. (1937) 'Tweedeeling in het oud-Balische dorp', *Mededelingen van de Kirtya Liefrinck-van der Tuuk*, 5, 45–71.
Guermonprez, J-F. (1987) *Les Pandé de Bali: la formation d'une caste et la valeur d'un titre*, Paris: École Française d'Extréme-Orient.
—— (1990) 'On the elusive Balinese village: hierarchy and values versus political models', *RIMA*, 24, 55–89.
Hanna, W.A. (1976) *Bali Profile: People, events, circumstances, 1001–1976*, New York: American Universities Field Staff.
Hardacre, H. (1986) *Kurozumikyo and the New Religions of Japan*, Princeton: Princeton University Press.
Hefner, R. (1997) 'Islamization and democratization in Indonesia', in Hefner, R. and Horvatich, P. (eds), *Islam in an Era of Nation-States*, Honolulu: University of Hawai'i Press.
—— (2000) *Civil Islam: Muslims and democratization in Indonesia*, Princeton: Princeton University Press.
Hill, H. (ed.) (1994) *Indonesia's New Order: the dynamics of socio-economic transformation*, St Leonards: Allen and Unwin.
Hobsbawm, E. and Ranger, T. (eds) (1983) *The Invention of Tradition*, Cambridge: Cambridge University Press.
Holt, C. (1967) *Art in Indonesia: continuities and change*, Ithaca: Cornell University Press.
Hooykaas, C. (1974) *Cosmogony and Creation in Balinese Tradition*, The Hague: Martinus Nijhoff.
—— (1978) *The Balinese Poem Basur: an introduction to magic*, The Hague: Martinus Nijhoff.
Hough, B. (1999) 'Education for the performing arts: contesting and mediating identity in contemporary Bali', in Rubinstein, R. and Connor, L. (eds), *Staying Local in the Global Village: Bali in the twentieth century*, Honolulu: University of Hawai'i Press.

Howe, L. (1981) 'The social determination of knowledge: Maurice Bloch and Balinese time', *Man*, 16, 220–34
—— (1983) 'An introduction to the study of traditional Balinese architecture', *Archipel*, 25, 137–58.
—— (1984) 'Gods, people, spirits and witches', *BKI*, 140, 193–222.
—— (1987) 'Caste in Bali and India: levels of comparison', in Holy, L. (ed.), *Comparative Anthropology*, Oxford: Blackwell.
—— (1989a) 'Peace and violence in Bali: culture and social organization', in Howell, S. and Willis, R. (eds), *Societies at Peace: anthropological perspectives*, London: Routledge.
—— (1989b) 'Hierarchy and equality: variation in Balinese social organisation', *BKI*, 145, 47–71.
—— (1991) 'Rice, ideology and the legitimation of hierarchy in Bali', *Man*, 26, 445–467.
—— (2000) 'Risk, ritual and performance', *JRAI*, 6, 63–79.
—— (2001) *Hinduism and Hierarchy in Bali*, Oxford: James Currey; Santa Fe: School of American Research Press.
—— (2002) 'The red temple and the invisible priest, or why the people of a Balinese village decided not to join Warga Pasek', *RIMA*, 36, 115–42.
—— (2004) 'Balinese cremation', in Davies, D. and Mates, L. (eds), *The Encyclopaedia of Cremation*, Aldershot: Ashgate.
Hunter, T. (1988) 'Balinese language: historical background and contemporary state', unpublished thesis, University of Michigan, Ann Arbor.
Jendra, I.W. (1996) *Variasi Bahasa Kedudukan dan Peran Bhagawan Sri Sathya Sai Baba dalam Agama Hindu*. Surabaya: Paramita.
Jensen, G. and Suryani, L.K. (1992) *The Balinese People: A reinvestigation of character*, Singapore: Oxford University Press.
Kahin, G.M. (1952) *Nationalism and Revolution in Indonesia*, Ithaca: Cornell University Press.
Keeler, W. (1983) 'Shame and stage fright in Java', *Ethos*, 11, 152–65.
—— (1987) *Javanese Shadow Plays, Javanese Selves*, Princeton: Princeton University Press.
Keesing, R. (1987) 'Anthropology as interpretive quest', *Current Anthropology*, 28, 161–76.
—— (1989) 'Exotic readings of cultural texts', *Current Anthropology*, 30, 459–79.
Kent, A. (2000) 'Creating divine unity: Chinese recruitment in the Sathya Sai Baba movement of Malaysia', *Journal of Contemporary Religion*, 15, 5–27.
—— (2004) *Divinity and Diversity: a Hindu revitalization movement in Malaysia*, Honolulu: University of Hawai'i Press.
King, V.T. and Wilder, W.D. (2003) *Modern Anthropology of Southeast Asia*, London: RoutledgeCurzon.
Kipp, R. and Rodgers, S. (eds) (1987) *Indonesian Religions in Transition*, Tucson: University of Arizona Press.
Klass, M. (1991) *Singing with Sai Baba: The politics of revitalization in Trinidad*, Boulder: Westview.
Klinken, G. (2001) 'The Maluku wars: bringing society back in', *Indonesia*, 71, 1–26.
Korn, V.E. (1932) *Het Adatrecht van Bali*, s'Gravenhage: G.Naeff.
—— (1933) *De Dorpsrepubliek Tnganan Pagringsingan*, Mees: Santpoort.
Legge, J.D. (1972) *Sukarno, a Political Biography*, Harmondsworth: Penguin Books.
Leigh, B. (1991) 'Making the Indonesian state: the role of school texts', *RIMA*, 25, 17–43.

Lekkerkerker, C. (1926) 'De Kastenmaatschappij in Britisch-Indie en op Bali', *Mensch en Maatschappij*, 2, 175–213, 300–34.
Lev, D.S. (1966) *The Transition to Guided Democracy: Indonesian politics, 1957–1959*, Ithaca: Cornell Modern Indonesia Project.
McKean, P. (1973) 'Cultural involution: tourists, Balinese and the process of modernization in an anthropological perspective', unpublished thesis, Brown University.
McPhee, C. (1947) *A House in Bali*, New York: Doubleday.
MacRae, G. (1999) 'Acting global, thinking local in a Balinese tourist town', in Rubinstein, R. and Connor, L. (eds), *Staying Local in the Global Village: Bali in the twentieth century*, Honolulu: University of Hawai'i Press.
Meillassoux, C. (1973) 'Are there castes in India?', *Economy & Society*, 2, 89–111.
Mencher, J. (1974) 'The caste system upside down', *Current Anthropology*, 15, 463–93.
Moertono, S. (1968) *State and Statecraft in Old Java: A study of the later Mataram period*, Ithaca: Cornell Modern Indonesia Project.
Morfit, M. (1986) 'Pancasila orthodoxy', in MacAndrews, C. (ed.), *Central Government and Local Development in Indonesia*, Singapore: Oxford University Press.
Parker, L. (1992a) 'The creation of Indonesian citizens in Balinese primary schools', *RIMA*, 26, 42–70.
—— (1992b) 'The quality of schooling in a Balinese village', *Indonesia*, 54, 95–116.
—— (1997) 'Engendering schoolchildren in Bali', *JRAI*, 3, 497–516.
Parry, J. (1979) *Caste and Kinship in Kangra*, London: Routledge and Kegan Paul.
—— (1980) 'Ghosts, greed and sin: the occupational identity of the Benares funeral priests', *Man*, 15, 88–111.
—— (1989) 'The end of the body', in Feher, M., Naddoff, R. and Tazi, N. (eds), *Fragments for a History of the Human Body* (Part 3), New York: Zone.
Pemberton, J. (1994) *On the Subject of 'Java'*, Ithaca: Cornell University Press.
Persoon, G. (1998) 'Isolated groups or indigenous peoples: Indonesia and the international discourse', *BKI*, 154, 281–304.
Picard, M. (1990a) '"Cultural tourism" in Bali: cultural performances as tourist attraction', *Indonesia*, 49, 37–74.
—— (1990b) 'Kebalian orang Bali: tourism and the uses of "Balinese culture" in New Order Indonesia', *RIMA*, 24, 1–37.
—— (1996) *Bali: Cultural tourism and touristic culture*, Singapore: Archipelago Press.
—— (1997) 'Cultural tourism, nation-building and regional culture: the making of a Balinese identity', in Picard, M. and Wood, R.E. (eds), *Tourism, Ethnicity and the State in Asian and Pacific Societies*, Honolulu: University of Hawai'i Press.
—— (1999) 'The discourse of Kebalian: transcultural constructions of Balinese identity', in Rubinstein, R. and Connor, L. (eds), *Staying Local in the Global village: Bali in the twentieth century*, Honolulu: University of Hawai'i Press.
Pitana, I.G. (1997) 'In search of difference: origin groups, status and identity in contemporary Bali' unpublished thesis, Australian National University.
—— (1999) 'Status struggles and the priesthood in contemporary Bali', in Rubinstein, R. and Connor, L. (eds), *Staying Local in the Global Village: Bali in the twentieth century*, Honolulu: University of Hawai'i Press.
Poffenberger, M. and Zurbuchen, M. (1980) 'The economics of village Bali: three perspectives', *Economic Development and Cultural Change*, 29, 91–133.
Pollmann, T. (1990) 'Margaret Mead's Balinese: the fitting symbols of the American dream', *Indonesia*, 49, 1–35.

Punyatmadja, I.B.O. (1976) *Pancha Cradha*, Denpasar: Parisada Hindu Dharma Pusat.
Quigley, D. (1993) *The Interpretation of Caste*, Oxford: Clarendon Press.
Raheja, G.G. (1988) *The Poison in the Gift*, Chicago: Chicago University Press.
Ramstedt, M. (1995) 'Preliminary reflections on an ambiguous relationship: agama Hindu Bali vis-a-vis Hindu Dharma Indonesia', paper presented at the Bali in the Late Twentieth Century conference, Sydney University, 3–7 July.
Rassers, W.H. (1922) *De Panji Roman*, Antwerp: de Vos-van Kleef.
Reeve, D. (1985) *Golkar of Indonesia: An alternative to the party system*, Singapore: Oxford University Press.
Richter, L.K. (1989) *The Politics of Tourism in Asia*, Honolulu: University of Hawai'i Press.
Ricklefs, M. (1974) *Jogjakarta under Sultan Mangkubumi, 1749–1792*, London: Oxford University Press.
—— (1981) *A History of Modern Indonesia*, London: Macmillan.
Robinson, G. (1992) 'The economic foundations of political conflict in Bali, 1950–1965', *Indonesia*, 54, 59–93.
—— (1995) *The Dark Side of Paradise: Political violence in Bali*, Ithaca: Cornell University Press.
Robison, R. (1986) *Indonesia: The rise of capital*, Sydney: Allen & Unwin.
Rubinstein, R. (1991) 'The Brahmana according to their babad', in Geertz, H. (ed.), *State and Society in Bali*. Leiden: Koninklijk Instituut voor Taal-, Land- en Volkenkunde.
—— (1995) 'Brahmana networks: cohesion and division in the 1990s', paper presented at the Bali in the Late Twentieth Century conference, Sydney University, 3–7 July.
Ruddick, A. (1986) 'Charmed lives: illness, healing power and gender in a Balinese village', unpublished thesis, Brown University.
Sahlins, M. (1974) *Stone Age Economics*. London: Tavistock.
Said, E. (1978) *Orientalism*, London: Routledge and Kegan Paul.
Santikarma, D. (2001) 'The power of "Balinese Culture"', in Ramseyer, U. and Tisna, I Gusti Raka Panji (eds), *Bali: Living in two worlds,* Basle: Museum der Kulturen.
Santri, R. (1993) *Kasta dalam Hindu: Kesalahpahaman berabad-abad*, Denpasar, Bali: Yayasan Dharma Naradha.
Schefold, R. (1998), 'The domestication of culture: nation-building and ethnic diversity in Indonesia', *BKI*, 154, 259–80.
Schiller, A. (1997) *Small Sacrifices: Religious change and cultural identity among the Ngaju of Indonesia*, Oxford: Oxford University Press.
Schrauwers, A. (2000) *Colonial 'Reformation' in the Highlands of Central Sulawesi, Indonesia, 1892–1995*. Toronto: University of Toronto Press.
Schrieke, B. (1957) *Ruler and Realm in Early Java*, The Hague: W. van Hoeve.
Schulte Nordholt, H. (1986) *Bali: colonial conceptions and political change, 1700–1940*, Erasmus University: Comparative Asian Studies Programme.
—— (1988) 'Een Balische dynastie: hierarchie en conflict in de negara Mengwi 1700–1940', unpublished thesis, Free University of Amsterdam.
—— (1991a) 'Temple and authority in south Bali, 1900–1980', in Geertz, H. (ed.), *State and Society in Bali*, Leiden: Koninklijk Instuut voor de Taal-, Land- en Volkenkunde.
—— (1991b) *State, Village and Ritual in Bali*. Amsterdam: University Press.
—— (1992) 'Origin, descent and destruction: text and context in Balinese representations of the past', *Indonesia*, 54, 27–58.
—— (1993) 'Leadership and the limits of political control. A Balinese "response" to Clifford Geertz', *Social Anthropology*, 1, 291–307.

Schulte Nordholt, H. (1996) *The Spell of Power: A history of Balinese politics, 1650–1940*, Leiden: Koninklijk Instituut voor de Taal-, Land- en Volkenkunde.
Schwarz, A. (1994) *A Nation in Waiting: Indonesia in the 1990s*, St. Leonards: Allen and Unwin.
Sellato, B. (1995) 'Culture, history, politics and the emergence of provincial identities in Kalimantan', in Charas, M. (ed.), *Beyond the State: essays in spatial structuralism in insular Southeast Asia*. Paris, CNRS: Lasima.
Shiraishi, T. (1990) *An Age in Motion: Popular radicalism in Java, 1912–1926*, Ithaca: Cornell University Press.
Siegel, J. (2001) 'Suharto, witches', *Indonesia*, 71, 27–78.
Spyer, P. (2000) *The Memory of Trade: Modernity's entanglements on an eastern Indonesian island*, Durham: Duke University Press.
Stephen, M. (2001) 'Barong and Rangda in the context of Balinese religion', *RIMA*, 35, 137–93.
—— (2002) 'Returning to original form: a central dynamic in Balinese religion', *BKI*, 158, 61–94.
—— (2005) *Desire, Divine and Demonic: Balinese mysticism in the paintings of I Ketut Budiana and I Gusti Nyoman Mirdiana*, Honolulu: University of Hawai'i Press.
Stoler, A. (1985) *Capitalism and Confrontation in Sumatra's Plantation Belt, 1870–1979*, New Haven: Yale University Press.
Stuart-Fox, D. (2002) *Pura Besakih: Temple, religion and society in Bali*, Leiden: Koninklijk Instituut voor Taal-, Land- en Volkenkunde.
Suasta, P. (2001) 'Between holy waters and highways' in Ramseyer, U. and Tisna, I Gusti Raka Panji (eds), *Bali: living in two worlds*, Basle: Museum der Kulturen.
—— and Connor, L. (1999) 'Democratic mobilization and political authoritarianism: tourism developments in Bali', in Rubinstein, R. and Connor, L. (eds), *Staying Local in the Global Village: Bali in the Twentieth Century*. Honolulu: University of Hawai'i Press.
Sukarno (1965) *Sukarno, An Autobiography (as told to Cindy Adams)*, Hong Kong: Gunung Agung.
Supartha, W. (ed) (1994) *Memahami Aliran Kepercayaan*, Denpasar: PT Bali Post.
Suryadinata, L. (1989) *Military Ascendancy and Political Culture*, Athens, Ohio: Ohio University Centre for International Studies.
Sutton, R. (1995) 'Performing arts and cultural politics in south Sulawesi', *BKI*, 151, 672–99.
Swellengrebel, J.L. (1960) 'Introduction', in Swellengrebel, J.L. (ed.), *Bali: studies in life, thought and ritual*, The Hague: W. van Hoeve.
Tambiah, S.J. (1985) 'A reformulation of Geertz's conception of the theatre state', in *Culture, Thought and Action: An anthropological perspective*, Cambridge, MA: Harvard University Press.
Taylor, P.M. (1994) 'The *nusantara* concept of culture: local traditions and national identity as expressed in Indonesia's museums', in Taylor, P.M. (ed.), *Fragile Traditions: Indonesian art in jeopardy*, Honolulu: University of Hawaii Press.
Thomas, N. (1989) *Out of Time: History and evolution in anthropological discourse*, Cambridge: Cambridge University Press.
—— (1994) *Colonialism's Culture: Anthropology, travel and government*, Cambridge: Polity Press.
Titib, I.M. (1994) *Ketuhanan dalam Weda*, Denpasar: P.T. Pustaka Manikgeni.

Tsing, A.L. (1990) 'Gender and performance in Meratus dispute settlement', in Atkinson, J.M. and Errington, S. (eds), *Power and Difference: gender in island Southeast Asia*. Stanford: Stanford University Press.
—— (1993) *In the Realm of the Diamond Queen*, Princeton: Princeton University Press.
Upadeca (1968) *Upadeca: tentang ajaran-ajaran agama Hindu*, Denpasar: Parisada Hindu Dharma.
Urry, J. (1990) *The Tourist Gaze*, London: Sage.
van den Berghe, P.L. (1980) 'Tourism as ethnic relations: a case study of Cuzco, Peru', *Ethnic and Racial Studies*, 3, 375–92.
van der Kraan, A. (1983) 'Bali: slavery and slave trade', in Reid, A. (ed.), *Slavery, Bondage and Dependency in Southeast Asia*, St Lucia: University of Queensland Press.
van Eck, R. (1876) *Eerste Proeve van een Balineesch–Hollandsch Woordenboek*, Utrecht: Kemink en Zoon.
van Leur, J.C. (1955) *Indonesian Trade and Society*, The Hague: W. van Hoeve.
Vickers, A. (1987) 'Hinduism and Islam in Indonesia: Bali and the Pasisir', *Indonesia*, 44, 31–58.
—— (1989) *Bali, A Paradise Created*, Berkeley: Periplus.
—— (1991) 'Ritual written: the song of the Ligya, or the killing of the rhinoceros', in Geertz, H. (ed.), *State and Society in Bali*. Leiden: Koninklijk Instituut voor Taal-, Land- en Volkenkunde.
—— (1996) 'Modernity and being *moderen*: an introduction', in Vickers, A. (ed.), *Being Modern in Bali: image and change*, New Haven: Yale University Southeast Asia Studies.
Volkman, T.A. (1985) *Feasts of Honour: Ritual and change in the Toraja highlands*, Urbana: University of Illinois Press.
—— (1987) 'Mortuary tourism in Tana Toraja', in Kipp, R.S. and Rodgers, S. (eds), *Indonesian Religions in Transition*, Tucson: University of Arizona Press.
—— (1990) 'Visions and revisions: Toraja culture and the tourist gaze', *American Ethnologist*, 17, 91–110.
Warren, C. (1993) *Adat and Dinas: Balinese communities in the Indonesian state*, Kuala Lumpur: Oxford University Press.
—— (1998) 'Tanah Lot: the cultural and environmental politics of resort development in Bali', in Hirsch, P. and Warren, C. (eds), *The Politics of Environment in Southeast Asia: Resources and resistance*, London: Routledge.
Waterson, R. (1990) *The Living House: An anthropology of architecture in South-East Asia*, Singapore: Oxford University Press.
Weber, M. (1985; first published in 1930) *The Protestant Ethic and the Spirit of Capitalism*, London: Unwin.
Wenban, G. (1993) 'Golkar's election victory: neither smooth nor fair', *Inside Indonesia*, 37, 12–14.
Wiana, I.K. (1992) *Sembahyang menurut Hindu*, Denpasar: Yayasan Dharma Naradha.
—— (1995) *Yajna dan Bhakti dari sudut pandang Hindu*, Denpasar: P.T. Pustaka Manikgeni.
Wiener, M. (1995) *Visible and Invisible Realms: power, magic and colonial conquest in Bali*, Chicago: Chicago University Press.
Wikan, U. (1987) 'Public grace and private fears: gaiety, offense and sorcery in north Bali', *Ethos*, 15, 337–65
—— (1990) *Managing Turbulent Hearts: A Balinese formula for living*, Chicago: Chicago University Press.

Wikan, U. (1992) 'Beyond the words: the power of resonance', *American Ethnologist*, 19, 460–82.
Wood, R. (1997) 'Tourism and the state: ethnic options and constructions of otherness', in Picard, M. and Wood, R.E. (eds), *Tourism, Ethnicity and the State in Asian and Pacific Societies*, Honolulu: University of Hawai'i Press.
Worsley, P.J. (1972) *Babad Buleleng*, The Hague: Martinus Nijhoff.
—— (1979) 'Preliminary remarks on the concept of kingship in the Babad Buleleng', in Reid, A. and Castles, L. (eds), *Pre-colonial State Systems in Southeast Asia*, Kuala Lumpur: Royal Asiatic Society.
Yamashita, S. (2003) *Bali and Beyond: Explorations in the anthropology of tourism*, Oxford: Berghahn Books.
Yampolsky, P. (1995) 'Forces of change in the regional performing arts in Indonesia', *BKI*, 151, 700–25.
Zurbuchen, M. (1987) *The Language of Balinese Shadow Theatre*, Princeton: Princeton University Press.

Index

Page numbers in *italics* indicate illustrations.

Aceh 31
Adams, K. M. 133
adat (indigenous religion) 57, 64, 72–4, 93, 94, 99–100, 103, 106, 137, 138, 139
agama (religion) 63, 64, 74, 91, 108, 137, 138, 139
agama Hindu 65, 66, 71, 72, 92–5, 104, 105, 106–8, 138
agriculture 9, 73
Agung eruption 8, 29
aliran kepercyaan ('streams of belief') 74, 95
alus (delicate, refined, formal) 40, 43, 113, 124
Ambon 31
anak agung (descent group) x, 111–12, 114, 115, 118
anak jaba (outsiders) 13, 112–13
anak jero (insiders) 13, 111–13
anak sakti (powerful people) 42, 43
ancestors: approval by 123; revelations of 126–7; temple system 14–15; wrath of 51
animal sacrifice 6–7, 69–72, 107
anthropologists 28, 34
army, the 29, 30
artificial culture 141–3
'arts industry' 141–2
Atkinson, Jane 91

Baba (Sri Saytha Sai Baba) 96, 98–9, 103, 109–10
babad (dynastic chronicles) 15, 117–18, 122–3
Babad Pasek 128
babies 58–9
badé (cremation towers) 60, 61, 66, *78*
Bahasa Indonesia 140
Bailey, F. 121

Bali Arts and Cultural Newsletter 6
Bali Arts Festival 142–3
balian (healer) 44–5, 52
Balinese interaction: Geertz 39–40; Wikan 40–2
Balinese personhood: Geertz on 31–2
'Balineseness' 138–9
'Balinisation of Bali': Dutch colonial control 18–21, 139
banjar (hamlet) 11, 16, 34
Barth, F. 123
Bateson, Gregory 28, 38
Baum, Vicki 27
Besakih *89*
black magic 40
bodily excuviae: use in witchcraft 49
bohemians 27
bombing (October 2002) 1–4, 144; rituals 6–7
books: religious 93
Boon, J. 122, 124
Brahmana category x, 12, 13–14, 22–3, 94, 111–12, 116
Burginese 133
buta-kala spirits 51, 69, 70–1

Carrier, J. 39
caste hierarchy: Balinese interpretations 116–20; challenge to 126–30; criteria 116; Dutch reforms 20–4; linguistic etiquette 113–14; naming system 111–12; organisation 7–8, 12–15; political and economic elite 114–15; reform 94; and Sai Baba 99–100; and wealth 121–5
catur warna 12–14, 94, 116, 119
centrality 16
ceremonies: after Kuta bombing 6–7; animal sacrifice 69–72; classification

58–62; debate on 72–4; marriage 59, *86, 87*; preparation of food *84*; reforms of 65–9; Sai Baba 98–9; significance 36; temple ceremony *83*; tooth-filing 59–60, *85 see also* rituals
character: of the Balinese 38–9
charity work 97
children 58–9
Christianity 132
classification: caste system 12–15
cockfighting 48, 70, *77*
coffee shop *81*
cokorda x, 111, 112, 114
Cokorda Pemayun palace *81*
colonial oppression 21–4
colonial period: societal structure 7–8
commodification: of culture 4, 143
'commoners' 13, 14, 16, 24, 64, 112–13
communism 140
communists 29, 30
compounds 10–11, *12*, 16, 113
conflicts 29–30, 31
Connor, L. 34, 66
'contest states' 32–3
Corong village 44–8, *81, 83*
cosmological principles 9–12, 69–70
Covarrubias, Miguel 27
cremation (*ngabén*) 60–1
cremation towers (*badé*) 60, 61, 66, *78*, 114
cross-caste marriages 114, 119
cultural diversity 141
cultural objects 131–2, 136
cultural tourism 135–6, 142
culture: appreciation of 26; idea of 5; image of 4–5; Indonesian 140–3; preservation of 18–21, 26; 'selling' of 1–2; terms for 139; Toraja 133–4; and tourism 131–2, 134–8; uniqueness 2–3

dance performances 136–8, 141–2
death rituals 60–1
debt slavery 35
Degung Santikarma 6–7
Denpasar 8, *88*
désa (villages) 9, 10–11, *13*
Déwa 44–5
Déwa Agung 117–18, 126
districts (*kecamatan*) 127
drama performances 136–8
Dumont, Louis 12, 121
Dutch colonial control 18–27, 117, 122, 132
dynastic chronicles (*babad*) 15, 117–18, 122–3

elections (1999) 31
elite rulers 8, 14, 24, 34–5, 37
emotional disturbance 51–2
environmental impact: of tourism 5–6, *90*, 144–5
equality 63, 100, 102, 113, 126, 128
essentialist constructions 39
ethnic identity 3, 5, 141; *kebalian* 108–10, 138–9
ethnic relations 73
etiquette 32, 40–2, 43–4, 46, 55, 113–14
'exotic Bali' 25–7, 26

families 10
farming 9, 73
fear 43; Balinese character 38–9
fines 35
food preparation *84*
functions: classification 119

gambling 61, 70, 73, 105
garbage disposal *90*
Geertz, Clifford: Balinese character 38–9; Balinese interaction 39–40; caste ascription 116; Dutch colonial policy 20; interpretation 31–2; king 35; *negara* 32–4; ritual 36; title system 115, 125; wealth 121
Geertz, Hildred 50
genealogies 117–18, 122–3
'gentry' 13, 14, 15, 16, 24, 64, 111–13, 126
geographical features 8–9
ghosts (*tonya*) 48 *see also* spirits (*buta-kala*)
Golkar (*Golongan Karya*, functional groups) 30–1
Goris, Roelof 20

hamlet (*banjar*) 11, 16, 34
Hare Krishna 57–8, 74, *88*, 95, 105–6
healers (*balian*) 44–5, 52
herbal medicines 52
hierarchy: Balinese interpretations 116–20; challenge to 126–30; Dutch reforms 20–4; linguistic etiquette 113–14; naming system 111–12; organisation 7–8, 12–15; political and economic elite 114–15; prevalence 15–16; reform 94; and Sai Baba 99–100; social 7–8, 12–15; and wealth 121–5
high priests (*pedanda*) 12, 22–3, 42, 43, 52, 66, 92, 127, 129

Hindu–Buddhist culture 20–21
Hinduism 5, 9, 57–8, 64, 65, 92, 104, 108
Hindus 107
house compounds 10–11, *12*, 16, 113
households 10

ica (gift, blessing, laughter) 53–4
identity 132–3, 138–9
ideological principles 30
illness 51, 52
image: of Bali 4–5, 25–7, 29
independence 29, 91
Indian influence 21
Indonesian national culture 140–3
infrastructure 5–6, 17, 145
insiders (*anak jero*) 13, 111–13
invasions: Dutch 18–19; Javanese 117, 138; spirit 51, 70–1
Islam 20, 63, 91

Japanese occupation 29
Javanese, the 1, 13, 20, 25, 33, 40, 105, 117
Jensen, G. 46

kaja–kelod axis 9–10
Kam, Garrett 6
kangin–kauh axis 10
karma 72
kasar (rough, informal) 40, 113, 124
kasta (hierarchy) 116–17
kawitan temples 14–15
kebalian (ethnic identity) 108–10, 138–9
kebudayaan (culture) 2–3
Kent, A. 101
kerohanian (spirituality) 105
Ketiman 47
killings: of migrants 1
kinship associations (*warga*) 126–30
Krause, Gregor 27
Kuta 8, *89*
Kuta bomb 1–4, 144; rituals 6–7

labour: unpaid 23, 24
land ownership 34
language hierarchy 113–14
laughter 40–1, 51, 52–4
leaders (*raja*) 7, 33
légong dance 136
lek (stage fright or shame) 40
léyak (witches) *see* witches
linguistic etiquette 7, 46, 113–14
living areas 10–11, *12*
Lombok 31

McKean, Philip 135
McPhee, Colin 27
MacRae, G. 34
magic lore 42–3
Makassarese 133
mapandes (tooth-filing) 59–60, *85*
markets *76*
marriages: ceremony (*masakapan*) 59, *86*, *87*; cross-caste 114, 119
martial arts 74
mass ritual 36–7
Mead, Margaret 27, 28, 38
meditation 103, 104, 109
Megawati Sukarnoputri 5, 31
men: young 73
meritocratic ideology 120
migrants: Indonesian 1, 3
Ministry of Religion 64, 65
miracles 96, 101
mobility, status 121–5
mother–child interaction: Mead's observations 28, 38
Muslim political parties 29, 30, 140–1
Muslims 1, 9, 107

naming system 111–12
national culture 132, 140–3
national unity 91
nationalism 140
nationalists 29
nawa sangga (template for offerings) 10, *11*, 69–70
negara (pre-colonial Balinese state): Geertz's study 32–7
nelubulanin: rite of 58–9
New Order (*Orde Baru*) 30, 141
ngabén (cremation) 60–1
ngulapin (ritual) 52
Nieuwenkamp, W.O.J. 27
Nusa Dua 8
nyambutin: rite of 58–9

'occidentalism' 39
occupation: Japanese 29
offerings *84*, *85*, 93
Oka, Ibu Gedong 119
Orde Baru (New Order) 30, 141
outsiders (*anak jaba*) 13, 112–13

pacalangan (vigilantes) 3
palaces *81*
Pancasila (ideological principles) 30, 64, 91, 106
Pandé groups 126, 127

160 Index

Parisada Hindu Dharma Bali (later *Indonesia*) 65, 92, 94, 127
Parry, J. 40
Pasek groups 126, 127–8
patron–client relationships 22, 33–5
patulangan (sarcophagus) 60, 61, *79*, *80*
peasants 24, 26, 34, 35
pedanda (high priests) 12, 22–3, 52, 92, 127, 129
performances: cultural 141–2
Person, Time and Conduct in Bali 31–2
Picard, Michel 26, 27, 131, 134, 135, 137, 139, 143
Pitana, I. G. 129
poisoning 49
political activity 30, 144–5
political factionalism 29
population 9
possession: by spirits 51, 70–1
potency (*sakti*) see *sakti*
poverty 8, 24, 26, 27, 68, 144
power: and wealth 121, 124
powerful people (*anak sakti*) 42, 43
priests 5, 7, 58, 60, 96, 97, 99–100 *see also* high priests (*pedanda*)
privileges 114
processions *83*
'protestantisation': of Balinese Hinduism 7
public identities 46
Pudja, Géde 119
Pujung village *76*, 130
pupatan atrocities 18–19, 26
purification rituals 6–7, 58, 66, 69–72, 99

Raffles, Sir Thomas Stamford 18, 25
Ramayana ballet (*sendratari* dance-drama) 142–3
rank *see* caste hierarchy
Rassers, W.H. 20
reforms: caste hierarchy 20–4, 94; religious 6–7; of rituals 65–9
regencies (*kabupaten*) 127
relative status deprivation 120
religion, Balinese: *agama* and *adat* 137; *agama Hindu see agama Hindu*; general 56–7; new 62–5, 95–6; rituals *see* rituals; state-imposed 95–6
religious belief 4, 103–4
religious identity 107–10
religious movements: Hare Krishna 57–8, 74, *88*, 95, 105–6; interest in 106; Sri Sathya Sai Baba 57–8, 95, 96–104, 107, 108–10
religious reform 6–7

republican forces 29
rice 17, 52, 54, 57, 60
rice fields 5, 8, 9, 10, 26, 29, *75*
riots 5
rites of passage (*manusa yadnya*) 58–61
ritual action: debate on 56; practical issues 72–4
ritual slaughter 6–7, 69–72, 107
rituals 10, 36–7, 52, 62–3, 93, 94–5, 103–4, 132 *see also* ceremonies
Robinson, G. 34
rubbish disposal *90*

Sahlins, M. 35
Sai Baba *see* Sri Sathya Sai Baba
Sai Baba temple *88*
sakti (potency or supernatural power) 42, 43, 104–6, 124, 125
Sanghyang Widi 92–3
Sanur 8
sarcophagus (*patulangan*) 60, 61, *79*, *80*, 114
Satria category 12, 13–14, 23, 111
Schulte Nordholt, H. 34
sendratari dance-drama (Ramayana ballet) 142–3
'sex tourists' 20
Shiraishi, T. 63
shrines *89*
singing 98
'sinking status' 117–18
sistim kasta 116–17
social change 63
socialism: of Sukarno 30
society (19th century): structure 7
sorcery 40–50
spatial layout 9–12
speech patterns 113–14
Spies, Walter 20, 27, 28
spirit mediums 123, 126–7
spirits (*buta-kala*) 48, 51–2, 69, 70–1
spirituality (*kerohanian*) 74, 105
spy network 24
Sri Sathya Sai Baba 57–8, 72, 74, 95, 96–104, 107, 108–10
state, the: and cultural diversity 141–2; and religion 64–5
state control 30
status 113; and wealth 121–5
status assertion 59, 61, 67, 68, 95, 121–5
'steady state' 28, 38
subordination 15–16
Sudra category x, 13–14, 23, 94, 112, 118
Suharto 30, 31, 140, 141
Sukarno 29, 30, 65, 140

Sulawesi 132–3
supernatural power (*sakti*) 42, 43, 104–6, 124, 125
Suryani, L.K. 46
Suryani, Professor 4

Taman Budaya Sulawesi 133
temple system 14–15
temple thefts 3
temples 11–12, 16, *87, 88*
terrorist attack 1–4, 144
'theatre states' 32–3, 34
time: Geertz's assertions 32
title system 111–16, 124, 125
tonya (ghosts) 48
tooth-filing (*mapandes*) 59–60, *85*
Toraja people 132–3, 141
tourism 2–6, 17, 26–7, 131–8, 139, 142–5
tourists *90*
towns 16–17
Tri Hita Karana 4
Triwangsa 13, 23, 111
twice-born priests (*pandita dwijati*) 128, 129

Ubud 8
Ujung Pandang 133
unemployment 73
unity, national 140
urbanisation 17

Van Bloemen Waanders, P.L. 25
Van den Bergh, P.L. 131
vegetarianism 103, 106
Vickers, A. 2, 28
vigilantes 3
village rule 34
villages (*désa*) 9, 10–11, *13*; and new religions 106–7
violence 51–2
volcanoes 8

walled compounds 10–11, *12*, 16, 113
war 36–7
warga (kinship associations) 126–30
Warga Pandé 126, 127
Warga Pasek 126, 127–8, 130
warna categories 12–13, 116
warna–kasta ideologies 118–20
water shortages 17
wealth: and hierarchical status 121–5
Wésia category 12, 13–14, 23, 111
Wikan, Unni 38, 39, 40–2, 49, 51, 52, 53
witchcraft 40–50
witches (*léyak*) 43, 45–6, 48, 49–50
women: *agama Hindu* 93; and fear 45; leaders 33; processions *83*; status 14, 15; workers *75*
women's groups 30
woodcarvings *75*